MASTERING GENEALOGICAL DOCUMENTATION

NATIONAL GENEALOGICAL SOCIETY
SPECIAL TOPICS SERIES

MASTERING GENEALOGICAL DOCUMENTATION

Thomas W. Jones

NATIONAL GENEALOGICAL SOCIETY SPECIAL TOPICS SERIES
MASTERING GENEALOGICAL DOCUMENTATION

NGS Special Publication No. 122
ISBN No. 978-1-935815-24-2

Printed in the United States on acid-free, 30 percent post-consumer recycled paper

Cover photos contributed by the author; courtesy of Karen Mauer Jones; and with permission of Bible Baptist Church, Galway, New York. Author's photo courtesy of Shelley Lewis.

10 9 8 7 6 5 4 3 2 1

PUBLISHED BY
National Genealogical Society
3108 Columbia Pike, Suite 300
Arlington, VA 22204-4370

Contents

List of Tables

List of Figures

Preface

Documentation has an underlying logic that genealogists can apply consistently. This textbook teaches that logic. You—a genealogy researcher, student, or novice—will learn how to apply reasoning to your documentation, including citing sources for which no model exists. You will learn how to document your sources conventionally with artistry, clarity, conciseness, completeness, and competence.

Each chapter in this book builds on prior chapters. Chapters 1–6 explain concepts applying to all genealogical documentation. Chapters 7–12 discuss elements of citation content. Chapters 13–16 cover principles for documenting varieties of images and online content. Chapter 17 pulls the logic together.

Each chapter's narrative explains your options and their rationales. Narrative and tables in several chapters compare the options, recommend some of them, and discourage using others. End-of-chapter exercises—160 of them—help you learn how to make and apply logical choices for documentation content, structure, and polish. Working through the exercises, checking the answers at the back of the book, and understanding them helps you master the knowledge and skills that the chapters explain. The more you practice, the more proficient you become.

Many of the exercises refer you to an article in appendix A. Read its narrative and documentation together. By understanding what and how citations document a narrative, you increase your learning.

The genealogy field's research, writing, and documentation standards provide this book's framework. Emerging in the early twentieth century, they evolved as "common understandings," and then began diverging. In the late 1990s, under the leadership of the Board for Certification of Genealogists (BCG), twenty highly qualified genealogists codified the standards. BCG published them in 2000. More than a decade later, twenty-six leading genealogists, after public input, updated the standards. BCG published the revision in 2014.[1]

1. For the publications, see Board for Certification of Genealogists, *The BCG Genealogical Standards Manual* (New York: Turner, 2000). Also, Board for Certification of Genealogists, *Genealogy Standards* (Nashville, Tenn.: Ancestry.com, 2014). For the standards' evolution, see Thomas W. Jones, "Roots of Today's Standards for Amateur and Professional Genealogy," *Crossroads* 11 (Spring 2016): 4–9.

Within the broad flexibility that the standards enable, this book emphasizes that crafting genealogical documentation is a decision-making process. You have options for documentation content, structure, and polish. The book discusses those options, including those that are substandard, but it also acknowledges long-standing conventions and my own preferences.

This book does not "re-invent the wheel." It is not a reference book providing models for citing kinds of sources. It does not discuss guidelines for myriad source types. For that, you need *Evidence Explained*, by Elizabeth Shown Mills.

Mastering Genealogical Documentation discusses principles and logic underlying choices that genealogists consider about what information to include in—and to exclude from—their documentation and how to arrange and finalize citation content. For further guidelines, models, and deeper understandings, this book frequently refers you to *The Chicago Manual of Style* and *Evidence Explained*. If you learn nothing else here, it will be that those two references are indispensable tools for documenting your work.[2]

Most of this book, as is typical of textbooks, is written in the third person. The words "researcher" and "genealogist" refer to you, this book's reader. "Readers" refers to anyone who uses *your* genealogical work, people who will read and analyze your citations, understand what your sources are, and sometimes track them down. They inevitably will include people you do not know. You want to communicate with them as clearly as you can.

For their careful readings of drafts of this book and helpful feedback, I thank Laura Murphy DeGrazia, CG, FGBS; Darrell Jackson, CG; Jordan Jones; and Elizabeth Shown Mills, CG, CGL, FASG, FNGS.[3] I am grateful to the Board for Certification of Genealogists for its permission to quote extensively from *Genealogy Standards*. I especially thank countless online genealogy students and those in classrooms in Birmingham, Boston, Detroit, Eugene, New York, Pittsburgh, and Salt Lake City—you know who you are—for helping me understand what emerging and advancing genealogists want and need to learn about genealogical documentation. Most of all, I thank Elizabeth Shown Mills, who has graciously guided and mentored me for decades, and from whom I still have much to learn.

Thomas W. Jones
1 March 2017

2. I have no financial interest in any resource this book mentions, except the *National Genealogical Society Quarterly*, which I coedit, and *Mastering Genealogical Proof* (Arlington, Va.: National Genealogical Society, 2013), which I wrote.

3. The words *Certified Genealogist* are a registered certification mark, and the designations *CG, CGL,* and *Certified Genealogical Lecturer* are service marks of the Board for Certification of Genealogists®. The postnominal *FASG* designates fellows of the American Society of Genealogists, who are elected on the basis of their published genealogical scholarship. The initials *FNGS* identify genealogists who have been named fellows of the National Genealogical Society for their service to the society or the field, and the initials *FGBS* designates fellows of the New York Genealogical and Biographical Society.

Chapter 1

The Purpose and Nature of Genealogical Documentation

> *"Documentation[:] The sources supporting genealogical conclusions and proof, citations to those sources, the genealogist's comments about them, and formatting showing the connections between the sources and specific statements and conclusions."*[1]

On different days three genealogists visit a museum. Each sees the same painting. They study it carefully, learning all they can about it from their inspection, its labeling, and the exhibition catalog. A few days later they tell their spouses, clearly, completely, and accurately, about the painting, what it shows, and how to find it within the museum's maze of galleries. The three descriptions provide similar information, but each is unique. Which one is correct?

The answer, obviously, is that all three descriptions could be "correct." Of course they differ. Each description fits the individual genealogist's and the respective spouse's interests in the painting and artist, their knowledge of the museum, and their conversation's context. Each genealogist chooses words and phrasing reflecting those factors. Even though the descriptions differ, each communicates—clearly, completely, and accurately—information that the genealogist wants to share and the spouse wants to know about the painting's qualities and location.

Just as differing descriptions of a painting and its location can be correct, other descriptions can be wrong. The genealogist might, for example, forget the artist's name, misremember the painting's title or content, confuse it with another painting, or omit part of the route for finding it. Any of those errors—miscommunications—could cause confusion or misunderstanding about the painting's qualities and its location.

This allegory applies not just to descriptions of art but also to descriptions of genealogical sources. Citations—the biggest part of genealogical documentation and the most important—are source descriptions. When they are clear and complete, they remind researchers of each source they have seen, those sources' qualities, and their locations. They document the research. Citations convey similar information to genealogists' readers. They meet both parties' needs. Just as three genealogists will describe a

1. Board for Certification of Genealogists [BCG], *Genealogy Standards* (Nashville, Tenn.: Ancestry.com, 2014), 67 (glossary definition of "documentation").

work of art and its location differently, their citations to the same source can vary. Despite varying, they all can be correct.

Correct does not mean *identical*. Like any description, citations vary from researcher to researcher, from source to source, and from context to context. They can differ from published models and templates. A citation's differences from other citations or citation models do not make it wrong. Regardless of variation, citations are right when they clearly, completely, and accurately describe sources. Documentation that varies to reflect different sources and contexts will serve researchers' purposes and meet their readers' needs more aptly than documentation that rigidly follows models.

Why document?

Without documentation, perfectly accurate and totally false family histories—or charts, reports, trees, or output from genealogy software—look the same. They offer no easy way to distinguish painstaking research and reasoning from its opposite. An absence of documentation prevents recognizing accuracy and detecting errors. Facing an undocumented family tree, how can anyone—including its compiler—know that it gives correct information?

Believable information about past generations is documented. Documentation can appear in a researcher's work, but documentation appears mostly in citations. Describing a source, a citation reflects the researcher's understanding of that source's qualities and location. The citation describes that understanding.

Serious researchers *want* to document their work, for at least four reasons:

- Citing a source requires researchers to analyze it thoroughly. This analysis helps them understand the source in depth, giving them a research advantage. Understanding a source's purpose, governance, and history helps researchers learn more about the people the source names than when they focus only on what the source says about those people. Researchers who habitually cite sources get more evidence from them.
- Documentation shows researchers and consumers of their work—now and in the future—the quantity and quality of the sources supporting their conclusions. When documentation shows that thorough underlying research yielded credible sources supporting the researcher's conclusions, it validates the researcher's work. Such documentation can show that a family's history is correct—that it accurately reflects events, identities, and relationships as they were in the past.
- When researchers need to reexamine a source, a clear and complete citation helps them turn to it. Such documentation helps them avoid repeating prior research.
- Habitual documentation prevents genealogists from accidentally committing plagiarism—implying that someone else's belief, idea, or

conclusion is their own. For this reason, genealogists document not only their research but also other output, including class and lecture handouts. They cite others' physical and intellectual property that they have used. That documentation includes any required permissions.

The presence of documentation does not by itself establish accuracy. Genealogical information can be poorly documented, obscuring the researcher's sources, or it can be well documented with poor sources. If the work is poorly documented, readers cannot tell whether it does or does not rest on likely accurate sources. If it is well documented, readers can see the research's qualities. They look for specific qualities in finished research:

- The research was reasonably thorough—it included the sources that most competent genealogists would consult when researching the same question in the same geopolitical and chronological context.
- At least some information supporting each conclusion came from eyewitnesses.
- At least some of the records supporting each conclusion were original records, not manual copies, abstracts, indexes, translations, and the like.
- Whenever possible, eyewitness information and original records replaced any relevant hearsay information, derivative records, or authored narratives.[2]

Documentation should enable readers to assess those qualities' presence or absence. When documentation consistently shows their presence, readers understand that the researcher's conclusions likely are sound, suggesting that the genealogist's conclusions are credible.

Documentation lies at the heart of respectable genealogy. Incomplete or absent documentation makes a family compilation, history, or report untrustworthy. Therefore, all serious genealogists thoroughly document their work.

"Right" documentation

Documentation is "right" when it achieves three purposes:[3]

- It communicates source qualities. Some qualities—eyewitness information and contemporaneous recording, for example—are consistent with accuracy. Other qualities—hearsay information, delayed recording, manual copying, or an undocumented narrative, for example—suggest error. Whatever a source's relevant qualities are, documentation should show them.
- Documentation tells where to view a source. This is handy, if not essential, for researchers wanting to review or reexamine sources. Information about a source's location also helps editors, reviewers, and readers who need or want to see what the researcher saw.

2. BCG, *Genealogy Standards*, 31, for standard 51, "Research scope."
3. Ibid., 6, for standard 3, "[Documentation] Purposes."

- Documentation shows research scope, enabling researchers and their readers to assess how research findings meet the standard of "reasonably exhaustive research."[4]

Genealogy standard 3 says this succinctly:

> Citations, narrative text, and connections between the two enable genealogists and others to *(a)* assess the credibility of each source or image a genealogist used, *(b)* locate that source or image, and *(c)* understand the research scope.[5]

Documentation and citations meet the standard of "complete [and] accurate" when knowledgable readers understand all three points as the researcher intended.[6] In other words, citations and other documentation elements facilitate clear communication between researcher and reader.

"Wrong" documentation

Documentation is "wrong" when it miscommunicates. This causes readers to understand something different from what the researcher intended, or it befuddles them. This can happen when the documentation omits information, or when it provides confusing or misleading information.

Miscommunication most often occurs when a researcher incompletely understands the source's characteristics. People cannot adequately describe something they do not understand. When researchers do not fully understand a source, they struggle to describe—to cite—it. A citation resulting from misunderstanding will fail to describe or communicate clearly.

Faced with citing a source they do not fully understand, researchers might try to follow a model or template. Partial understanding, however, can lead them to blindly follow an example that does not suit their source. Also, a template-creator's sources could have different characteristics or contexts from a researcher's sources, even when they seem similar. Alternatively, no model could exist, or the closest model might not be what the researcher's source requires. Rigidly following models can generate citations that mislead rather than citations that describe sources clearly, completely, and accurately.

Because sources differ, citation content and formats vary with the source. Random variations, however, cause confusion. Readers expect citation differences to reflect source and context variations. When inconsistencies do not reflect different source characteristics or contexts, the citation miscommunicates. Communication breakdown makes documentation "wrong."

4. BCG, *Genealogy Standards*, 1, for the first element of the Genealogical Proof Standard.
5. Ibid., 6, for standard 3 "[Documentation] Purposes." Quoted here with permission from BCG.
6. Ibid., 1, for the second element of the Genealogical Proof Standard.

Effective documentation requires flexibility

Genealogical documentation is hard, but not for the reasons that many family historians think. Some believe that properly documenting their research requires them to memorize and apply dozens or hundreds of rules. Some might believe that each category of source has just one correct citation format and that any deviation is wrong, but they are hard-pressed to figure out what that one format is.

Such beliefs are false. The genealogy field uses three outstanding reference works for its documentation guidelines—*The Chicago Manual of Style, Evidence Explained,* and *Genealogy Standards.*[7] All three are indispensable to serious family historians. *Chicago*'s principles and models focus on published work and archived manuscripts. It emphasizes general documentation principles more than *Evidence Explained,* which adapts *Chicago*'s principles to meet genealogy's stringent standards and extends the coverage to myriad unpublished source types. *Genealogy Standards*—a form of user guide for the genealogy field—provides six broad standards for documentation, as well as standards for genealogical research and writing. With tools like these, no genealogist needs to memorize any guideline.[8]

Although all three books give guidance for documenting research and citing sources, none of them emphasizes ironclad rules. Providing numerous and varying citation models, *The Chicago Manual of Style* and *Evidence Explained* repeatedly encourage researcher flexibility:

> "None of our recommendations are meant to foreclose breaking or bending rules."[9]
>
> "Rules and regulations such as these . . . cannot be endowed with the fixity of rock-ribbed law. They . . . must be applied with a certain degree of elasticity."[10]
>
> "Citation is an art, not a science," and "we are free to improvise."[11]
>
> "Like most of the 885 pages in *Evidence Explained,* the examples in this QuickLesson are 'food for thought,' not rigid rules. They . . . are offered

7. *The Chicago Manual of Style,* 16th ed. (Chicago: University of Chicago Press, 2010). A digital version of the manual is available online. See *The Chicago Manual of Style Online* (http://www.chicagomanualofstyle.org/home.html : 20 February 2017). Also, Elizabeth Shown Mills, *Evidence Explained: Citing History Sources from Artifacts to Cyberspace,* 3rd ed. (Baltimore: Genealogical Publishing, 2015). Also, BCG, *Genealogy Standards.* Besides their book formats, *Evidence Explained* and *Genealogy Standards* are available as Kindle e-books.

8. For a recent statement of the field's adoption of these manuals, and its rejection of other citation style guides, see BCG, *Genealogy Standards,* 8, for standard 6, "[Documentation] Format," and footnote 8.

9. *Chicago Manual of Style,* xii.

10. Ibid., xii–xiii, citing the manual's first edition (1906).

11. Mills, *Evidence Explained,* 41, for sect. 2.1 "Art vs. Science."

> to help you think through what you are using and the manner in which those sources and their quality can be most-clearly identified."[12]

Similarly, *Genealogy Standards* refers to citations as descriptions of four or five "facets of each cited source."[13] The manual's six documentation standards—all broad—do not prescribe a specific citation structure.

The Chicago Manual of Style and *Evidence Explained* provide guidelines and examples, not models and templates for researchers to slavishly copy. Given the great variety of genealogical sources, and variations within them, blindly copying examples is a good way to create citations that do not achieve their purposes of describing clearly and completely. When the model does not fit the source exactly, rigidly following it leads to communication breakdown. Flexibility in crafting citations—like flexibility in speaking and writing—is essential for documentation to communicate clearly and effectively.

Effective documentation requires knowledge

Genealogists use and cite published and unpublished materials of many kinds. They include mostly governmental, religious, and privately-held artifacts, narratives, and records, all unpublished. They also include published articles, books, microfilm, trees, and websites. Dating across centuries, genealogical sources use modern and not-so-modern forms of many languages, even within one community. They appear in archaic and modern varieties of handwritten and printed alphabets.

Especially when compared with other research fields, which use and cite mostly modern published articles and books, the range of genealogical resources is daunting. Their near-infinite variety requires genealogists to develop far greater understanding of source material—and, thus, citation options—than practitioners in most other research fields.

Genealogy's citation guide, *Evidence Explained,* "covers citations for the full array of materials used by genealogists."[14] It helps researchers understand sources and make decisions about citing them. Updated in 2015, *Evidence Explained* provides thousands of sample citations in some nine hundred pages. "QuickCheck Models" appear on easy-to-find gray pages. White pages discuss sources and provide further sample citations. Those discussions could be the planet's single most comprehensive guide to genealogical source materials and their idiosyncrasies.

---

12. Elizabeth Shown Mills, "Options—not 'More Rules to Memorize'," in "QuickLesson 19," *Evidence Explained: Historical Analysis, Citation and Source Usage* (http://www.evidenceexplained.com/content/quicklesson-19-layered-citations-work-layered-clothing : viewed 20 February 2017).
13. BCG, *Genealogy Standards,* 7–8, for standard 5, "Citation elements."
14. Ibid., 8, for standard 6, "[Citation] Format."

Despite the white pages' importance, *Evidence Explained*'s gray pages tempt many researchers to use them exclusively. Those pages seem to provide a quick and easy way to create a citation: researchers can find a seemingly apt model on a gray page and substitute information from the source they want to cite.

Using a model in this way subjects the genealogist to pitfalls. By copying a model or plugging data into a template, researchers bypass in-depth understanding of their sources. They miss opportunities to learn more about people mentioned in those sources. Furthermore, if *Evidence Explained*'s model does not cite a source identical to the researcher's, it could provide elements or details that the researcher's citation does not need. It also could omit those that the researcher's citation does need.

These are not shortcomings of *Evidence Explained*. It could not possibly provide a sample citation for every source a genealogist might consult. *Evidence Explained* also could not provide an in-depth explanation of every source's governance, provenance, and use. Any shortcomings are those of researchers who expect genealogical documentation to be as easy as copying a model. It is far more complex.

Researchers could begin with *Evidence Explained*'s white pages, but it would be just a starting point. Researchers benefit from studying their sources in context, comparing and contrasting them with similar sources. They learn about laws and regulations relevant to their sources. They read archival guides to their research materials. They study offline and online guides to genealogical sources, like those listed in this book's "Reading and Source List 2" (p. 216). Researchers who engage in these activities learn much about their sources—more than one book could possibly tell them. They also will learn more about the people that sources name than they would learn from what sources say.

Researchers can carry only so much of this knowledge in their heads. Experienced researchers study their sources as they encounter them. They also research their sources, learning about how and why they were created, their provenance through the years, and the laws, regulations, and customs governing their creation, use, and preservation. Such learning is a normal part of genealogical research. This book's later chapters will expand these points.

Effective documentation requires decision making

Researchers crafting one genealogy citation might have to make dozens of decisions. They must decide what to document and what to not document, what to include in a citation and what to exclude, and how to sequence the citation elements. They must choose words and formats that clearly communicate their source's qualities and location. Making those decisions requires knowledge of sources and their contexts. It also requires knowledge of citations and the context where their citations will appear.

Most citations vary in format. Citation models, like those in *Evidence Explained*, provide themes for citing different kinds of sources. Researchers create variations of those themes when they adapt models to differing sources. The author of *Evidence Explained* says it well:

> As budding artists, we learn the principles—from color and form to shape and texture. Once we have mastered the basics, we are free to improvise. Through that improvisation, we capture the uniqueness of each subject or setting.[15]

Tailoring a citation model to accurately describe a specific source can require different words, different elements, and different sequences from an apt model, if one exists. The researcher, wanting to communicate clearly, completely, and accurately, chooses carefully and wisely.

People like right-wrong contrasts and having rules to follow. They dislike decision making. Yet, crafting effective documentation requires decisions on a source-by-source and citation-by-citation basis. That decision-making can be hard, but it also offers a measure of creative freedom.

Limits of creativity

Crafting and polishing documentation requires knowledge, flexibility, decision making, and artistic license, but it is not free-form. If documentation were entirely idiosyncratic, no one except perhaps one researcher with a good memory would understand it. Communication would not occur. To facilitate communication between researchers and readers, documentation conventions have evolved over centuries of writing about research. These customs make communication easier and more efficient.

Only one citation convention is inviolable—"Communicate clearly." When following a convention risks impairing communication between researcher and reader, the researcher should improvise. Italicizing publication titles, for example, is one of the longest standing and most consistently applied citation conventions. In some contexts, however, italicizing a publication title can confuse or mislead readers—for example, when the title appears in an italicized context like a pull quote or in a chapter title in another publication's citation. In both cases, using "reverse italics," de-italicizing the title, will minimize confusion.

Citation software

Citation software, including templates in genealogy computer programs, can be time savers and time eaters. Software and templates, of course, do

15. Mills, *Evidence Explained*, 41, for sect. 2.1, "Art vs. Science."

not have the human attributes this chapter describes—flexibility, knowledge, decision-making capability, and creativity. In addition, some software lacks the flexibility for researchers to cite unique or varying sources clearly, completely, and accurately.

This book does not discourage the use of citation software, templates in genealogy programs, and citations written by website designers. Those media provide a convenient way to record and store citation data. They might save time, and their output can be helpful. *The Chicago Manual of Style,* however, warns readers about them:

> The variety of sources . . . nearly always precludes an acceptable result from software alone. Authors are therefore strongly encouraged to review their citations for consistency, accuracy, and completeness.[16]

That review is human intervention. Most machine-produced citations need—at a minimum—tweaking and polishing. This requires the human attributes this chapter describes. The entire book advocates flexibility. It describes the contexts and principles affecting documentation decisions; it provides the knowledge needed to construct, edit, and finalize citations; and it discusses the boundaries of documentation creativity.

This book emphasizes creating citations "from scratch," rather than filling forms. Manually creating citations helps researchers understand their sources, get optimal value from them, understand the people they are researching, and fully document their research. The same knowledge and skills help users of machine-generated citations tweak their citations to meet the field's standards today and for generations to come.

This book

Most of this textbook, like *Evidence Explained,* focuses on citation conventions for genealogists. Both books also encourage flexibility in crafting citations. *Evidence Explained* provides guidance mostly on a source-category basis, and it focuses on capturing information for citations while examining sources.[17] *Mastering Genealogical Documentation* emphasizes the documentation that researchers create in their research plans, working notes, works in progress, and finished products. *Evidence Explained* primarily is a reference book, and *Mastering Genealogical Documentation* is a textbook, not a reference book. Readers will find its guidelines and examples consistent with *Evidence Explained, The Chicago Manual of Style,* and *Genealogy Standards.*

---

16. *Chicago Manual of Style,* 1660, for sect. 14.13, "Source citation software."

17. Mills, "Evidence Explained vs. Traditional Citation Guides," table, *Evidence Explained: Historical Analysis, Citation & Source Usage.* (https://evidenceexplained.com/ : viewed 20 February 2017).

Unlike *The Chicago Manual of Style* and *Evidence Explained, Mastering Genealogical Documentation* is not organized by source categories. Readers would not look here for guidance on how to cite a specific source or kind of source. *Mastering Genealogical Documentation* is organized primarily by general documentation purposes, source and citation contexts, and citation elements and structures. Applying the genealogy field's published standards, it highlights principles of citing sources and documenting family-history research. It emphasizes patterns and logic in genealogical documentation. This book's purpose is to help researchers describe all kinds of genealogical sources clearly, completely, and accurately, including sources for which no model exists.

Documenting genealogical research requires specialized knowledge and skill. Researchers must understand every source they use. Then, considering options for each citation component, they choose the best alternative for the respective source, the genealogical work they are creating, and the people who will use it. Finally, they assemble their choices into a citation and polish it.

Genealogical documentation, like genealogical research, benefits from commonsense reasoning and flexibility more than it does from following rules. The benefits multiply when the researcher understands the underlying rationales. Students using this textbook will learn those principles. They also will learn how to learn about their sources well enough to describe them. The exercises at the end of each chapter will help students gain understanding of how to create conventional citations with artistry, clarity, completeness, conciseness, and competence.

Chapter 1 exercises

1. What is a citation?
2. What are the purposes of citations?
3. Why should genealogists want to document their research?
4. What is the meaningful difference between poor documentation and documentation with poor sources?
5. How does "right" documentation differ from "wrong" documentation?
6. How do researchers learn about their sources?
7. What are the risks of blindly using citation models and templates?
8. What are the genealogy field's primary guides to documentation?
9. What is the major difference between *Mastering Genealogical Documentation* and *Evidence Explained*?

Chapter 2

Noncitation Aspects of Genealogical Documentation

> *"Documentation is fundamental to planning and executing genealogical research, collecting and recording data, and compiling research results."* [1]

Documenting research is more than citing sources. When researchers document, they use citations plus some combination of written explanation, tables, family charts, and images to show their research scope, to establish the bases for their conclusions, and to credit others whose work or property they have used. To accomplish these purposes, documentation has four components:

1. *Sources* and specific information within them comprise researchers' supporting materials.
2. *Citations* describe researchers' sources. They show source qualities and locations. They also show the locations of specific information items within sources. One citation describes one source.
3. *Narrative* in footnotes or elsewhere can discuss sources, their content, and their qualities. Tables and other enhancements also can show the researchers' assessments and interpretations of source content and qualities.
4. *Formatting,* a written work's visual and spatial features, shows connections between researchers' citations and specific statements, images, and conclusions.

None of these components documents by itself. All four work together to support a genealogist's work. Contexts presenting genealogical conclusions need those components' support.

What to document and not to document

Genealogy standard 1 describes what researchers should document:

> Genealogists use citations to identify the sources of all substantive information and images they gather, use, or plan to gather or use, except

1. Board for Certification of Genealogists [BCG], "Standards for Documenting," *Genealogy Standards* (Nashville, Tenn.: Ancestry.com, 2014), 5. Quoted here with BCG's permission.

> sources of "common knowledge" beyond dispute, such as the years of major historical events.[2]

The Chicago Manual of Style gives a similar guideline:

> Ethics, copyright laws, and courtesy to readers require authors to identify the sources of direct quotations or paraphrases and of any facts or opinions not generally known or easily checked.[3]

Under these guidelines, what researchers should document seems clear:

- Sources—records, narratives, artifacts, charts, and images—that the researcher plans to use (documented in research plans) or has consulted (documented in works in progress and final products)
- Sources and information produced by individual people, governments, religious organizations, businesses, and any other entity
- Electronic sources, besides those in print
- Sources of all quotations of others' words
- Sources of all paraphrases, summaries, and translations of someone else's beliefs, ideas, opinions, or words
- Sources of facts, ideas, opinions, and conclusions that do not arise from the researcher's personal beliefs, experiences, observations, and reasoning

Less clear is what researchers need *not* document. "Common knowledge," "generally known," and "easily checked" are subjective concepts. They also are context and experience specific. For example, the five elements of the Genealogy Proof Standard might be common knowledge among genealogists but not among genealogy clients. Similarly, a genealogist might be able to "easily check" a death date, but the deceased person's descendant might find it difficult. An experienced reader of a field's published research will have firmer grasp on what does not need to be documented than someone with less literacy in the field's published research.

Given these ambiguities and variables, deciding what *not* to document requires caution. The consequences of a wrong decision to omit attribution could be severe, whether the decision is conscious or accidental. Where doubt exists, the wisest course is to document. Providing too much documentation always is wiser than providing too little.

When to document

Genealogy standard 4 delineates genealogical contexts requiring documentation:

---

2. BCG, *Genealogy Standards*, 5, for standard 1, "[Documentation] Scope." Quoted here with permission.

3. *The Chicago Manual of Style*, 16th ed. (Chicago: University of Chicago Press, 2010), 655, for sect. 14.1, "The purpose of source citations."

> Genealogists place citations in research plans, logs, notes, works in progress, and similar materials. They use them in classroom and lecture materials. They also use citations, usually in footnotes, in all kinds of finished genealogical-research products, including articles, blogs, books, case studies, charts and forms, educational materials, family histories, other kinds of histories, lineage-society applications, reports, and various kinds of written projects.[4]

Thus, genealogists document when they plan research, as they gather information and evidence from sources, and while they are compiling or writing family histories and charts and trees in any format. They also document as they prepare to teach others about genealogy and in their writings about genealogy. Only genealogical fiction requires no documentation.[5]

Where to document

When genealogists document specific statements, facts, quotations, and the like, they usually cite the sources in reference notes. Reference notes support facts and statements, but they do not intrude into them or intermingle with them.

Reference notes typically are grouped, even in electronic publications. They can run across page bottoms, appear at ends of printed works and electronic files, or follow chapters or sections within a work. As a group, reference notes show the scope of the research supporting the researcher's statements or data. Grouping of reference notes also accommodates readers who want to read the notes separately from the content they document.

Genealogy standard 4, quoted above, says genealogists "use citations, usually in footnotes." Footnotes are reference notes, one or more, at the bottoms of pages. Footnotes appear in most paginated genealogical output, as they do in this book.

The advantage of footnotes, compared to other citation placements, is that they lie near the information they document. After reading a statement, or a series of statements, readers can glance at the bottom of the page to see the researcher's sources and their qualities. They can see a statement and its documentation nearly simultaneously.[6] Readers of footnoted works need not hunt for a reference note, turn pages, or click through links to find it.

Experienced readers of genealogical works prefer footnotes because they are convenient. Inexperienced readers, however, might dislike glancing back and forth between data or narrative and the supporting footnotes. With practice, readers can become adept at reading text and its footnoted

---

4. BCG, *Genealogy Standards*, 6–7, for standard 4, "Citation uses." Quoted here with permission.

5. For a notable example, see Elizabeth Shown Mills, *Isle of Canes: A Novel* (Provo, Utah: Ancestry, 2004).

6. *Chicago Manual of Style*, 673, for sect. 14.39, "Footnotes—pros and cons."

documentation nearly simultaneously. Once accustomed to footnotes, readers miss them in works where reference notes are not at the pages' bottoms.

Genealogists have options besides footnotes for their reference notes' placement. Each option has advantages and disadvantages, but in paginated works footnotes usually have fewer shortcomings than other options.

The options differ by the location of citations within the genealogist's work:

- *At the end of a work.* Citations can appear at the ends of works in progress and finished works, including articles, blog postings, books, class handouts, conference syllabus materials, family trees or charts, or genealogical reports for a client or the researcher's files. The content flows from page to page. This endnote option physically separates citations from the information that they document, requiring readers to turn pages back and forth to see the writer's documentation for specific statements. This can become so irritating that the reader ignores the documentation.[7]
- *Within a work.* Researchers can place citations after a work's chapters, parts, or sections. These citations appear near the respective statements that they document, but the sections separate groups of citations. Readers must turn pages while reading to find the documentation, and they might have difficulty finding the group pertaining to a specific chapter or section. In most cases, finding citations at the end of a work is easier than finding citations among several groupings within it.[8]
- *At the beginning of a work.* Researchers rarely choose this option, which appears in some genealogical reports. At a report's beginning a "sources consulted" reference list shows research scope, but it does not document statements within the report. Item-specific documentation requires researchers who begin a printed report with a source list to also use footnotes or endnotes referring back to listed sources.
- *On or within an image, container, or artifact.* Researchers use this option to document stand-alone items, including digital images, photocopies, and printouts. Genealogy standard 8 recommends that these citations or digital metadata be "firmly attached," and it advises genealogists to "prevent mechanical or digital separation of citations from [what] . . . they document."[9]

Genealogists today rarely use in-text reference notes—placing citations, or abbreviated citations, in parentheses after each documented statement. *The Chicago Manual of Style* calls this system "Author-Date References."[10]

7. In 1996 "requests of readers" led the *National Genealogical Society Quarterly* to drop endnotes in favor of footnotes. See Elizabeth Shown Mills and Gary B. Mills, "Sources: You Can't Miss them Now!" in *National Genealogical Society Quarterly* 84 (March 1996): 3.
8. *Chicago Manual of Style*, 673, for sect. 14.40, "Endnotes—pros and cons."
9. BCG, *Genealogy Standards*, 9, for standard 8, "Separation Safeguards."
10. "Documentation II: Author-Date References," *Chicago Manual of Style*, 785–810.

Other popular style guides, like that of the American Psychological Association(APA), prescribe a similar system.[11]

In-text citations work well when all, or nearly all, the researcher's citations refer to published articles and books. Such sources are fairly homogeneous and have concise citation formats. They abound in most academic and scientific writing about research.

The in-text citation system does not work well in fields like genealogy, although genealogy is scholarly and scientific. Genealogical sources are extraordinarily diverse, making them complicated to describe and cite. When genealogy publications did use in-text citations, a line or two of citation often would follow one sentence after another. The citations were closely tied to statements they documented, but their placement made the content hard to follow. Scholarly genealogical journals dropped in-text citations by the mid-1990s. One editor gave the reason:

> In the interests of making the *Register* easier to read . . . footnotes will replace the references that have hitherto been embedded in the text. Readers will no longer have to tangle with or hurdle over long titles that interfere with the progress of sentences.[12]

Today, genealogy standard 6 categorizes in-text citations among "nonstandard styles for genealogical writing."[13]

Documentation mechanics

Citations support genealogists' proof statements, proof summaries, and proof arguments—points along a continuum of complexity. Proof statements are statements of fact or specific data items, like dates, places, and relationships. They require no explanation because their documentation makes their validity obvious. Genealogists assemble proof statements into proof summaries, which are lists or narratives stating support for a conclusion. Genealogists assemble proof statements and proof summaries into proof arguments defending solutions to complex genealogical problems.[14]

Proof statements, summaries, and arguments can stand alone, or they can be components of a longer work, like a blog, case study, family history, online tree, or output of a genealogy computer program. Genealogists document their work, whether it is a specific item, like an image or quotation a researcher has used, research notes, or a short or long narrative.

11. *Publication Manual of the American Psychological Association*, 6th ed. (Washington, D.C.: American Psychological Association, 2010).

12. Jane Fletcher Fiske, "An Editorial," *The New England Historical and Genealogical* Register 148 (January 1994): 5.

13. BCG, *Genealogy Standards*, 8, for standard 6, "Format," and footnote 8.

14. For distinctions among proof statements, proof summaries, and proof arguments, see ibid., 32–33 (for standard 53, "Selection of appropriate options)" and 72–73 (glossary definitions). Also, Thomas W. Jones, *Mastering Genealogical Proof* (Arlington, Va.: National Genealogical Society, 2013), 84–89.

That documentation can stand alone, or it can work in tandem with other documentation. Stand-alone and in-tandem documentation frequently are mixed in the same genealogical work.

Stand-alone documentation usually applies to data items (like dates, places, and relationships), images (like personal photocopies or maps in a narrative), and a researcher's paraphrases, quotations, and statements of fact, including proof statements. One citation can document the item or statement. If the footnote contains more than one citation, each citation documents the statement or data item. Rather than complementing each other, such citations corroborate each another.

Citations also can document in tandem. The researcher makes a statement or provides a data item that no source documents in its entirety—for example, one source might document someone's month of birth and another might complement it by documenting the year. Within the work or the accompanying footnote, the researcher describes how each source supports the statement.

Documentation occurs in tandem most often in genealogy products, or sections in the form of proof summaries and arguments. Both forms present a series of points leading to and supporting a conclusion. Authors of proof arguments group some or all the points into proof summaries, which lead to and support a further conclusion. Citations in proof summaries and arguments document each point, perhaps some alone and others in tandem. All the citations together, along with the author's reasoning, support the conclusion. No citation alone supports a conclusion from a proof summary or argument, but each plays a role by documenting and strengthening points that support and lead to the conclusion.

Documenting digitally

The placement of reference notes can be a nonissue in contexts with hyperlinks. Writers in digital environments have the same options for placing reference notes as writers in print environments. Hyperlinks, however, give further options.

Hyperlinks in digital works minimize the shortcomings of citation placement at the end of a work or grouped within it. Readers of electronic files with hyperlinks need not glance at the bottom of a screen or scroll down to see the writer's support. Instead, they can click or touch a link or move a mouse or pointer over a number or symbol to reveal the reference note supporting a statement or fact. When they click again or move their pointer elsewhere, they return to the body of the work. Linking to reference notes within a document is preferable to linking externally, because changes in an external target's location or digital address can require ongoing maintenance of the links.

Linking to images of sources can interest and help readers, but images without citations are problematic. Citations distill a source's attributes into a clear and concise description that readers can digest and assess. An image with no citation requires readers to repeat the researcher's struggle with reading old handwriting, analyzing the source, and understanding its meaning, contexts, and provenance. Also, hyperlinks to external images will fail after the image's location or digital address changes.

Reference notes and their numbers

Reference notes are numbered in the order a researcher uses them to document a genealogical work. Genealogical and word-processing programs can do this numbering automatically. The numbers help researchers and readers locate the documentation for any fact or statement. Whether a genealogical work is electronic or printed, reference-note numbers signal the presence of documentation. The absence of reference-note numbers can signal the opposite.

In-text note numbers

Citations can appear at the bottoms of pages or the end of a work, interspersed between chapters or sections, or as hyperlinks. Regardless, reference-note numbers connect specific statements to most, if not all, of their respective documentation. Software typically superscripts in-text note numbers. They usually appear in an upright regular typeface, like the number at the end of this paragraph. In the reference note itself—like the ones at the bottom of this page—the note numbers "are normally full size, not raised, and followed by a period."[15]

Readers use the numbers to identify the researcher's sources and footnoted comments about them. Note-number 15 at the end of the preceding paragraph, for example, refers to footnote 15, at the bottom of this page. That reference note cites the source and information item documenting the paragraph's last two sentences, including the quotation.

Each reference-note number in a researcher's work refers to one corresponding reference note. The numbers do not refer to citations, sources, or other repeated content within a reference note. For this reason, each note number appears only once in a section of a genealogical work—even if the same source or citation is used more than once in that section.[16]

In this book, for example, each chapter's footnotes start with note 1, and the ensuing footnotes are numbered consecutively throughout the chapter. This chapter contains twenty-five footnotes citing information from eight sources. The same numbering pattern appears in each chapter's narrative

15. *Chicago Manual of Style*, 665, for sect. 14.19, "Numbers in text versus numbers in notes."

16. Ibid., 667, for sect. 14.23, "Multiple citations and multiple references."

and footnotes. Software's insert-reference feature ensures that reference-note numbers remain sequential when an author rearranges the text containing them. When preparing a final product, authors and editors work to ensure that corresponding numbers in text and footnotes appear on the same page. Software does that task imperfectly.

Articles, blogs, chapters, and reports typically use one set of numbers. Authors may number reference notes consecutively throughout a book or electronic publication, but only if it contains no chapters or other divisions.[17]

Note-number placement

The placement of reference-note numbers in a genealogical work helps genealogical writers meet genealogy standard 2:

> The specificity of these connections [between citations and statements, facts, images, and conclusions] leaves no question about the basis or source of each statement, fact, image, or conclusion.[18]

In family trees and charts, researchers attach note numbers to data items. In narratives, however, they have options for note-number placement.

Following standard 2, some genealogists might place note numbers midsentence immediately after the words the corresponding citation documents. Midsentence note numbers interfere with readability, however, and they can distract readers. Note numbers in narratives typically appear at the ends of sentences and clauses. They usually follow all punctuation.[19]

In most cases midsentence note numbers are avoidable. Writers often can place the number at the end of a sentence and still meet standard 2. In other instances they can reword the sentence to avoid placing a number midsentence.

End-of-sentence placement is needed especially when one sentence states several facts, each with its own source, like this example:

> Thomas was in enlistee Nathaniel's birth county—Herkimer—in 1813, when Nathaniel probably was a young child.[20]

This sentence refers to three facts—Thomas's appearance in Herkimer County in 1813, Nathaniel's birth there, and Nathaniel's age in 1813. If the author had not previously documented any of those facts, he might put

17. *Chicago Manual of Style,* 666, for sect. 14.20, "Sequencing of note numbers and symbols."

18. BCG, *Genealogy Standards,* 6, for standard 2, "Specificity."

19. *Chicago Manual of Style,* 666, for sect. 14.21, "Placement of note number." For further guidance, see Elizabeth Shown Mills *Evidence Explained,* 3rd ed. (Baltimore: Genealogical Publishing, 2015), 63–64, for sect. 2.42, "Reference Numbers, Placement of."

20. Example from Thomas W. Jones, "Too Few Sources to Solve a Family Mystery? Some Greenfields in Central and Western New York," *National Genealogical Society Quarterly* 103 (June 2015): 85–103, at p. 93.

three note numbers in that sentence, but where would they go? Putting a number after "Thomas was," "Herkimer," and "child" would be inelegant and unnecessary, if not disruptive and potentially confusing. A single footnote with its number at the end of the sentence would be clearer and cleaner. With finessing, it would meet genealogy standard 2. The single footnote would contain three citations, each describing a source:

- One citation would describe the record of Thomas's witnessing an inventory of a Herkimer County estate in 1813.
- Another citation would describe Nathaniel's enlistment record, which gives his county of birth.
- A third citation would describe the 1830 census giving evidence of Nathaniel's year of birth.

If readers would understand which source documents which fact, the single footnote, containing three citations, would meet genealogy standard 2. More likely, however, readers would not be able to easily match each fact to its source, or vice versa. In that case, a few words added to each citation makes those connections clear:

> For Thomas in 1813, see [citation to estate inventory]. For Nathaniel's birthplace, see [citation to enlistment record]. For his age, see [citation to 1830 census].

Placing a note number within a sentence sometimes works better than placing it at the sentence's end, but midsentence placement usually is unnecessary. A midsentence note number appears about once in every twenty to thirty pages or so in the *National Genealogical Society Quarterly*.

Reference-note content

Researchers and compilers of documented family histories and genealogical articles and charts physically separate the family story or chart from most of its documentation. They also make the family content distinct from the documentation content. The family portion consists of data items or narrative paragraphs, perhaps enhanced with charts, figures, lists, and tables. The documentation portion consists of reference notes containing citations that support the family portion and any discussion of the cited sources. When the family portion excessively mentions sources, or the reference notes discuss family members, the work loses its structure. Readers will find it difficult to follow.

Reference notes can contain discussion, besides citations, but discussion usually is restricted to information about a source cited in the respective reference note. Reference notes containing discussion, with or without citations, are discursive notes. Discussion in reference notes usually takes the form of grammatical sentences. Researchers usually do not attach the sentences to the citations with a semicolon or other punctuation.

Documented family histories, reports, and trees are most effective when they relegate citations and most discussions of sources to the documentation section. They reserve all other discussion for the family data or narrative. Any discussion of sources in the story should be essential to the story.

Before placing discussion unrelated to a source in a reference note, researchers should consider integrating that narrative into the family information. If the discussion seems too tangential or awkward to integrate, the writer should consider deleting it or using it elsewhere, rather than putting the material in a reference note. Effective compilers minimize discussions in reference notes, when those discussions do not pertain to cited sources.[21]

No guideline says a reference note should contain only one citation or describe only one source. Reference notes often contain two or more citations.[22] Researchers sometimes string a series of citations together, joining them with semicolons. That practice, however, makes citations hard to distinguish and reference notes difficult to digest.

Separating citations with periods, like sentences, helps readers see citations separately. Even more effective is the practice of adding a word or phrase to the fronts of citations after the first one in a reference note. Compare these two examples, both citing the same two sources:

> Norwich, town records 2:134, "Josiah Burton Died March 19th. 1814 aged – 72 years," recorded on 1 January 1844; "Died," *Spooner's Vermont Journal*, 4 April 1814, page 3, col. 4.
>
> Norwich, town records 2:134, "Josiah Burton Died March 19th. 1814 aged – 72 years," recorded on 1 January 1844. Also, "Died," *Spooner's Vermont Journal*, 4 April 1814, page 3, col. 4.

Setting each citation into its own sentence and adding a short word contribute a bit more clarity.

Tables, figures, and other enhancements

Genealogists documenting their work use reference-note numbers, but they often use reference-note *letters* in accompanying charts, figures, tables, and other enhancements. There, documentation begins with reference-note letter *a* and continues alphabetically. The lettered reference notes will appear at the bottom of the enhancement. Depending on the enhancement's size and placement, its reference notes might or might not appear at the bottom of a page.[23] For an example, see figure 1.

Lettering notes in tables and figures avoids confusion between documentation for a the main body of a work and documentation for its enhancements.

21. *Chicago Manual of Style*, 682, for sect. 14.51, "Avoiding overlong notes."

22. Ibid., 682–83, for sect. 14.52, "Several citations in one note."

23. Ibid., 148, for sect. 3.77, "Notes to specific parts of a table." The manual says "letters are generally preferred" in tables, but it allows symbols and numbers.

Figure 1

Example of a Figure with Reference-Note Letters

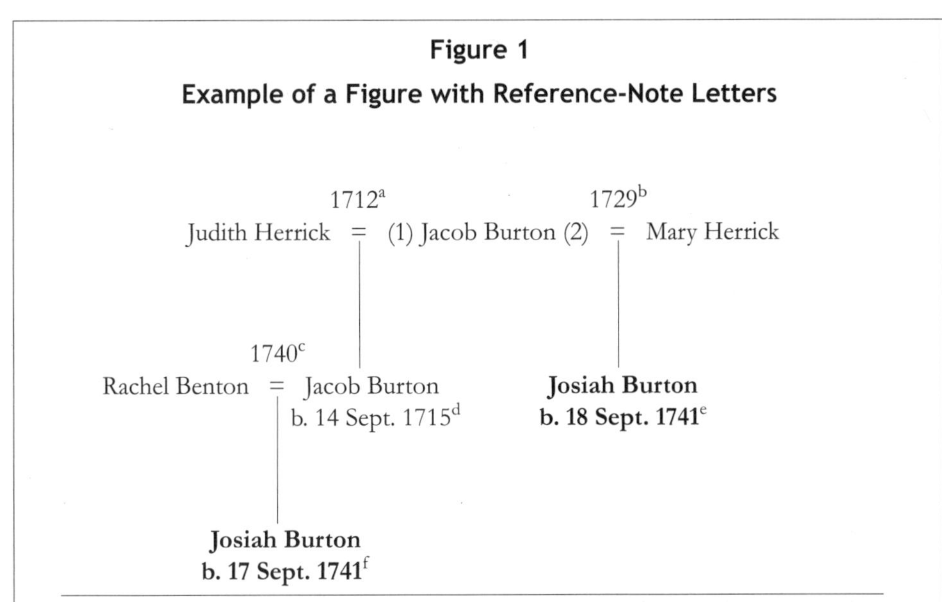

a. Preston, Conn., Births Marriage Death Record 1:89, Jacob Burton-Judith Herrick marriage, 11 June 1712; Town Clerk, Preston; microfilm,1311,194, Family History Library (FHL), Salt Lake City.

b. Preston, Births Marriage Death Record 1:89, Jacob Burton-Mary Herrick marriage, 25 August 1729. Also North Church (Preston), records 1:254, Jacob Burton-Mary Herrick marriage, [day unspecified] August 1729; Connecticut State Library (CSL), Hartford; FHL microfilm 4,374.

c. Tolland, Conn., vital records 1:133, Burton-Benton marriage, 6 November 1740; Town Clerk, Tolland; FHL microfilm 1,376,026, item 1. Also, Coventry, Conn., Miscellaneous Town Records 1692–1840, p. 408, "Burtin"-Benton marriage, [no day] November 1740; CSL; FHL microfilm 1,376,123, item 2.

d. Preston, Births Marriage Death Record 1:89, birth of Jacob Burton, son of Jacob and Judith, 15 September 1715.

e. Preston, Births Marriage Death Record 1:89, birth of Josiah Burton, son of Jacob and Mary, 18 September 1741.

f. Coventry, Conn., Miscellaneous Town Records 1692–1840, p. 408, birth of Josiah "Burtin," son of Jacob and Rachel, 17 September 1741; CSL; FHL microfilm 1,376,123, item 2. This Josiah, the subject of this article, married, first, Mary Leonard and, second, Abigail Colburn. See North Church, records 1:261, Burton-Leonard marriage, 10 April 1765. Also, Sharon, Vt., Vital Records 1:27, Burton-Colburn marriage, 23 June 1785; Town Hall, Sharon; FHL microfilm 28,906.

Note: From Thomas W. Jones, "'In the County of Cumberland and the Province of New York': Clarifying Josiah Burton's Identity, Relationships, and Activities," *New York Genealogical and Biographical Record* 147 (April 2016): 88.

Lettering also facilitates creating the enhancements as files separate from the file containing the work's body and documentation.[24] An author or editor often does not know exactly where a table or figure will appear until late in the production process—problematic timing for numbering and citation changes.

Some documented tables and figures do not need reference-note letters, numbers, or symbols to show their documentation. For examples, see appendix A.

With phrases like "See table 1," the author's work refers readers to a chart, figure, or table.[25] Such references to documented enhancements can substitute for documentation within a work's family portion.

24. Ibid., 63, for sect. 2.23, "Separate files for illustrations, captions, and tables."
25. Ibid. 64, for sect. 2.27, "Text references and callouts to tables and illustrations."

Conclusion

In this chapter you learned how citations and explanations help document genealogical writing, what to document and what not to document, and when and where to document. You also learned that documentation is a general concept describing how genealogists show that their source material supports their conclusions.

The biggest part of documentation is source citation. Each citation describes a source clearly, completely, accurately, and as concisely as possible. Creating such a description requires decisions based on documentation principles. The remainder of this book will discuss those principles and decisions, the options that researchers have, and source features that help researchers choose the best option for each source, context, and audience.

Chapter 2 exercises

10. What are the four components of genealogical documentation?
11. What should genealogists document?
12. In what kinds of written works do genealogists provide documentation?
13. Why do experienced genealogical readers prefer footnotes over endnotes?
14. When are endnotes a good choice?
15. In the Greenfield article in this book's appendix A, find examples of citations documenting the following:
    a. Specific data items (dates, places, and relationships)
    b. Statements of fact (more than dates, places, and relationships)
    c. Quotations
    d. Paraphrases
    e. Elements within a table or figure
16. Dissect footnote 1 in the Greenfield article:
    a. How many citations does the footnote contain?
    b. What devices did the researcher use for separating the citations?
    c. Which respective data item or statement of fact does each citation document?
    d. What noncitation components does this footnote contain?
    e. What are those components' roles within the footnote?

17. Dissect Greenfield footnote 58 like you dissected footnote 1:
    a. How many citations does the footnote contain?
    b. What devices did the researcher use for separating the citations?
    c. Which respective data item or statement of fact does each citation document?
    d. What noncitation components does this footnote contain?
    e. What are those components' roles within the footnote?
18. Why is note-number 58 in the Greenfield article's narrative not at the end of the sentence?
19. How many citations does Greenfield footnote 31 contain? How are they separated? What noncitation content does this footnote contain? Why might the author have chosen to include that content in the citation?
20. In the Greenfield article's narrative portion, what examples do you find of mentioning or discussing sources? Why are these discussions not in the footnotes?
21. Which sentences in the two following paragraphs need documenting?

    Three years later Mary married the widower Fred Guker. Marinda might have brought them together. The marriage might never have occurred had Mary not walked to Red Bud through the snow with two children.

    Mary and her brother, Jacob, apparently never reconciled. In 1921 some fifty guests attended the fiftieth-anniversary celebration of Jacob and his wife, Lena. Coming from St. Clair County and St. Louis, most were Lena's relatives. Not one represented Jacob's side of the family.

22. Below are two undocumented paragraphs. Within them, place note numbers 1–7 at the ends of sentences, or groups of sentences, requiring documentation. Below the two paragraphs are seven citations in random order. Number them to correspond with the seven note numbers you placed in the two paragraphs.

    In 1767 Archibald Greenfield bequeathed to "my grandson James Greenfield the Son of Starr Archibald Greenfield a Silver Spoon." This grandson's birth, on 7 January 1752[/3], was recorded at Lyme. The date is consistent with the calculated birth year of James Greenfield who died at the town of Russia, New York, on 15 January 1812 "in the 59 year of his age." Nonetheless, these men of one name and similar age are distinguishable.

    James Greenfield, "aged 92 years, a soldier of the Revolution," died at Lyme on 26 November 1843. Living there in 1832 at age eighty, he applied for a pension. Citing Lyme's town records, he said he had lived there since his birth, on 7 January 1752. He recalled serving five terms during the war, totaling twenty-nine months while based at Lyme. Other Lyme-native veterans confirmed that James was born there and "ever since lived there." He received the pension in Connecticut through September 1843.

? "U.S., Revolutionary War Pensioners, 1801–1815, 1818–1872," *Ancestry* (http://ancestry.com/search/db.aspx?dbid=1116 : viewed 20 February 2017) > T718: 1818–1872 > 08: Revolutionary War, 1831–1848 > image 90, Treasury Department pension payment ledger for 1831–48, p. 99, James Greenfield.

? "U.S., Revolutionary War Pension and Bounty-Land Warrant Application Files, 1800–1900," *Ancestry* (http://search.ancestry.com/search/db.aspx?dbid=1995 : viewed 20 February 2017) > G > Graham, Joseph–Gregory, Joseph > Greenelsh, Edward–Greenslit, John > image 131, James Greenfield, claim for a pension, 6 August 1832, in James Greenfield pension application file S13192.

? "U.S., Revolutionary War Pension and Bounty-Land Warrant Application Files, 1800–1900," *Ancestry* (http://search.ancestry.com/search/db.aspx?dbid=1995 : viewed 20 February 2017) > G > Graham, Joseph–Gregory, Joseph > Greenelsh, Edward–Greenslit, John > image 147, Seth Miner, deposition, 15 December 1832; image 149, John Mather, deposition, 7 December 1832; and image 151, John Lay, deposition, 8 December 1832, in James Greenfield pension application file S13192.

? "Died," *People's Advocate* (New London, Conn.), 13 December 1843, page 3, col. 3.

? Essex Co., Mass., Probate Records (Old Series Books) 45, fols. 255–56, will of Archibald Greenfield, 1 November 1767, proved on 4 September 1769; Registry of Probate, Salem, Mass.; microfilm 875,028, Family History Library, Salt Lake City.

? *Find A Grave* (http://www.findagrave.com/cgi-bin/fg.cgi : viewed 20 February 2017), memorial 20981767, for James Greenfield gravestone (Century Cemetery, Russia, N.Y.), digital image, 13 May 2011, by Steve Staruch.

? Lyme, Conn., vital records 1:65, James Greenfield birth, 7 January 1752[/3]; Town Clerk, Lyme; microfilm 1,311,111, Family History Library, Salt Lake City.

Chapter 3

Citation Settings, Forms, and Shortcuts

> *"Genealogists use humanities-style citations (notes plus bibliography), a style designed for heavy users of manuscript materials."*[1]

> *"Once they cite a source completely, genealogists may use a short-form citation or 'ibid.,' when appropriate, to refer back to a complete citation documenting the source of a statement, fact, image, or conclusion in the same finished product."*[2]

A citation is a description of a source. One citation describes one source. Genealogists' citations appear in three settings: in reference notes, as source labels, and in reference lists. Reference notes and source labels have similar purposes, and their citations use a similar form. Reference lists have a distinctly different purpose, and their citations use a different form.

Citation forms and their differences have evolved over centuries of use in academia, publishing, and writing. *The Chicago Manual of Style* spells them out, and *Evidence Explained* applies them to its explanations and examples. These citation forms and differences appear in documented genealogical works, online and off.

Reference notes

Individual reference-note citations document specific facts, images, statements, and conclusions. They also credit people and entities whose words, ideas, or intellectual or physical property a researcher has used. To serve these purposes, reference-note citations not only describe sources, they usually point to specific information within sources. Together, reference notes show the scope of research supporting a conclusion.

Genealogical and word-processing software arranges reference notes in the sequence that researchers use them to document a narrative or other portrayal of facts or data. Software also numbers the reference notes in that sequence. Reference-note citations do not appear alphabetically,

1. Board for Certification of Genealogists [BCG], *Genealogy Standards* (Nashville, Tenn.: Ancestry.com, 2014), 8, for standard 6, "Format." Quoted here with permission.
2. Ibid., 9, standard 7, for "Shortcuts." Quoted here with permission.

categorically, or chronologically. Therefore, personal names appear in reference-note citations in the order they appear in the cited sources. Thus, most Western names appear given-name first in reference-note citations.

Researchers format reference-note citations like sentences with no verbs. Each citation begins with a capital letter and ends with a period. Otherwise, only proper nouns and titles are capitalized. Like sentences, reference-note citations contain no internal periods, except those after abbreviations and within URLs. A period with a space after it signifies the end of either an abbreviation or a citation. Also, as in standard English-language sentences, commas in citations separate items in series, and semicolons group segments and separate those groups. Reference-note citations appear in footnotes throughout this book and the article in appendix A.

Genealogists use reference-note citations when they want to document specific statements or facts or to give credit to others. These citations are common in articles, books, and digital publications, including family histories.

Shortened reference-note citations

When researchers cite a source in a reference note for the first time in an article, chapter, or other genealogy work, they cite the source in full. In other words, they fully identify the cited source's qualities and location. They provide the full citation only once in that work, however. This book follows that practice within each chapter.

After a source's first citation, researchers cite a shortened version of the prior citation. They do this even if information-item specifics differ. See table 1 for an example.

Shortened reference-note citations use abbreviated titles, author's surnames only, and cities or counties without states when the state is unambiguous. Shortened citations omit information about the publication, repository, and medium through which the researcher viewed the source. They leave enough information to *(a)* trigger the reader's memory of the prior full reference-note citation and *(b)* point to the source's information

Table 1

Full and Shortened Reference-Note Citations to Different Parts of One Source

13. Norwich, Vt., town records 1:271, Jacob Burton death, 12 July 1798; Town Hall, Norwich, Vt.

26. Norwich, town records 1:3, town meeting minutes, 14 March 1769, Josiah Burton.

29. Norwich, town records 1:264, Zerviah Burton birth, 7 September 1767.

Table 2

Full and Shortened Reference-Note Citations to the Same Source

FULL CITATION	SHORTENED CITATION
1. William Adams Simonds, *Edison: His Life, His Work, His Genius* (New York: Bobbs-Merrill, 1937), 337.	11. Simonds, *Edison*, 410.
2. "Brevities," *Quincy Daily Whig* (Quincy, Ill.), 5 October 1882, page 8, col. 4.	12. "Brevities," 5 October 1882, page 8, col. 4.
3. "Katruska Family Tree," *Ancestry* (http://trees.ancestry.com/tree/2384160 : viewed 20 February 2017).	13. "Katruska Family Tree."
4. Anne Bruner Eales and Robert M. Kvasnicka, *Guide to Genealogical Research in the National Archives of the United States* (Washington, D.C.: NARA, 2000), 26.	14. Eales and Kvasnicka, *Guide to Genealogical Research*, 197.
5. Jeanne Larzalere Bloom, CG, untitled report to Thomas W. Jones, 16 October 2011; files of Thomas W. Jones, Fairfax, Va.	15. Bloom, report to Jones.
6. J. J. Moran and Sons [undertakers], untitled mortuary record card, case no. 7927, 9 January 1940, George W. Edison; Moran and Goebel Funeral Home, Decatur, Ill.	16. Moran and Sons, untitled mortuary record card, no. 7927, George W. Edison.
7. "Family Record," printed form containing handwritten entries on both sides, likely 1920 or later and from a family Bible; photocopy from Howard Elting, Clinton, Utah; files of Thomas W. Jones, Fairfax, Va.	17. "Family Record," photocopy from Elting.

item documenting the statement or fact to which the shortened citation is attached. Table 2 shows examples. *The Chicago Manual of Style* and *Evidence Explained* provide further information about shortened citations.[3]

Reference-note citation shortcuts

Reference notes can be long. In heavily documented works like family histories, they also can be numerous. Too many footnotes can overwhelm a page, obscuring the researcher's work. To avoid these issues, researchers have options, besides shortened citations, for reducing the space that

3. *The Chicago Manual of Style*, 16th ed. (Chicago: University of Chicago Press, 2010), 667–69, for sects. 14.24–14.28 under "Shortened Citations." Also, Elizabeth Shown Mills *Evidence Explained*, 3rd ed. (Baltimore: Genealogical Publishing, 2015), 64–66, for sects. 2.43–2.45, "Short Citations."

footnotes might occupy. These options apply to both full and shortened reference-note citations.

Abbreviating in running text is uncommon, but in footnotes researchers abbreviate extensively. Initialisms (formed from a phrase, like *GPS* for *Genealogical Proof Standard*) and acronyms (pronounceable initialisms, like *NARA*) do not contain a period. Letters in initialisms can be all capitalized (like *BCG*) or mixed (like *ICAPGen*). Abbreviations typically end with a period. Researchers capitalize the first letter of abbreviations representing proper nouns (like *Va.* for *Virginia*). Otherwise, they lowercase abbreviations that are not initialisms or acronyms (like *vol.* for *volume*).[4]

This book, for example, uses the abbreviation *s.v.* in its citations to dictionary entries. Those letters abbreviate the Latin words *sub verbo*, meaning *under the word*. Since most people do not look up words in a dictionary or encyclopedia by the page number, researchers can use the *s.v.* abbreviation (not italicized in citations) to refer readers to a specific alphabetized entry.[5]

Many abbreviations are standard, like those for states and months. *The Chicago Manual of Style* (*CMOS*) shows standard abbreviations of months and traditional and modern United States Postal Service (USPS) abbreviations of states.[6] *CMOS* recommends putting periods after abbreviations of months and to use modern USPS state abbreviations (initialisms, like *NY*). Many researchers and editors, however, still prefer traditional USPS abbreviations for states (like *N.Y.*) *CMOS* provides an entire chapter on abbreviating, including standard abbreviations for Canadian provinces and foreign countries.[7]

Most readers will understand the word a standard abbreviation represents. For lists of standard abbreviations for citations, see *The Chicago Manual of Style* and *Evidence Explained*.[8] Without ever spelling out the abbreviated word, researchers can use familiar abbreviations in footnotes without confusing readers.

Researchers also can abbreviate words that appear repeatedly in their citations—for example, *enumeration district*, *family*, and *population schedule* in census citations. If the full word is transparent to the readership—*Township* abbreviated as *Twp.*, for example—the researcher can use the abbreviation

---

4. For these definitions and more on abbreviations, acronyms, initialisms, and other shortened forms of words, see *Chicago Manual of Style*, 487–529, for chapter 10, "Abbreviations."

5. Ibid., 755, for sect. 14.247, "Dictionaries and encyclopedias." *S.v.* is italicized here because of the convention of italicizing references to a word rather than to its meaning. See ibid., 366, for sect. 7.58, "Words and phrases used as words."

6. Ibid., 503, for sect. 10.40, "Months," and 498, for sect. 10.28, "US states and territories."

7. Ibid., 487–529, for chapter 10, "Abbreviations," including 499, for sect. 10.29, "Canadian provinces and territories," and 500, for sects. 10.32–10.33, "Names of Countries."

8. Ibid., 504–10, for sect. 10.43, "Scholarly Abbreviations." Also, Mills, *Evidence Explained*, 72, for sect. 2.56, "Abbreviations, Standard."

unannounced. If readers might not understand a fairly obvious abbreviation, the researcher can announce it subtly by spelling out the word at its first appearance and abbreviating it thereafter. Researchers also can introduce an abbreviation by putting it in parentheses after the word or phrase—for example, *population schedule (pop. sch.)*—and using the abbreviation thereafter.

Researchers may devise initialisms for publishers and repositories that they frequently cite, even when those publishers and repositories do not use them. Whether the initialism is well known or devised, the researcher spells out the name and announces the initialism in parentheses before using the initialism alone. The third paragraph before this one contains two examples of announcing an initialism—for *CMOS* and *USPS*.

Abridging inclusive numbers—ranges of pages, years, or other numbers—also helps researchers shorten footnotes. The second number often can be shortened without causing confusion—for example, *pp. 127–31* and *1801–6*. *The Chicago Manual of Style* gives specific guidelines and options.[9]

Researchers also can shorten footnotes by avoiding repetition and omitting words. If, for example, a source's corporate author and publisher, or its corporate author and title, are the same, the corporate name need not appear in the citation's author field. The first citation in this chapter's footnote 3 shows such an omission. The book's author and publisher (University of Chicago Press) are the same.

Genealogists also can omit generic words and abbreviations, like *Company*, *Ltd.*, and *Publishers*, from publisher names in citations. The second citation in this chapter's footnote 3, for example, omits *Company* from *Genealogical Publishing Company*.

When citing a series of sources—for example, a series of city directories or tax rolls—researchers can save space by combining the citations. This avoids repeating information that appears in each item in the series. This example combines into one citation nine sequential tax lists in separate booklets:

> Virginia Auditor of Public Accounts, Land Tax Records, Cumberland Co., Va., Holman's dist.; 1787, p. 18; 1788, p. 18; 1789, p. 15; 1790, p. 17; 1791, p. 20; 1792, p. 24; 1793, p. 23; 1794, p. 6; and 1795, p. 22; all for John Woodson pltr.; Land Tax microfilm 82, Library of Virginia, Richmond.[10]

Ibid., an abbreviation of a Latin word meaning *in the same place*, also helps shorten footnotes. It is best used only in final or near-final drafts. When consecutive citations are partially or fully identical in one or more reference

9. Ibid., 482–84, for sects. 9.58–9.63, "Inclusive Numbers."

10. Adapted from B. Darrell Jackson, "Which John Woodson Served in the 4th Virginia Regiment of Foot, 1776–1778?" *National Genealogical Society Quarterly* 104 (June 2016): 125–38, for p. 129, footnote 16.

notes, *ibid.* replaces the duplicate information after the first citation. *Ibid.* is not italicized in citations.

Researchers should not use *ibid.* when the preceding reference note contains more than one citation, because readers might not see at a glance which citation the *ibid.* refers to. Researchers who use more than one sequential *ibid.* to document statements in a paragraph could have inserted unnecessary in-text note numbers. One note number at or near the end of the paragraph often would suffice.

This chapter's footnotes 5–9 use *ibid.* in citations. *The Chicago Manual of Style* and *Evidence Explained* provide further detail about this convention.[11]

Modern genealogists rarely, if ever, use cross-references in reference notes because they inconvenience readers by requiring them to turn back and forth to locate the referenced citation. Such cross-references include abbreviated Latin words like *infra* (referring to a citation below), *loc. cit.* or *op. cit.* (referring to a previous citation but not the one immediately above), and *supra* (also referring to a prior citation). Genealogists instead use shortened citations with enough information to remind readers of the prior full citation.

Inconsistency is a risk when using abbreviations, inclusive numbers, *ibid.*, and other acceptable conventions for shortening reference notes. For example, spelling out a U.S. state in one citation and abbreviating it or another state in another citation when referencing a location is an inconsistency. Using a traditional abbreviation in one citation and a modern abbreviation in another also is an inconsistency. Researchers should avoid such inconsistencies because they can impair communication between themselves and their readers by signaling meaningful differences where none exist.

Consistently abbreviating, however, does not mean abbreviating a word every time it appears. Different sources call for different decisions. A researcher would not abbreviate *Virginia* in *Library of Virginia,* for example, if the library spells out the word in its name. Differences exist for reasons; inconsistencies are accidental or random. Common sense helps researchers avoid meaningless inconsistencies while shortening their footnotes as much as possible.

Source labels

Genealogists sometimes need to label a stand-alone source or container outside a broader context. These include family artifacts, documents, and photographs. They also include individual photocopies, photographs, or printouts, or source abstracts or transcriptions.

11. *Chicago Manual of Style*, 669, for sect. 14.29, "'Ibid.'" Also, Mills, *Evidence Explained*, 415, for "use of ibid."

Genealogists affix physical or virtual labels to these items or to their containers. Per genealogy standard 8, the labels are "firmly attached."[12] Ideally these labels appear on the front of the copy, image, or container. Copies and images can be digitally shrunk to create space for the label. A label on the front reduces the possibility of loss during subsequent copying of fronts only.

Source-label citations use a sentence-style format resembling that of full reference-note citations. Most source-label citations, however, do not point to a specific item within the source, unless doing so is meaningful. *Evidence Explained* provides further information about source labels.[13]

Reference lists

Unlike reference *notes*, reference *lists*—also called bibliographies and source lists—do not document specific statements, facts, or conclusions. Instead, they show groups of sources. These include lists of sources a researcher consulted, lists of references related to a topic, and reading lists. Because their purpose is to show a group of sources, reference-*list* citations—unlike reference-*note* citations—usually do not point to specific pages or items.

Genealogists most often use reference lists in teaching materials, like class handouts, conference syllabus materials, research guides, and textbooks. Authors of family histories and reports might provide one or more source lists showing the scope of research underlying the work.

Journal articles rarely include reference lists. Reference notes in articles provide full details and show the underlying research scope. Articles can, however, include a reference list when an article's readers would benefit.

Researchers use paragraph-style formatting for reference-list citations. Citation elements begin with capital letters and end with periods, like sentences within a paragraph. The usual rules of English-language capitalization apply. For examples, see table 3 and this book's "Reading and Source List."

Reference-list citations, like paragraphs, usually are indented. The usual indent for a reference-list citation is a hanging indent, also called "flush-and-hang style." The citation's first line begins at the left margin and its remaining lines are indented.[14] This format makes the citation's first word prominent, a convenience when scanning an alphabetized list. Researchers and teachers may annotate reference lists. Annotations might, for example, summarize a source's focus or recommend it to readers for a specific reason.

12. BCG, *Genealogy Standards*, 9, for standard 8, "Separation Safeguards."
13. Mills, *Evidence Explained*, 67, for sect. 2.46, "Source Labels."
14. *Chicago Manual of* Style, 896–97, s.v. "flush-and-hang style" and "hanging indention."

Table 3

Reference-List Citations

Connecticut. Coventry. Miscellaneous Town Records, 1692–1840. Connecticut State Library, Hartford.

———. Tolland. Vital records. Town Clerk's Office, Tolland. Microfilm 1,376,026. Family History Library, Salt Lake City.

Find A Grave. Http://www.Findagrave.com : 2017.

Gilmore, George C. *New Hampshire Men at Bunker Hill: June 17, 1775*. Manchester, N.H.: John B. Clarke, 1899.

———. *The Last Fourteen Survivors of the Revolutionary Army*. Concord, N.H.: C. Evans, 1898.

Latham, Charles, Jr., ed. *The Life of Asa Burton Written by Himself*. Thetford, Vt.: First Congregational Church, 1973.

Reference lists most often appear in a single alphabetical sequence, based on the citation's first word. Researchers making this choice will cite the author's surname first. If a cited work has multiple authors, only the first author's name is cited surname first. *The Chicago Manual of Style* discusses alphabetization of complex surnames and foreign names.[15]

Rather than repeating an author's or creator's name in an alphabetically arranged list, researchers replace subsequent occurrences of the name with a three-em dash. They insert the em character or symbol (—) three times in place of the author's name.[16] This convention helps readers scan a list to locate a specific author or reference-list citation. Table 3 and this book's "Reading and Source List" show examples.

Researchers may group and sequence a reference list, if grouping makes it easier to use. They also can group reference lists to show what they want their lists to show. In other words, the list's sequence and any groupings within the list help readers and serve the researcher's purpose in providing the list. Possibilities include grouping by source type (books, journals, manuscripts, and the like), by repository (archives, courthouses, libraries, for example), geographic areas (cities, counties, regions, states, for example), or by surnames or families. Researchers also may rearrange elements within a reference-list citation to enable the citation's first word to group related citations together in an alphabetized list (by state, for example).

15. *Chicago Manual of* Style, 836–41, for sects. 16.71–16.87 under "Personal Names" and "Foreign Personal Names."

16. Ibid., 691–93, for sects. 14.63–14.67, under "The 3-Em Dash for Repeated Names in a Bibliography." Also, Mills, *Evidence Explained*, 325–26, for "Formatting note—Three-em dash."

Reference lists in digital and print publications usually are unnumbered. They can be numbered, however. Speakers and teachers, for example, may more easily refer to a specific reference-list citation by number than by the author's surname or the citation's first word.

Three citation forms

By subtracting words and sections and with some rearranging, researchers can use full reference-note citations to create shortened reference-note citations and reference-list citations, each for its respective setting. See table 4 for a comparison of the three forms' content, formatting, and uses. See table 5 for examples.

Conclusion

This chapter describes three citation forms for documenting genealogical works. Most of the remainder of *Mastering Genealogical Documentation* will emphasize one form—full reference-note citations. It will explain their elements and nuances, options for constructing them, and rationales for those options. Readers should be able to apply that information with no difficulty to shortened citations and reference-list citations.

Table 4

Comparison of Genealogy Citation Forms

<table>
<tr><th colspan="2">REFERENCE-NOTE CITATIONS</th><th rowspan="2">REFERENCE-LIST CITATIONS</th></tr>
<tr><th>FULL</th><th>SHORTENED</th></tr>
<tr><td>Used once, for first citation to a source</td><td>Used one or more times after first citation</td><td>Appear at end of book or handout</td></tr>
<tr><td colspan="2">Common in articles, books, and reports</td><td>Common in books and handouts</td></tr>
<tr><td colspan="2">Document statements and facts by pointing to specific information</td><td>Show research scope; do not point to specific information</td></tr>
<tr><td colspan="2">Sentence format</td><td>Paragraph format</td></tr>
<tr><td>Punctuated mostly with commas and semicolons</td><td>Punctuated mostly with commas</td><td>Punctuated mostly with periods</td></tr>
<tr><td>Contain all required elements</td><td>Trigger recall of prior long-form citation</td><td>Contain all elements except item of interest</td></tr>
<tr><td colspan="2">Sequenced as needed</td><td>Alphabetized; can be categorized</td></tr>
<tr><td>Author's given-name first</td><td>Author's surname only</td><td>First author's surname first</td></tr>
</table>

Table 5

Three Citation Forms for Two Sources

Source One

FULL REFERENCE-NOTE CITATION:

1. Barbara B. Ferris, *Connecticut Divorces: Superior Court Records for the Counties of New London, Tolland, and Windham; 1719–1910* (Bowie, Md.: Heritage, 2000), 431.

SHORTENED REFERENCE-NOTE CITATION:

11. Ferris, *Connecticut Divorces*, 208.

REFERENCE-LIST CITATION:

Ferris, Barbara B. *Connecticut Divorces: Superior Court Records for the Counties of New London, Tolland, and Windham; 1719–1910.* Bowie, Md.: Heritage, 2000.

Source Two

FULL REFERENCE-NOTE CITATION:

2. St. Clair Co., Ill., marriage licenses, numerically arranged, no. 4859, Brickey-Carr, 22 May 1856; Illinois Regional Archive, Carbondale; FHL microfilm 2,169,443.

SHORTENED REFERENCE-NOTE CITATION:

22. St. Clair Co., marriage licenses, no. 1605, Carr-Potter, 20 January 1846; FHL microfilm 2,169,354.

REFERENCE-LIST CITATION:

Illinois. St. Clair Co. Marriage licenses. Illinois Regional Archive, Carbondale. Microfilms 2,169,147–2,195,251, Family History Library, Salt Lake City.

Chapter 3 exercises

23. In the Greenfield article in this book's appendix A, footnote 1 announces three acronyms or initialisms and uses other abbreviations. What are the acronyms and initialisms, and what do all the abbreviations stand for?

24. In the Greenfield article, compare the second citation in footnote 18 (the atlas) with the last citation in footnote 35. What similarities and differences do you see between the full and the shortened reference-note citations?

25. Why is the last citation in Greenfield footnote 34 a shortened citation and not a full citation?

26. In the Greenfield article, compare the last citation in footnote 4 with the first citation in footnote 55. These full and shortened citations to the same source document different statements. What similarities and differences do you see between those citations?

27. Greenfield footnote 11 contains two *ibid*s. What does each of them refer to? What does each of them replace?

28. The first citation in footnote 22 omits the author's or creator's name. What is it, and why is it omitted?

29. Using this book's tables 1–5 as guides, convert each full reference-note citation below to *(a)* a shortened reference-note citation and *(b)* a reference-list citation:

    Jane Fletcher Fiske, transcr., *Rhode Island General Court of Trials: 1671–1704* (Boxford, Mass.: privately printed, 1998), 223.

    Gerald W. McFarland, *A Scattered People: An American Family Moves West* (New York: Pantheon, 1985), 26.

    "Died," *People's Advocate* (New London, Conn.), 13 December 1843, page 3, col. 3.

    Marya Myers and Donald W. James Jr., "The Family of William^{1} and Susannah (Martin) James of Portsmouth and Newport, Rhode Island: New Discoveries," *New England Historical and Genealogical Register* 147 (October 1993): 334, footnote 5.

    First Church of Christ (New London, Conn.), records 1:157, James Greenfield, 5 November 1738; Connecticut State Library (CSL); microfilm 1,011,944, Family History Library (FHL), Salt Lake City.

    Lyme, Conn., Land Records 6:70, Roulin-"Greenfeald" marriage, 1 May 1736, recorded on 17 December 1736; Town Clerk, Lyme; FHL microfilm 4,680.

    1790 U.S. census, Albany Co., N.Y., "Stephen Town," pp. 281 (Raymond Greenfield), 285 (Bethuel Greenfield), and 287 (Archibald Greenfield); microfilm M637, roll 6, National Archives and Records Administration (NARA).

    Find A Grave (http://www.findagrave.com/cgi-bin/fg.cgi : viewed 20 February 2017), memorial 20981767, for James Greenfield gravestone (Century Cemetery, Russia, N.Y.), digital image, 13 May 2011, by Steve Staruch.

    "Massachusetts, Town Clerk, Vital and Town Records, 1626–2001," *FamilySearch* (https://familysearch.org/search/collection/2061550 : 20 February 2017) > Essex > Salem > Marriages 1695–1815 vol 4 > image 25, Salem, Book of Marriages 4:44, Greenfield-Bacon, 31 May 1733, return "By the Rev^{d}. M^{r}. Wm Jenison."

Chapter 4

Assembling Components into Clear Citations

> *"Complete citations use a standard format to describe at least four facets of each cited source. . . . Complete citations to information items documenting specific statements, facts, images, and conclusions (reference-note citations) describe a fifth facet."*[1]

Genealogy standard 5, partially quoted above, says that reference-*list* citations describe at least four aspects of sources. It also says that full reference-*note* citations—those documenting specific statements, facts, images, and conclusions—describe those four aspects and one more. Subsequent chapters of *Mastering Genealogical Documentation* discuss each aspect, respectively, and its implications for documentation. This chapter focuses on identifying these five components in sources and options for sequencing them in citations.

Researching sources

Prerequisite to citing a source is understanding it. Besides researching people, genealogists research sources, going beyond what sources say about people the genealogists are investigating. Genealogists learn as much as they can about their sources. That knowledge increases their knowledge of the people they seek to understand. Source knowledge helps advance genealogical research and achieve its goals. Studying sources also helps genealogists craft citations that clearly, completely, and accurately describe the materials they consult.

Understanding sources includes knowing exactly what each source is, including its context and components. Understanding also includes knowing who created each source, when and why they created it, who provided the relevant information the source contains, and when and why they provided it. Gaining those understandings also means learning the source's purpose and history, including its location today. Genealogists gain this knowledge from *(a)* information within sources and *(b)* information written about sources. That information is beyond this book's scope. For guides to American genealogical sources, see this book's reading and source list 2.

---

1. Board for Certification of Genealogists [BCG], *Genealogy Standards* (Nashville, Tenn.: Ancestry.com, 2014), 7, for standard 5, "Citation Elements." Quoted here with permission.

Generic citations, provided by image publishers and research guides, are unlikely to provide all the needed information. Publisher-created citations can contain errors, contradictions, and omissions. Even when a generic citation is complete and accurate, it might not aptly describe exactly what the researcher is using or help them and their readers assess it.

Creators of generic citations often did not see what a researcher saw, and the researcher did not see the source cited as a generic model. Worse, simply copying someone else's citation or model without understanding their own sources costs researchers exactly what they seek. They bypass opportunities to understand the people they are researching.

Genealogists gather some source information before they examine sources. As they develop research plans, they examine library catalogs, archival finding aids, and other material—much of it online today. For example, Googling a National Archives microfilm publication number can lead to a descriptive pamphlet written by an archivist about the publication's content. The pamphlet will describe the microfilmed records and their purpose and history. It also will identify each microfilm roll's contents. That information, of course, is valid also for online images made from the microfilm. Gathering source information during the research-planning phase gives at least a partial understanding of a source's nature, purpose, and history.

Genealogists also develop their understanding of sources while examining them. At a minimum, this will reveal something the source says directly, implies, or does not say relevant to a research project. Examining a record, or an image of a record, can show who provided relevant information, when, and why.

Upon finding relevant information, the researcher determines how to describe its location within the source. That description often is a more direct path than the researcher's search. For a simple example, the researcher might consult a book's index to locate information within the book. The citation, however, shows the information's page number; it does not mention the index. Users of the citation can turn directly to the page, bypassing the index and any other stages of the original writer's research. Researchers usually can cite sources with stable numbering—pages, volumes, files, microfilm frames, and most online images, for example—more easily than unnumbered material. Citations usually describe the location of specific information, not how the researcher found it.

Source knowledge also comes from examining the context of relevant information. An item of interest can differ from surrounding items in a meaningful way, but researchers who do not examine them will miss that meaning. Researchers also might find useful information about a source at the beginning of a publication or series of records, or at its end, but they must look for it. Clicking on a link to an image of interest and looking at nothing else in the source can block researchers from meeting their goals. It also can prevent them from creating useful citations.

During research-planning and data collection phases, researchers try to gather all the information they need for citing their sources. Their research plans will include partial citations. After they examine a source, their research notes will include a complete citation.

Researchers write citations in research notes for their personal use. Those citations, often less structured and containing more information than citations in finished products, might include unhelpful details that later can be discarded. Research notes, however, should include all the detail needed to create a polished citation. When they do not, the researcher must revisit the source, information about the source, or both.

What to exclude from citations

Researchers studying sources learn much about them, much more than they need to structure a citation. They also learn much about the people they are researching. Some researchers succumb to the temptation to include many of those details in the citation. That is a mistake.

Citations differ from abstracts. Abstracts summarize a source's contents. They tell what is *within* a source. In contrast, citations tell *about* a source. A citation to a marriage record, for example, would give the names of the parties (perhaps only their surnames), and the date of marriage because this information helps readers understand what the source is and where to find the specific entry. A researcher would be unlikely to have a similarly valid reason to cite the names of the officiant and witnesses, the parties' residences, and their parents's names. Such details likely would appear in a researcher's family data or narrative.

Specifically, citations tell what a source is, its qualities as a container of genealogical evidence, where it can be consulted, and the location of specific information in it. Over-burdening a citation with details about the people it mentions makes it hard for the citation to meet its purposes.

A source can appear in several places or media. The same images of an online book, for example, can be in many libraries and one or more websites, enabling readers to view it wherever they have online access. Records in an archive or courthouse can be imaged on FamilySearch microfilm, which could be digitized and published online. When readers have many options for where to view a source, citing all the options can add useless information to a citation.

If a source is published, whether online or not, by definition it is available to the public in many places. Citations need show only that the source is published. (They do this by italicizing the source title and providing information about its publisher and place of publication.)

Expanding a citation to a publication with information specifying viewing locations and media is not customary, but it also is not wrong. Researchers can add information about media and viewing to basic citations. They do so in contexts like working notes, where additions could be useful, and finished products where readers would use the added information.

Citations in many genealogy works are long and numerous. To prevent footnotes from overwhelming the works that they document, genealogists strive for conciseness. They use the shortcuts that chapter 3 describes to make their citations as compact as possible. They avoid adding information to citations "just because it is there." By default, their citations answer genealogy standard 5's citation questions. Any additions meet the researcher's and the citation's purposes.

Identifying citation components

Genealogy standard 5 says reference-note citations describe five aspects of each cited source. Those aspects are answers to questions about each source a genealogist examines:

> *Who*—the person, agency, business, government, office, or religious body that authored, created, edited, produced, or was responsible for the source; or, if identified, the source's informant
>
> *What*—the source's title or name; if it is untitled, a clear item-specific description
>
> *When*—the date the source was created, published, last modified, or accessed; in some cases, if the source is unpublished, the date of the event it reports
>
> *Where[is]*—if unpublished, the source's physical location; if a published book, CD-ROM, microfilm, or newspaper, its place of publication; if an online resource, a stable URL . . . .
>
> *Wherein*—the specific location within the source where the information item can be found [*or where the researcher looked for relevant information but did not find it*], for example, page, image, or sequence number; or—if the source is unpublished—its box number, folder or collection name, or similar identifying information.[2]

Answers to these five questions provide raw material for citations. Researchers need those answers to craft citations that will be clear, complete, and accurate. Each answer becomes a component of the citation.

The second answer—to *What*—is the most important answer of the five. That answer, clearly and unambiguously, should leave no doubt in a reader's mind about what specific source and what kind of source the citation

---

2. BCG, *Genealogy Standards*, 7–8, for standard 5, "Citation Elements." Quoted here with permission. *Wherein* is shorthand for *Where within the source*. The coined word *Whereis*, which does not appear in *Genealogy Standards*, is the present author's shorthand for *Where is the source*.

describes. Standard 5 lists *What* second because its answer often is a citation's second element. Researchers must answer the *What* question first, however.

The answer to *What*, like the answers to all five questions, should be precise. The answer should describe exactly what the researcher consulted. Many genealogical sources have parts, groupings, and levels, complicating the formulation of a precise answer to the *What* question.

A probate file illustrates some complications of precisely answering the *What* question. Court officials gather papers related to a deceased person's estate, bundle them together, label the bundle, and file it in the courthouse with other bundles of probate papers. The papers in a bundle might include a will signed by a testator, a petition by a potential administrator, an inventory signed by assessors, and bills, receipts, and other petitions, most created by different people. The files could have been moved to a state archive or "loaned" to a local genealogical society. FamilySearch might have microfilmed the file. It also might have published online images of the microfilm and numbered the digital images.

After consulting the file, answering *What* can be complicated. The researcher's answer might be the entire file. More likely, the researcher is citing the source of a specific fact or quotation. If so, the answer will refer to a specific document within the file. If the researcher viewed the file online, that answer can include the name of the website—a publication—and an image number.

The "correct" answer to *What* is whatever the researcher used as documentation. For example, the dates a will was made and presented in court could support a researcher statement about when the testator died. In that case, the answer to *What* is the will. The citation would show whether the researcher used a published online image of the will or the manuscript filed in an archive or courthouse. When researchers understand each source, its context, and how they use it, that understanding helps them formulate clear and precise answers to the *What* question.

The *Who* question appears first in the list because its answer usually is a citation's first element. The answer to that question, however, depends on the answer to *What*, the second question. The source that is the researcher's focus also is the citation's focus.

For example, a different person might have created each document in a probate file. The answer to *Who* depends on what the researcher uses to document a statement or quotation. If the entire file provides the documentation, the answer to *Who* is the file's creator. That usually would be the county or probate district—a government—that created the file, not a specific court or person working for that government. If a record within the file provides the documentation, the answer to *Who* will be the name of the government or private person who created the record. If the researcher viewed an image of the file, *Who* could have a third answer—the name of the the entity that made the image.

Answers to question 3—*When*—are a bit easier to determine because most dates are obvious. Again, the answer to question 2—*What*—helps answer question 3. The papers in a file will bear different dates. If one paper documents the researcher's work, the date of that paper answers *When*. A digital image of that paper would have been created and viewed on later dates. Citing one or both those dates, as well as the paper's date, can add meaning and usefulness to the citation.

Question 4—*Whereis*—refers to where a source is today. If the source is a printed or online publication—available in many places—the answer refers to the publisher and its locale. If the source is unpublished, the answer is its location, usually an office, city, and state or province.

For example, if the researcher used a paper in an unpublished probate file, the answer to *Whereis* would be the office holding the file. That office might be part of the government that created the file, if it had not been moved elsewhere.

If a source was moved elsewhere, the answer to *Who* would name the record's original creator and the answer to *Whereis* would identify its present-day custodian. These answers also would reflect jurisdiction name and boundary changes. For example, a Virginia county could have created a probate file in the 1850s, which today resides in a West Virginia courthouse. The answer to *Who* is an extinct Virginia county government, and the answer to *Whereis* is a present-day West Virginia repository.

The answer to *Wherein* tells readers exactly where within the source is the item of information that the researcher used. If the source is paginated or chronologically arranged, that answer can be as simple as a page number or date—perhaps, but not necessarily, the same date that answers the *When* question.

Other answers to *Wherein* can be more complicated than a page or image number. When the researcher in person has viewed a paper in a file, the answer identifies the bundle, the box of filed bundles, and the office, city, and state or province. If the file is in a large archive, the answer to *Wherein* also can include names or numbers of some combination of record series, collection, and group. A numbered online image can be part of several nested levels of larger and larger image groupings. To make the image number useful, the answer to *Wherein* must identify each level.

Researchers can bypass question 5—*Wherein*—only when the entire source, the answer to *What,* documents the researcher's statement, quotation, or image. This might be the case, for example, if the source is a photograph or an isolated record, like a privately held passport or a certified typescript of an official record.

Once researchers have answered the five questions, they form the answers into a citation, as they might form phrases into a sentence. As in writing a sentence, the researcher has options for sequencing the segments. They choose the option that is easiest to read and seems to communicate most clearly.

Sequencing the components

Conventions exist for sequencing citation elements. Researchers, however, have the final decision. They have more flexibility with the placement of some components than with others. Ultimately, however, communicating clearly is more important than following any model or convention.

Sequencing by answer

Citations usually begin by answering genealogy standard 5's *Who* question and then its *What* question. Citations to publications often continue by answering *Whereis, When,* and *Wherein,* in that order. Citations to unpublished records most often answer *Whereis* last: *Who, What, When, Wherein,* and *Whereis.* Often those sequences can be improved. Variations are common, because researchers want their citations to be as clear as they can make them. See table 6 for examples and variants.

Researchers may omit the answer to *Who* when the same name also answers another question. For example, the name of a corporate author or creator, answering *Who,* can also be the source title or publisher's name.

If two or more people had different roles in producing a publication—author and editor—for example, the researcher can place one name before the answer to *What* and the other after it, like this citation fragment:

> Birdie Monk Holsclaw, "Proofreading and Indexing," *Professional Genealogy,* ed. Elizabeth Shown Mills.

The abbreviation *ed.* in this context means *edited by*. This sequencing shows that Holsclaw authored the chapter and Mills edited the book. If Mills's name and role preceded the book title—the typical place for the answer to *Who*—readers might not know whether Mills edited just the Holsclaw chapter or the entire book.

Mills's "Velcro principle"

One principle guiding sequencing of citation elements is Elizabeth Shown Mills's "Velcro Principle": "Don't separate what ought to be stuck

Table 6

Common Sequences of Answers to Citation Questions about Published and Unpublished Records

	PUBLISHED RECORDS
Who?	June A. James, translator
What?	*Early Church Records: St. John Lutheran Church; Red Bud, Illinois; 1855–1937*, 2 vols.
Whereis?	(Chester, Ill.: Randolph County Genealogical Society,
When?	2002),
Wherein?	1:78.
Who?	[Find A Grave (purposely omitted from the citation)]
What?	*Find A Grave*
Whereis?	(http://www.findagrave.com/cgi-bin/fg.cgi :
When?	viewed 20 February 2017),
Wherein?	memorial 114788840, Cordelia Ziegler gravestone (Our Redeemer Cemetery, St. Louis, Mo.), digital image, 2 August 2013, by Susan Ing.
Who?	[National Archives]
What?	*Passengers Lists of Vessels Arriving at New York, 1820–97*, microfilm publication M237, 95 rolls
Whereis?	(Washington, D.C.: National Archives,
When?	1962),
Wherein?	roll 74, chronologically arranged, 15 July 1848, ship *Bowditch* manifest.
	UNPUBLISHED RECORDS
Who?	St. Charles Co., Mo.,
What?	Deed Record U:
Wherein?	219–20, Berdolt to Gross,
When?	11 December 1848;
Whereis?	Register of Deeds, St. Charles, Mo.
Who?	Fred D. Guker and Fern M. Jehling,
What?	"Guckers," typescript,
When?	about 1968,
Wherein?	p. 3;
Whereis?	author's files, Monroe, N.Y.

together."[3] A date, for example (likely the answer to *When)* will follow—will be "stuck" to—the citation item that it dates.

The citation at the bottom of this page provides an example. Its website access date follows—is attached to—the website address. Similarly, the posting number and date follow the description of the posting. In this example Mills's Velcro principle trumps the *Who-What-When-Whereis-Wherein* sequence. The citation contains all five answers, but carefully arranging them avoids confusion about what each date refers to.

Other parts of citations besides dates—numbers of pages or images, or parts of books or files—usually should be attached to what they pertain to. Separating parts that "belong to" each other creates confusion about, for example, what a date or number refers to, or which part of a multilevel source a description portrays.

Exceptions to Mills's Velcro principle are allowable, of course. They should occur when they improve a citation's clarity and communication between researcher and reader.

The "Russian dolls" principle

Many sources involve a series of groups nested inside increasingly larger groups, similar to a set of Russian dolls. The nested groups' relationships can be clearest in a citation when the researcher lists them in sequence. That sequence might be specific-to-general or general-to-specific.

Citing a probate file shows the issues and illustrates the principle. The specific item could be an estate inventory. A clear, complete, and accurate answer to *Wherein* requires the researcher to identify the bundle of papers containing the inventory, the box or file containing that bundle, the collection of boxes or files, the office housing that collection, that office's city, and that city's state or province. The researcher could list those levels in a specific-to-general sequence, like a collection of Russian dolls, each nested inside the next larger. The citation would begin with the estate inventory, including its creators and date. It would proceed through increasingly larger levels and end with the name of the state or province. This specific-to-general example cites a dated paper in a file in a titled box at a courthouse:

> Frederick von Berum, report of sale, filed 6 May 1863; in Monroe Co., Ill., Bernum vs. Gross file; box A-4, Foreclosures 1859–1860; Circuit Court, Waterloo, Ill.

In other cases the opposite sequence—general-to-specific—might be clearest. For example, if the probate file is published online within a collection of probate files, the image of the estate inventory usually will have an image

3. Elizabeth Shown Mills, *Evidence Explained: Historical Analysis, Citation & Source Usage* (http://www.evidenceexplained.com/content/find-grave : viewed 20 February 2017), for "Find A Grave" discussion posting no. 29, 10 July 2013.

number. That number will be nested in a grouping of numbered images, which could be nested in a larger grouping, and so forth, leading back to the entire titled publication—a website. This example shows a general-to-specific sequence from a website through a numbered image:

> *FamilySearch* (https://familysearch.org/search/film/007607650 : viewed 20 February 2017), digital film no. 007607650, image 283, for [description of what image shows].

Answering *What*—telling readers what a source is—near a citation's beginning can help them understand the entire citation, especially if the source is a publication. The opposite, identifying a published source near the end of a citation, often is not a good idea. Beginning a citation with a page or image number also could cause confusion.

Descriptions of online sources with nested levels can be clear when the citations start with the collection and website titles (the broad level) and work down through increasingly specific levels to the image. Greater-than signs (>) connecting the levels show the declining greater-than relationship. This example ends with the image number and a description of the specific record that the image shows:

> "Missouri, County Marriage, Naturalization, and Court Records, 1800–1991," *FamilySearch* (https://familysearch.org/search/collection/2060668 : viewed 20 February 2017) > St. Louis > Marriage licenses 1913–1914 no 179693–187612 > image 403, for [description of what image shows].

No rule tells researchers when to use specific-to-general or general-to-specific "Russian Dolls" sequencing. Sources, their locations, and citation contexts vary. The researcher crafts the citation that best fits the circumstances, most clearly communicates the source's qualities to others, and tells them where to find it. In some cases, either choice works.

A bad choice, however, might be to mix levels of specificity, requiring readers to figure out the answers to the *Whereis* and *Wherein* questions. This is problematic when several levels are involved, like these:

> book or journal title
>
> series within the title
>
> sets of volumes within the series
>
> a numbered volume within the set
>
> a separately paginated issue or part within the volume
>
> a page within that issue or part

When, however, the number of levels is few—for example, just a book in a series—sequencing by levels of specificity is unnecessary. In all their citations, researchers arrange citation components in the way that provides the most clarity and is least likely to confuse readers.

Further guidance

Later chapters of *Mastering Genealogical Documentation* will discuss in depth the answers to the citation questions given by genealogy standard 5: *Who* (chapter 8), *What* (chapters 6–7), *When* (chapter 9), *Wherein* (chapters 10–11), and *Whereis* (chapter 12). In all cases, researchers—using reasoning and striving to communicate clearly—choose the most effective option.

Chapter 4 exercises

30. What questions must genealogy citations answer?
31. How does learning about sources advance genealogical research goals?
32. For each of the groups a–d of unsequenced citation elements complete tasks 1 and 2:

Task 1: Identify the citation question that each element answers.

Task 2: Using standard sequencing, Mills's "Velcro principle," the "Russian dolls principle," or a combination, sequence each group for a clear citation.

Example of completed task 1 (identify citation questions) :

- notes in author's files *(Whereis)*
- 11 July 1971 *(When)*
- interview by author *(What)*
- Susan K. Guker *(Who)*
- page 5 *(Wherein)*

Example of completed task 2 (rearrange for a citation):

- Susan K. Guker
- interview by author
- 11 July 1971
- page 5
- notes in author's files

Group *a* for reader tasks 1 and 2:

- Standard Certificate of Death no. 38796
- State of Illinois
- Department of Health, Springfield, Ill.
- Mary Margaretta Guker
- (1934)

Group *b* for reader tasks 1 and 2:

- searched on 20 February 2017
- search for "Jac* Gros*" in Illinois and Missouri
- http://search.ancestry.com/search/db.aspx?dbid=6742
- "1880 United States Federal Census," *Ancestry*

Group *c* for reader tasks 1 and 2:

- 313–14
- "Biographical," in *Portrait and Biographical Record of Randolph, Jackson, Perry, and Monroe Counties, Illinois*
- 1894
- Chicago: Biographical Publishing

Group *d* for reader tasks 1 and 2:

- Belleville, Ill.
- page 3, col. 1
- "Jacob Gross and Wife Wed Half Century: Freeburg Couple celebrate Golden Wedding at Singer Hall in that City Sunday," *Belleville News-Democrat*
- 1 August 1921

Chapter 5

Capitalization, Italics, Punctuation, and Other Citation Subtleties

> *"Genealogists' capitalization, grammar, spelling, punctuation, and word usage follow widely accepted conventions and rules."*[1]

Except for omitting verbs, writing citations is like writing sentences. Anyone who can capitalize and punctuate a sentence can capitalize and punctuate a citation. With few exceptions, their conventions are identical.

Conventional capitalization, punctuation, and similar features of writing and citing, though nearly unnoticeable, add meanings that readers understand. When used unconventionally, however, they can introduce confusion. The citation could fail in its purpose to describe clearly.

Citations are researcher creations. Like writers composing sentences, researchers choose their citations' capitalization and punctuation.[2] Readers understand that citations—except portions within quotation marks—reflect researcher decisions, not necessarily those of a cited source's author, editor, or publisher.

Citations follow common principles of capitalization and punctuation, regardless of what the source shows. Deviations from conventional capitalization, punctuation, and other writing subtleties are acceptable, but only when they improve a citation's clarity. When a deviation is accidental or random two problems arise: *(a)* part of the citation's meaning could change, and *(b)* readers could pay more attention to the unconventional capitalization or punctuation than the citation's content. To help genealogists avoid those issues, this chapter reviews—in alphabetical order—capitalization, punctuation, and other "spit and polish" conventions that appear in genealogy citations in American contexts.

---

1. Board for Certification of Genealogists [BCG], *Genealogy Standards* (Nashville, Tenn.: Ancestry.com, 2014), 36, for standard 63, "Technically correct writing."

2. *The Chicago Manual of Style*, 16th ed. (Chicago: University of Chicago Press, 2015), 621–22, for sect. 13.7, "Permissible changes to punctuation, capitalization, and spelling." Also, Elizabeth Shown Mills, *Evidence Explained*, 3rd ed. (Baltimore: Genealogical Publishing, 2010), 75–76, for "Corrections," and 90, for sect. 2.76, "Titles."

Apostrophes (')

By adding an apostrophe and the letter *s* to all singular nouns and plural nouns not ending in *s,* writers make those words possessive. This includes capitalized nouns and singular nouns ending with *s*:

children's

Tom's

Jones's

census's

Apostrophes added to plural nouns ending in *s* make them possessive:

the records' provenance

the counties' border

Apostrophe-plus-*s* similarly shows attribution except when the noun is capitalized:

genealogists' associations

Department of Veterans Affairs.[3]

Brackets [ ]

Square brackets surrounding a word or phrase show readers that the researcher has inserted the bracketed word or phrase within or after a title or a quotation. The brackets signal to readers that the bracketed word, phrase, or punctuation does not appear in the source:

"E. K. Stone jr. [and] Mrs. Cora E. Stone"

p. [8B], dwell. 206

dwell./fam. 131, Geo[.] W. Edison household

Commissioners Return [allowances to unpaid creditors], 24 Nov. 1821

Bracketed insertions in genealogy citations include the genealogist's translations of foreign-language titles:

Actes de Mariage pour 1845 [Register of marriages in 1845]

Brackets in citations and running text mark a parenthetical expression within a parenthetical expression:

(*Springfield, Missouri, 1913 Directory* [missing title page], pp. 175 and 645.)

A common usage of square brackets in citations and elsewhere is with the Latin word *sic,* the Latin word for *thus*:

"Injured by Falling Icycle [*sic*]," *Daily Inter Ocean,* Chicago. . . .

---

3. For these guidelines and more on possessives, see "Possessives," *Chicago Manual of Style,* 353-58, sects. 7.15–7.28.

Sic refers to an unusual word, spelling, illogical statement, or other anomaly in a quotation or title. Researchers place *sic* in square brackets immediately after the anomaly. The insertion assures readers that the anomaly does appear in the source and is not a researcher misreading or typing error. Researchers do not use *sic* to point out all spelling or wording anomalies. They use it only when readers might not understand that the original writer created the anomaly.[4]

Capitalization

Researchers capitalize the first word of a citation and all the names within it. This seems like a simple guideline, but ambiguities and complexities abound for capitalizing words that are neither personal names nor titles. Two general guidelines are helpful:

- Words used generically should not be capitalized. For example, *a county clerk* or *clerk of Knox County* would not be capitalized—they refer to any clerk. *Clerk of Knox County Jane Doe,* however, would be capitalized. In that example, it is a formal title.
- *Chicago* style, which the genealogy field has adopted, recommends a "down style" for capitalization. Genealogists, therefore, capitalize words only where capitalization is unambiguously required.[5]

For words with questionable capitalization, the researcher's first recourse should be a good recent dictionary, like *Merriam-Webster's Collegiate Dictionary,* 11th edition.[6] A dictionary entry is capitalized only when the word requires capitalization. Secondarily, *The Chicago Manual of Style* offers a chapter focused almost entirely on capitalization issues and nuances, including historical terms, names of offices and organizations, religious and military names and terms, and scientific terminology.[7]

American researchers conventionally use headline style in citations to capitalize titles cited with no quotation marks. In most cases, *headline style* means capitalizing a title's first and last words and all other words except articles (*a, an,* and *the*), four conjunctions (*and, but, nor,* and *or*), and most prepositions. *The Chicago Manual of Style* discusses variations and exceptions.[8]

Researchers often leave titles between quotation marks unchanged. They also can leave other titles unchanged, if the original capitalization does

4. Ibid., 642, for sect. 13.59, "'Sic.'"

5. Ibid., 387, for sect. 8.1, "Chicago's preference for the 'down' style."

6. *Merriam-Webster's Collegiate Dictionary,* 11th ed. (Springfield, Mass.: Merriam-Webster, 2004); also available as a Kindle e-book. For a recommendation of that dictionary and the dictionary from which it is abridged, see *Chicago Manual of Style,* 172, for sect. 2.51, "Choosing a dictionary and other reference works."

7. "Names and Terms," *Chicago Manual of Style,* 385–462.

8. Ibid., 448–51, for sects. 8.157, "Principles of headline-style capitalization," 8.158, "Examples of headline-style capitalization," 8.159, "Hyphenated compounds in headline-style titles," and 8.162, under "Subtitle capitalization."

not interfere with meaning or readability. All-caps capitalization, however, interferes with readability; titles in all-caps should be cited headline style.

Headline-style capitalization guidelines apply to titles and subtitles of publications or groups or parts of publications:

> *Annual Directory of the City of Wichita*
>
> "Freeburg Couple Celebrate Golden Wedding at Singer Hall"
>
> National Genealogical Society Special Topics Series

Citation segments cited headline-style also include titles and subtitles of unpublished records and narratives and the formal titles of containers and collections of records:

> Medical Certificate of Death
>
> "Essex County, MA: Probate File Papers, 1638–1881"
>
> Records of the Department of Veterans Affairs

Headline-style capitalization contrasts with sentence-style capitalization, used in prose writing. Prose writers capitalize each sentence's first word, names, and any proper nouns requiring capitalization, leaving all other words uncapitalized. Researchers use sentence-style capitalization for all citation segments except names, titles, and capitalized words within quotation marks:

> Frederick von Berum, special master, to S. L. Bryan, judge, report of sale, filed 6 May 1863; in Monroe Co., Foreclosures 1859–1860

In that partial citation, headline-style capitalization shows which citation segments are formal titles ("Foreclosures"), and sentence-style capitalization shows which segments are the researcher's words and descriptions ("special master," "judge," and "report of sale").

Usages of sentence-style capitalization in citations include:

- Descriptions of sources—for example, digital image, microfilm publication, warranty deed
- Descriptions that substitute for unwieldy or uninformative titles—for example, *1850 U.S. census* instead of *Seventh Census of the United States*
- Words or abbreviations that clarify people's roles—for example, *comp., ed., translator*
- Words that clarify a number's function—for example, *folio 72v, page 7, sheet 16B, table 6, vol. 17, 9 vols.*
- Translations of foreign-language titles, because the researcher's translation is not the source's title[9]—for example, *Actes de Mariage pour 1845 [Register of marriages in 1845]*

9. *Chicago Manual of Style*, 706, for sect. 14.108, "Translated title supplied by author or editor."

In today's world some businesses, people, and websites use names and titles with unconventional capitalization—for example, the title *Find A Grave* unnecessarily capitalizes the article *a*, and many *Find A Grave* contributors identify themselves with unconventionally capitalized pen names. Researchers modify such names only when the change improves a citation's effectiveness. When unconventional capitalization makes a name easy to recognize, citing it otherwise could be unwise.

Colons (:)

In prose writing, a colon at the end of a sentence "announces" that words or listed points will follow the sentence:

> Three points support this conclusion:

Colons conventionally appear in citations in three contexts:

- A colon separates a work's title from its subtitle—

  Genealogy and the Law: A Guide to Legal Sources

  "Inscriptions from Gravestones at Old Lyme, Conn.: From a Copy in the Possession of the New England Historic Genealogical Society,"

- A colon separates a volume designation from a page number. For example, *2:45* is shorthand for *volume 2, page 45*. This format is used for citing multivolume books and journals with volume numbers or letters—

  Deed Record U:219–20

  Descendants of Thomas Durfee, 2:416

  "Chicago Personals," *Electrical Worker* 1 (April 1893): 3

  When parenthetical information follows a volume designation, like the "Chicago Personals" example, a space conventionally follows the colon. If nothing intrudes between the volume designation and the colon, then no space is needed before or after the colon, like the first two examples.

- In a citation's publication details, a colon separates the publisher's location from its name or an online access date—

  (Arlington, Va.: National Genealogical Society, 2017)

  (http://www.ngsgenealogy.org/cs/ngsq_archives : viewed 20 February 2017)

In the latter example, a space conventionally precedes the colon to prevent accidentally adding it to the URL.

Commas (,)

Commas serve similar functions in sentences and citations:

- Commas separate citation components—

> Adams Co., Ill., Marriage Record 1:3, George Watkins and Minnie A. Edison, 24 January 1878
>
> "Dr. Edison Passed Away," *Quincy Daily Journal* (Quincy, Ill.), 11 March 1905, page 5, col. 5

- Commas separate words in a series. Genealogists, following advice in *The Chicago Manual of Style,* consistently place a comma before the final *and* in a series of three or more numbers, phrases, or words—[10]

> dwellings 456, 457, and 460
>
> For Sadie's mother, sister Mattie, and sister-in-law, see. . . .

- Commas set off asides and appositives from the rest of a sentence. Those commas always work in pairs. One partner precedes and the other partner follows the set-off number, word, or phrase—

> Milwaukee Co., Wisc., Registration of Marriages
>
> See, for example, "Katruska Family Tree"
>
> ages as four and fourteen, respectively, confirm 1866.
>
> Isaac W. Hammond, comp. and ed., . . .

- Commas set off opening and closing phrases:

> For only the date, see. . . .
>
> 2:416, also reports the Conway Springs residence.

- Commas separate two independent clauses joined by a conjunction. (An independent clause is a group of words that could be a stand-alone sentence, if it was not joined to another independent clause with a conjunction). This example of two independent clauses joined by a comma and a conjunction comes from a discursive footnote:

> Both censuses have 1 June enumeration dates, and Clara's household was visited on 19 July 1870 and 5 June 1880.

Genealogists use judgment in applying commas to break up long numbers, like those for *Find A Grave* memorials and Family History Library microfilms. *Find A Grave* memorial numbers include no commas. Family History Library microfilm boxes and films, however, include the commas, but its catalog does not, and the catalog's search engine does not accept them. As long as researchers' citations are consistent, they may include or omit those commas, follow the varying practices each source shows, or provide the most convenient option for themselves and their readers.

Dashes (– and —)

Writers use two kinds of dashes. In most fonts, en dashes are about double the width of hyphens, and em dashes are exactly twice the width of en dashes. Dashes do not appear on standard keyboards, but most typefaces

10. *Chicago Manual of Style,* 312–13, for sect. 6.18, "Serial Commas."

include them. Writers find them under their word processor's insert-symbol menu or in a similar location. They can easily create keyboard shortcuts—alt-n for the en dash, for example—to insert a dash where needed.

Genealogists use en dashes in citations to join words designating ranges of pages, volumes, years, and other inclusive numbers or words representing spans:

> February–June 1842
>
> *Springfield, Missouri, City Directory (1910–1911),* 159–60
>
> Annette Hughes and Minnie Lanahan, national nos. 380509–10

Writers also use en dashes to replace hyphens when an expression on one or both sides of the hyphen contains more than one word:

> unattributed family group sheet for George Edison–Ida Hall
>
> Springfield–Greene County Library
>
> NA–Washington

In the last example, the *NA* initialism represents two words, *National Archives*. A prior citation announced the initialism.

Genealogists use longer dashes, em dashes, on either side of a question mark to represent an unknown name, often a maiden name:

> Nelson, son of Jonathan and Mary ([—?—]) Ganoung
>
> [—?—] Welsh

Em dashes also set off parenthetical comments, like these from discursive reference notes:

> Ford's first name—initialized in the marriage record—was. . . .
>
> Marinda's oldest child—Howard, born on 26 March 1878—was eager.

Ellipsis dots (. . . and . . . .)

Ellipsis dots—three or four periods—show where a researcher has omitted words from a cited title or quotation. Researchers may choose to consistently place or omit spaces between the dots—an aesthetic choice. Three dots replace material omitted from a sentence's or title's middle:

> Case Files of Approved Pension Applications . . . , 1861–1934

Four dots replace omitted material that includes a sentence's end. In that case, no space precedes the first dot, signifying the sentence ended somewhere within the omitted words:

> William . . . removed to little Hoosack. . . . from thence to Pittstown. . . .

Readers understand that quotations are parts of longer passages. Writers, therefore, insert ellipsis dots at the beginning or end of quoted material only when they want to emphasize the omission of preceding or following words. For example, a writer who wants to convey a sense of "trailing off" may opt to use ellipsis points at the end of a quotation.

Greater-than signs (>)

Many publishers number online images as parts of a collection of sequentially numbered images. That collection might be part of a larger collection, which could be part of an even larger collection, and so forth up to the website level. The publishers list the names of those levels, usually above or below the image, to show a path to the image. They separate the levels' names with greater-than signs, signifying which level is greater than the next. Researchers can copy these paths and paste them into citations to show exactly where to turn to a numbered image by clicking through a series of drop-down menus, one for each level:

> "New York Passenger Lists, 1820–1957," *Ancestry* (http://www. ancestry.com/search/db.aspx?dbid=7488) > Roll > M237, 1820–1897 > Roll 074 > image 147.

In that example, the titled database (a publication part) and a titled website (a publication) comprise the largest level, which has its own URL. The URL points to a page with a series of drop-down menus enabling users of the citation to click through to the image. The collection is organized by *Date* and *Roll*. The above partial citation shows the path through the *Roll* option (referring to microfilm rolls used to create the online images). Under *Roll* are three options, including *M237, 1820–1897*. Under that level are 675 roll options, including *Roll 074*. Its level is a collection of 1,118 numbered images. Clicking *Roll 074* opens the collection at image number 1. Changing that number to 147 downloads the cited record.

Hyphens (-)

Hyphens have the same uses in citations and written narrative:

- Hyphens join words in a "phrasal adjective"—a group of words that in their entirety, but not individually, describe or modify a noun that follows the phrase. Writers coin phrasal adjectives, for example, *a dirt-poor-but-happy ancestor*. (When placed after the noun, however, the phrase becomes a dependent clause and would not be hyphenated—*an ancestor who was dirt poor but happy*). *The Chicago Manual of Style* discusses exceptions and nuances in creating hyphenated phrasal adjectives.[11]
- Hyphens join two closely related words that seem to be evolving from an open compound to a closed compound, as shown in a standard dictionary. (An open compound is two separate words often used together, like *half sister*. A closed compound is two formerly separate words now joined together, like *stepfather*.) When questioning the need for a hyphen between words, researchers check a standard dictionary to see

11. *Chicago Manual of Style*, 227–28, for sect. 5.91, "Phrasal adjectives."

if the words form an open compound, a closed compound, or a standard hyphenated compound (*great-niece*, for example).

- Researchers coin hyphenated words when joining them adds clarity or avoids confusion—for example, *old picture-collection* has a different meaning from *old-picture collection*, but the meaning of *genealogy documentation guide* is clear with no added hyphen. Researchers exercise discretion in coining hyphenated words. They hyphenate only when a hyphen adds clarity or avoids confusion better than rewording.
- Hyphens occasionally join a prefix to a root word—for example, *pre-Columbian*—but most words with prefixes are solid words—for example, *midcontinent, postwar*, and *premigration*. A standard dictionary's listing for the prefix and individual dictionary entries show few words for which the prefix should be hyphenated and many for which it should not.[12] Writers should not treat words with prefixes like compound words or phrasal adjectives, because a prefix is not a word. Researchers should hyphenate prefixes only when they have a specific reason for the hyphen, such as a capitalized root word—for example, *post-Reconstruction* era or *pre-British settlement*.

The Chicago Manual of Style provides an eight-page table on compound words and a two-page table on words with prefixes. Both cover cases that do and do not require hyphens.[13]

Italics

Italics—a typeface with slanted letters, *like this*—have a special purpose in citations: they mark titles of publications. Citations italicize the titles of all kinds of publications, including websites. They do not, however, italicize the titles of parts of publications—for example, articles, chapters, tables, or web pages. They also do not italicize the title of some publication series or the title of any unpublished source.

When citing, researchers should italicize no title except a publication title. Italics show readers that a series of words is a publication title. Italicizing any series of words that is not a publication title can unnecessarily break or complicate communication between author and reader.

Italics also are used conventionally for names of ships and other named vehicles—for example, the *Enola Gay*, HMS *Sir Galahad, Mayflower*, shallop *Betty*, USS *Scroggins*. Following convention, the vessel's descriptors or other designations are not italicized.

Italics rarely appear elsewhere in citations. *Ibid.*, discussed in chapter 3, is not italicized in citations. (It is italicized in this narrative because of the convention of italicizing a word discussed as a word.)

---

12. See, for example, *Merriam-Webster's Collegiate Dictionary*, 975–76, s.v. "pre-."

13. *Chicago Manual of Style*, 374–84, for sec. 7.85, "Hyphenation guide for compounds and words formed with prefixes."

One exception is the Latin word *sic,* meaning *thus.* Researchers conventionally italicize *sic,* but not other commonly used foreign words, including Latin words.[14] Writers in English do not italicize foreign words that appear in English-language dictionaries.

Researchers who translate titles of foreign-language publications to cite them in English-language contexts should not italicize their translations. A researcher's translation is not the publication's title. Italicizing it could confuse readers.

Numerals

Researchers use numerals more frequently in citations than in running text, where they often are spelled out. For clarity, researchers use arabic numerals to cite roman numerals in sources (volume numbers, for example), except when citing introductory page numbers. Letters with ordinal numbers (4th, for example) conventionally are not superscripted except when quoting.

Parentheses ( )

In citations to published books, journals, websites, and other publications, parentheses serve the specific function of grouping publication details separately from the rest of the citation:

> *Find A Grave* (https://www.findagrave.com/)
>
> *A History of the Starr Family of New England* (Hartford, Conn.: Case, Lockwood, and Brainard, 1879)
>
> *New England Historical and Genealogical Register* 45 (October 1891): 309
>
> "Died," *People's Advocate* (New London, Conn.), 13 December 1843

Parentheses can serve the same function in citations that they fill in written narrative. They surround a word or phrase that restates or amplifies the words the parenthetical expression follows without affecting the overall context's grammatical structure or meaning:

> Congregational Church (Montville, Conn., formerly New London North Parish), records 3:25 (separately numbered section at front of volume)
>
> Duck River Cemetery (Old Lyme, Conn.), Sarah DeWolf gravestone

Because parenthetical phrases "belong to" the words they follow, no punctuation immediately precedes parenthetical expressions, including those citing publication details. When a comma is needed, it follows the closing parenthesis.

---

14. *Chicago Manual of Style,* 365, for sect. 7.53, "Roman for Latin words and abbreviations."

Periods (.)

Single periods in citations have no function different from their functions in narrative writing. Periods show where sentences end, and they show where citations end. Other periods in citations follow abbreviations and appear within URLs.

Periods separate citation components in reference-*list* citations, which are formatted like paragraphs. Periods should not separate citation components in reference-*note* citations, which are formatted like stand-alone sentences.

Quotation marks, double and single (" " and ' ')

Single quotation marks resemble apostrophes, and double quotation marks resemble pairs of apostrophes. In polished publication contexts, both kinds of quotation marks are "curly" (not straight up and down), but their precise appearance varies with the writer's font. Most word-processing software defaults to curly quotation marks or a variant (as in this book). Changing a setting can make it a default.

Quotation marks appear in pairs—one before a word or series of words, and its partner after. Writers use double quotation marks in all contexts but one. When a quotation appears within another quotation, a pair of single quotation marks separate the inner quotation from the surrounding material.

Researchers use quotation marks around titles of *parts* of publications. These include book chapters, journal articles, and websites' titled web pages. Parts of publications also include titled figures, illustrations, and tables.

Only the title of an entire publication is italicized; only quotation marks identify its parts. Readers can glance at a citation to a part of a publication and see immediately which citation component is the publication title and which component is the title of a part of the publication:

> "Captains and Masters of Ships," *The Refugees of 1776 from Long Island to Connecticut*
>
> "Died," *People's Advocate*
>
> "Genealogical Notes from early Wills," *Newport Historical Magazine*
>
> "1880 United States Federal Census," *Ancestry.com*

Quotation marks in citations identify titles of unpublished narratives:

> "Snell families in New England and descendants," manuscript, 1939
>
> "The True Story of 'Black Bart,' King of the Caribbean Pirates"

Researchers also use quotation marks in citations on either side of a word or series of words that a researcher wants to show exactly as the original writer created it:

> digital image by "LadyGoshen."
>
> Land Records 6:70, Roulin-"Greenfeald" marriage
>
> return "By the Rev^{d}. M^{r}. Wm Jenison." This record is a copy made before 2 September 1815 from "the second volume of marriages births and deaths."

Semicolons (;)

The much-maligned semicolon serves an indispensable function in citations.[15] In sentences and in citations semicolons group together related phrases. At the same time, they separate each group from other groups.

There is no better option. Attempting to separate parts of a reference-note citation with periods would wrongly signal that one citation has ended and another is beginning. Internal periods would break a single citation into two or more citations. Commas also would not work. A long string of citation components all separated with commas, as if they are equal or equally related, challenges comprehension.

Some locations in a citation are logical places for a semicolon:

- Between the part of the citation describing an unpublished source and the part describing the repository holding it—

  > interview by author, 11 July 1971; notes in author's files

- Between the part of the citation describing an underlying source and the part describing the medium through which the researcher viewed it (or through which the reader can most easily view it)—

  > 1900 U.S. census, St. Louis, Mo., ED 6, Ward 1, p. 5A, Andrew Clark household; NARA microfilm T623, roll 889

- Between a citation's parts describing, respectively, a bundle, series, collection, record group, or other grouping in a courthouse or large archive—

  > Jacob Gross, questionnaire 3–447, 23 November 1903; in Jacob Gross (Pvt., Co. K, 149th Ill. Inf., Civil War) pension no. W.C. A5-19-26; Case Files of Approved Pension Applications . . . , 1861–1934; Civil War and Later Pension Files; Record Group 15: Department of Veterans Affairs; National Archives, Washington, D.C.

15. For an example of maligning, see Kurt Vonnegut, "Here is a lesson in creative writing," in *A Man without a Country*, ed. Daniel Simon (New York: Seven Stories, 2005), 23. He wrote, "First rule: Do not use semicolons. . . . All they do is show you've been to college." For another, see John O'Callaghan, "The semicolon; and its faults," *The Economist*, 26 March 2016, p. 14.

Researchers decide where to place semicolons grouping a citation's parts. Their goal is both to break the citation into digestible chunks and show the relationship of elements within the citation.

Semicolons are most helpful in citations with several parts or a series of nested levels:

> Frederick von Berum, special master, to S. L. Bryan, judge, report of sale, filed 6 May 1863; in Monroe Co., Foreclosures 1859–1860, box A-4, Berum vs. Gross; Circuit Court, Waterloo, Illinois.
>
> James M. Gucker, a history of the Brickey family from his experiences and memories of conversations with his mother, Marinda (Brickey) Gucker, undated; digital typescript dated November 2010 by Patrice Parres Oliver; Gucker folder 3, author's files.

Slashes (/)

Slashes in genealogy citations appear most often in cited URLs. Researchers copy URLs exactly as they appear in a web browser. They may, however, remove the beginning, end, or both from some URLs, including slashes, without impairing their functionality.

In citations and elsewhere, genealogists also use slashes in pre-1752 "double dates." They cite these recorded dates with a slash—for example, *12 February 1748/9*. They may double a pre-1752 year for January, February, and March dates when the original record keeper did not. In that case, square brackets surround the added slash and year—for example, *27 January 1749[/50]*.

Using a slash in a date to mean anything other than colonial double-dating will confuse readers accustomed to pre-1752 double dates. For those genealogists, a slash between years does not refer to a two-year span or imply that either of two years might be correct. Instead, en-dashes connect a span of years *(1752–53)*, and the word *or* clearly identifies alternatives *(1752 or 1753)*.

Conclusion

Capitalization, italics, and other details add clarity and polish to citations. In working notes and personal databases, they would not matter unless their absence or unconventional usage confused or misled the researcher. These details are important in genealogical material that is shared, however, because they enhance the functionality of researchers' citations to communicate clearly with readers.

Chapter 5 exercises

33. In the Greenfield article in appendix A, footnotes 8, 18, 30, 65, 88, and 89, what are the functions of the paired square brackets and the content between them?
34. For the citations in Greenfield footnotes 2, 3, 10, and 23, explain why the capitalized and uncapitalized words appear the way they do.
35. In Greenfield footnote 18, line 8, what are the punctuation marks around *tons* and why are they there?
36. For the citations in Greenfield footnote 22, explain why the capitalized and uncapitalized words appear as they do.
37. What is the purpose of the colons in the citations in Greenfield footnote 30?
38. In Greenfield footnote 1, what are the functions of the commas and semicolons in the first citation?
39. In Greenfield footnotes 3 and 72, what are the functions of the ellipsis dots?
40. Explain the greater-than signs in Greenfield footnote 71.
41. What is the first footnote in the Greenfield article that cites a publication title? How can you easily find it?
42. What are the functions of the dashes, hyphens, and semicolons in Greenfield footnote 23?
43. What are the functions of the parentheses in the citations in Greenfield footnotes 1, 2, 3, 4, and 17?
44. What are the purposes of the quotation marks in the citations in Greenfield footnote 18?
45. What are the purposes of the slashes in the citations in Greenfield footnote 7?
46. Punctuate and capitalize these citations:

    randolph co ill birth record 1 120 no 1537 edgar f guker county clerk chester ill fhl microfilm 973995

    st michael s roman catholic church paderborn ill deaths marriages unpaginated 1871 marriages no 4 gross-hausman 3 august 1871 diocese of belleville belleville ill

    1900 us census city of st louis mo pop sch ed 6 sheet 5a dwell 76 fam 102 andrew clark household nara microfilm t623 roll 889

Chapter 6

Determining a Source's Publication Status

> *"Publish . . . : to make generally known . . . to disseminate to the public . . . to produce or release for distribution."*[1]
>
> *"To publish a work is to distribute copies . . . to the public."*[2]

Understanding what a source is begins with understanding whether it is published or not. *"Is this source a publication"* is among the first questions researchers ask about a source. With experience, they habitually—nearly unconsciously—ask and answer this question. The answer clears their path to describing the source in a citation.

Researchers determine a source's publication status because citations to published and unpublished sources differ greatly. Citing a publication as if it were unpublished, or vice versa, would mislead readers. The citation would fail to communicate.

The words *publication* and *publish* refer to availability and distribution to the public. The intent of publication is to make some quantity of a work generally available to people who want a copy, usually—not always—for a price. *Publishers* handle a publication's initial distribution, if not further distributions. They also handle any purchases related to the distributions.

This description of publication might seem clear, but genealogists use many kinds of published and unpublished materials. Some are hard to distinguish. Some books and microfilms, for example, are published, but others are not. Some sources have both a published and an unpublished form, and some have more than one published form.

This chapter discusses these variations and more. It gives genealogists knowledge that will help them determine whether to cite a genealogical source as published, unpublished, or both.

---

1. *Merriam-Webster's Collegiate Dictionary*, 11th ed. (Springfield, Mass: Merriam-Webster, 2004), s.v. "publish," definitions 1 a, 2 a, and 2 b.

2. "U.S. Copyright Office Definitions," *Copyright.gov* (https://copyright.gov/help/faq/definitions.html : viewed on 20 February 2017).

Published or unpublished: the basics

In past centuries publications and unpublished materials lay on either side of a "great divide." Private and public libraries housed publications, while archives and record creators held unpublished material. Little doubt existed about what was published and what was not. Reflecting this long-standing difference, formats for citing publications evolved differently from those for citing unpublished material.

Today the distinctions between published and unpublished sources are complex. Websites publish images of vast quantities of material. Part of that material was previously published offline, part was never previously published, and part was originally unpublished and then published offline. Other images appear offline, some in publications and others in unpublished media. Websites function as libraries in some regards and as publishers in others. Brick-and-mortar libraries can house unpublished materials, besides publications. Archives can hold books and periodicals, besides unique manuscripts. Some libraries and archives also produce images in unpublished media, publications, or both.

The similar appearances of unpublished and published images of previously unpublished and published material, as well as the variety of organizations publishing images, create challenges for genealogists crafting citations. To describe a source clearly, they must understand its origin and history. If the source is imaged, they must unravel the permutations of publication statuses, processes, and entities behind it. This starts with understanding basic distinctions between what is published and what is not.

Published works and media

Publishers produce material for distribution to the public for personal ownership or access, usually for a price. Only the quantity of physical publications limits their availability to people who request or purchase them. Quantity, however, is not a factor for online publications.

Publishers range in size and complexity from private individuals to mega-corporations. Publishers can disseminate home-printed or digital family trees at no charge, sell subscriptions to huge databases for thousands of dollars, or anything in between. Any person or business that makes a supply of written, imaged, or recorded material available to the public, for individual ownership or personal access, has published it.

Publication media have diversified since the fifteenth century, when publishers first distributed printed books.[3] Traditional publications include

3. Frederic G. Kilgour, *The Evolution of the Book* (New York: Oxford University Press, 1998), 93.

books, which people and libraries purchase. They also include journals, magazines, and newspapers, for which people and libraries pay subscription fees.

In the middle of the twentieth century, companies began publishing images in a medium generically called *microform*. These publications show images of pages reduced to widths of 35 millimeters (about 1.4 inches) and smaller. Varieties include microfilm, microfiche, and microcards.[4] Reading them requires machines with lighting, magnification, and mechanisms to adjust focus and move images through the focal area. Many materials published in commercial microform were previously published in print. Like most published books, most microform publications have prices listed in commercial catalogs. Genealogists and libraries desiring microform publications purchase them, just like they purchase published books.

Later in the twentieth century, publishers began selling digital content on CD-ROMs. Library patrons and purchasers at home could view the contents on personal computers. These publications contain family information, indexes, digital images of records, and other material that had not been published elsewhere. They also show images—often searchable—of previously published books, journals, and magazines.

In the late twentieth century, individuals, archives, businesses, religious groups, and other commercial and nonprofit organizations began publishing genealogical information on the Internet. Some of this material is original content written or compiled exclusively for online publication—for example, blogs, record transcriptions, and family trees. Other online publications provide images made from previously published books, journals, magazines, and newspapers, and from microfilm and CD-ROM publications.

Virtually all online material is published.[5] Whether it is free or requires a subscription, any researcher who wants to use it can access it without visiting a designated repository. *The Chicago Manual of Style* notes that online materials are published and copyrighted:

> *Anything* posted on the Internet is "published" in the sense of copyright and must be treated as such for the purposes of complete citations and clearance of permissions, if relevant. [Italics are in the original.][6]

---

4. For more information about microforms, see South Carolina Department of Archives and History, *Microfilm and Microforms*, public records information leaflet no. 7, PDF (rm .sc.gov/leaflets/Documents/SEVEN.pdf : accessed 20 February 2017).

5. Elizabeth Shown Mills, *QuickSheet: Citing Online Historical Resources Evidence! Style*, laminated folder (Baltimore: Genealogical Publishing, 2005); also revised edition (2007). Also, Elizabeth Shown Mills, *Evidence Explained*, 3rd. ed. (Baltimore: Genealogical Publishing, 2015), 50–51, for sect. 2.18, "Citing Published vs. Unpublished Materials." The exception is password-protected material accessible only to a small private group.

6. *The Chicago Manual of Style*, 16th ed. (Chicago: University of Chicago Press, 2010), 658, for sect. 14.9, "Authority and permanence [of electronic resources]."

Print, microform, CD-ROM, and Internet publications come to many places where researchers can study them. They can come also to researchers' homes. Because of publications' wide distribution and availability, citations to publications reference the source's publisher, not the place the researcher used the source. Readers can use this information to consult the researcher's source and examine it in a location convenient to themselves.

Unpublished works and media

Unpublished sources are unique or nearly so. No person or business has made them available to the public in quantities. An unpublished source comes neither to the public individually nor to many places where they can consult it. Researchers must go to a designated site or sites to use an unpublished source. Because unpublished sources are not widely distributed, citations to them—unlike citations to publications—name the repository where a researcher consulted the unpublished source.

Unpublished sources use some of the same media as publications. For example, officials customarily enter or copy business, governmental, and religious records into hardbound or softbound books. Many of those books have titles, but they are not publications. They have no publisher or distributor. Researchers must consult them at a facility holding them.

In 1938 the Genealogical Society of Utah (GSU, now FamilySearch) began microfilming records of genealogical value.[7] It created the films for research, not commercial, purposes. The films, now numbering over 2.4 million, are available for viewing at the Family History Library (FHL), in Salt Lake City.[8] FamilySearch makes the films available on short-term, extended, or permanent loan to 4,745 FamilySearch Centers and affiliate libraries around the world.[9] Researchers must go to one of those centers or libraries to view the microfilm. FamilySearch does not distribute the films to the public for private ownership or access. The public cannot own them or subscribe to them. Therefore, microfilms created by GSU and FamilySearch are unpublished.[10]

Other organizations besides FamilySearch have produced unpublished microfilm collections. They include archives, businesses, educational and religious organizations, and membership societies. Each creates microfilm for preservation or research purposes. They do not give away or sell

7. "Genealogical Society of Utah," *FamilySearch Research Wiki* (https://familysearch.org/wiki/en/Genealogical_Society_of_Utah : viewed 20 February 2017).

8. "Family History Library Catalog," *FamilySearch* (https://familysearch.org/locations/saltlakecity-library : viewed 20 February 2017).

9. "About FamilySearch," *FamilySearch* (https://familysearch.org/about : viewed on 20 February 2017).

10. Robert Raymond (Deputy to FamilySearch Chief Genealogical Officer) to author, e-mail, 27 April 2016; author's files. For a similar view, see Mills, *Evidence Explained*, 53–54, for sect. 2.24, "FHL, GSU, LDS, and *FamilySearch*."

the microfilm rolls in any quantity that would justify calling them "published." Any distribution is through interlibrary loan or a similar lending program, not by purchase or gift.

A notable example is the "U.S. Newspaper Program," a project sponsored by the National Endowment for the Humanities from 1982 to 2011. The project microfilmed American newspapers dating from the 1700s forward. A repository in each state holds the respective state's microfilm, unpublished, resulting from this project.[11]

Published-unpublished hybrids

Hybrids are sources having characteristics of both published and unpublished material. They differ from published images of previously unpublished material, and vice versa. Those are distinct sources, not hybrids, and they are common. Hybrids are rare.

One hybrid that genealogists encounter is a family Bible record. The Bible is a publication. It had a publisher and a price. Someone purchased it for personal ownership and took it home. Within the Bible, however, are family pages, where someone wrote records, filling perhaps several pages in longhand. Those records are unique; they exist nowhere else. Researchers can see the published Bible in many places or purchase the same edition. To see the unpublished record within one published Bible, however, they would have to visit the repository holding it.

A similar hybrid is a published family history with handwritten corrections and additions. Researchers can consult the family history in many places or purchase it, but they can see the annotations in only one place.

Hybrids include some court record books, legal case files, and pension application files. Each contains unique handwritten records. Some, however, also contain clippings from newspapers—publications.

Each of those examples is a single source. Because the family record is part of the family Bible, citing two sources could mislead. Researchers who see one source should cite one source. Because the published Bible is the predominate "mass" of the source, researchers choose the format for citing publications. Citing the published Bible, they append information about the unique family record, its location within the Bible, and that Bible's location.

Similarly, if the mass of a court file is unpublished manuscript material, researchers would choose the format for citing unpublished material. Citing the unpublished file, they identify the published item within it as a clipping, removed from a publication.

11. "U.S. Newspaper Program," *National Endowment for the Humanities* (https://www.neh.gov/us-newspaper-program : viewed on 20 February 2017).

Extremely rare books resemble hybrids. Long ago a publisher distributed a quantity of books, probably for a price, to libraries and private individuals. Today, however, few copies survive. Citing a rare publication as if it were widely available is not helpful. Though technically the book is a publication, a useful citation would identify its repository, as if the book was not published.

Not related to publication status

A source's medium does not determine its publication status. Many books are published, for example, and many are unpublished. The same is true of microfilms.

Copyright—or its absence—also does not affect publication status. Copyright protects creators of unpublished material just like it protects creators of publications. Publication does not depend on formal application for copyright. The presence or absence of copyright registration plays no role in how a researcher cites a source.

The presence or absence of pricing also does not determine publication status. Free material can be published, and unpublished material can be sold. Commercial availability plays no role in a source's publication status.

Image and website complications

An imaging of a source, whether published or not, complicates citing it. The image can appear in an unpublished medium (like preservation microfilm), a published medium (like the Internet) or both. Each imaging creates a new incarnation—the source appears in a new form. Given that sources and images are either published or not, four combinations of image-source pairings are possible:

1. *Published images made from a previously published source*—for example, *(a)* online images made from a family history previously published as a book; *(b)* commercial microfilm images showing a newspaper; and *(c)* online images of a census previously published on microfilm.
2. *Unpublished images made from a previously published source*—for example, a library's preservation microfilm of a family history previously published as a book, or a newspaper's private digital archive of its printed issues.
3. *Published images made from a previously unpublished source*—for example, online images made directly from a pension application file.
4. *Unpublished images made from a previously unpublished source*—for example, an archive's preservation microfilm of an agricultural census.

Further permutations arise from successive imaging. A common scenario is the online publication of images from published or unpublished microfilm of a published or unpublished underlying source.

Further complications arise from the roles that websites can simultaneously fill:

- They function as libraries when they make previously published material available to the public, but they function as publishers when they publish images of previously unpublished manuscript material.
- The name of the publisher who produced a website and the name of the the website—the publication—often are the same.
- The name of the creator of website content and its publisher, title, or both can be the same.

Those simultaneous roles are typical of websites but not unique to them. Brick-and-mortar libraries can publish, for example, and offline publishers can house libraries. Newspaper publishers and titles often have the same name. Similarly, a book's publisher can also be its creator—as is typical of many institutionally produced works. (For example, the University of Chicago Press created the content for *The Chicago Manual of Style* and then published it.)

Conclusion

This chapter provides an overview of the publication of genealogical research materials. It describes characteristics distinguishing published from unpublished material and how publications have been produced. It also provides examples of various kinds of published and unpublished sources and hybrids. It explains complications in determining a source's publication status—factors that researchers should consider, especially when they consult images.

Researchers can apply this chapter's information to help them determine whether each source they use is published or unpublished. They do this by gathering information from and about their sources. This includes learning how the sources were produced and distributed, including any imaging between the source's creation and the researcher's use. This information-gathering can be as simple as turning to a book's title page or as complicated as finding information about a source outside the source itself. This book's chapters 7, 8, and 12–16 describe or point to resources where researchers can gather the information they need.

The knowledge researchers gain about their source's publication status helps them cite their sources clearly and effectively. Researchers have options for crafting those citations. Choosing the best option requires them to recognize whether a source they consulted, any of its prior incarnations, and its images were published or not. It also requires them to understand the various roles that online and offline publishers might have filled to create and provide the material that genealogists use.

Chapter 6 exercises

Following conventional guidelines, all citations to publication titles include italicized words. Conversely, most citations with no italics (except for *sic* and ship names) refer to unpublished sources. The exceptions include citations where a researcher substituted a description for the publication's official title—for example, citing a National Archives microfilm publication as "1850 U.S. census" instead of *Seventh Census of the United States, 1850.*

Using this information, examine the citations in this book's appendix A. For each kind of source listed below, find at least two citation examples.

47. Published book
48. Published microfilm
49. Unpublished microfilm
50. Unpublished material viewed on-site
51. Unpublished material in personal files
52. Previously unpublished material viewed as published images
53. Source material created for online publication

Chapter 7

Issues in Citing Source Titles, Descriptions, or Both

> "What—*the source's title or name; if it is untitled, a clear item-specific description*"[1]

Genealogy standard 5, quoted partially above, says the researcher's answer to *What is the source* is a citation "facet." Although that answer is most citations' second component, researchers address it first. Their answer helps them with questions about their sources' other facets.

A citation's answer to the *What* question tells readers exactly what source a researcher used. Readers should not need to repeat the genealogist's research to gain that understanding. From a citation, sometimes with added explanation, readers should be able to see at a glance whether a source is published or not. They also should be able to see whether the source has a meaningful title or not. Third, they should be able to see whether the source, as a whole, is a narrative or a record:

- Narratives combine accounts of various events into a prose format. They usually are based on several sources from which an author has formed conclusions existing nowhere else. Nearly all narratives' titles are unique. Examples include family histories in articles and books.
- Records document or memorialize events, often soon after they occurred. Examples include land deeds, tax rolls, and vital records. Groups of the same kind of record usually are bound or filed together. Many records will have the same title because their titles often are generic descriptions of their content.

If the genealogist's source is a record, the citation should help readers understand whether it is an original record or derived from a prior record. Such derivatives include abstracts, indexes, keyboarded database entries, and translations.

Citations often answer the *What* question with a source's title. In many cases, the source title clearly and completely answers the question. Italicization or its absence usually shows whether a source is published or not. The title's content shows whether the source is a narrative or a record. If it is a record, its title or descriptive words show whether the record is original or derivative.

---

1. Board for Certification of Genealogists, *Genealogy Standards* (Nashville, Tenn.: Ancestry.com, 2014), 7, for standard 5, "Citation Elements." Quoted here with permission.

Sometimes, however, a source's title does not communicate what it and its characteristics are. Some titles are hidden. They also can be misleading, illogical, or cryptic. Unpublished sources might have no title. Sources with titles can also have subtitles. This chapter covers these issues and more. It addresses options for clearly and completely answering the *What* question in genealogical citations. The answers should show readers whether a cited source is published or unpublished, titled or not, and a narrative or an original or derivative record.

The process of answering the *What* citation question begins with determining what the source is. Unlike sources in most research fields, those in genealogy seem infinite in their variety. See figure 2 for some of the myriad possibilities.

Titles of print publications

A published book's title usually appears on its front cover and title page. The title also could appear on the book's spine, its copyright page, and an otherwise empty page preceding the title page. Usually the identical title appears in each place. If a published book's title varies or is in question, researchers check library catalogs or *WorldCat.org* to see how libraries have cataloged the book. Because readers use catalogs to find cited books, differences between cited titles and cataloged titles can create confusion about the researcher's sources.

If a book's title has a subtitle, researchers may cite both. They conventionally separate title and subtitle with a colon, and any further subtitles with semicolons. Researchers sometimes cite several subtitles to distinguish among books with identical publishers, titles, and strings of nearly identical subtitles. A subtitle, for example, could be the only distinction between two Bibles. The last subtitle distinguishes these two examples:

> *The Holy Bible Containing the Old and New Testaments: Translated out of the Original Tongues; And with the Former Translations Diligently Compared and Revised by His Majesty's Special Command; Appointed to be Read in Churches*

> *The Holy Bible Containing the Old and New Testaments: Translated out of the Original Tongues; And with the Former Translations Diligently Compared and Revised by His Majesty's Special Command; Appointed to be Read in Churches; Authorized King James Version*

Periodical print publications—journals, magazines, newsletters, and newspapers—usually have no dedicated title page or copyright page, and some have no spine or cover. These publications usually have a masthead or nameplate announcing their official title. Periodicals occasionally have subtitles. Citations conventionally set off periodical subtitles with colons, as they do with book subtitles:

> *OnBoard: Newsletter of the Board for Certification of Genealogists*

Figure 2

Some Varieties of Sources for Genealogical Documentation

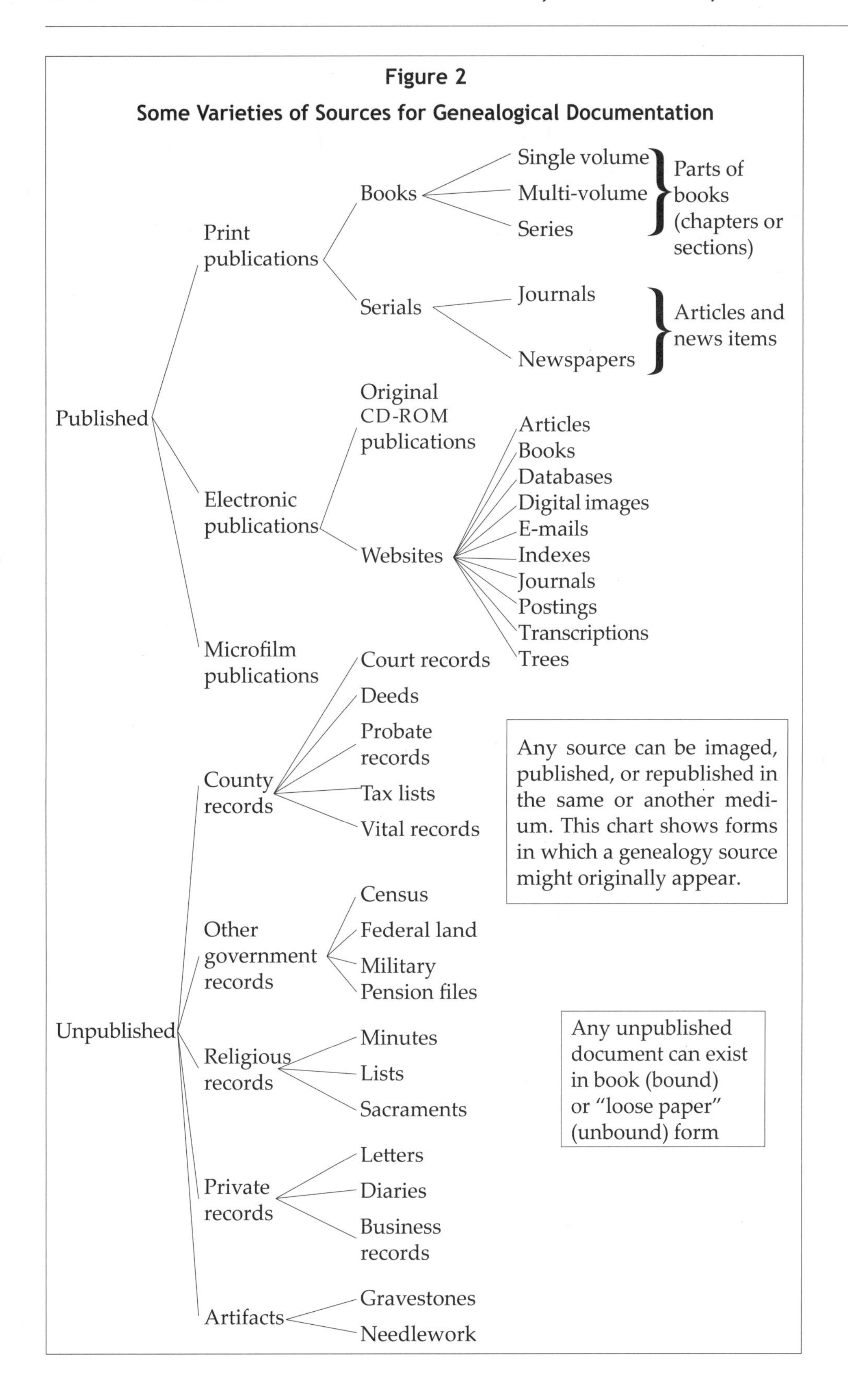

Parts of print publications

Besides citing an entire print publication as a source, researchers may cite the title of a publication's part. Print-publication parts can be major sections, like book chapters, journal articles, or newspaper items. They also could be small parts, including figures, sections, and tables.

Researchers always cite article titles, unless the article has no title. Citing a part of a published book, however, is optional. Researchers cite titles of chapters, sections, tables, and figures in books when they believe the information is useful or helpful to themselves or their readers.

Researchers citing or referring to entire publications typically show the title and any subtitles in italics. When citing titled parts of publications, they put those titles between quotation marks and do not italicize them. In traditional citations, the part's title precedes the whole publication's title:

> "Dilley of Northern Virginia and Ohio: A Proposed Solution Hanging on a Single Word," *The American Genealogist*
>
> "The Genealogical Proof Standard: How Simple Can It Be?" *OnBoard: Newsletter of the Board for Certification of Genealogists*
>
> "Issues in Citing Source Titles, Descriptions, or Both," in *Mastering Genealogical Documentation*

In those examples, the title of the part and the title of the publication, together, answer the *What* citation question.

Citing the title of a publication's part before the title of the publication is common, but the opposite sequence is not wrong. Putting a publication title first can help genealogists who use a master-source citation template to cite various parts of publications. The title of the part will appear later in the citation, after publication details:

> *Ancestry* [publication details], "New York, Tax Assessment Rolls of Real and Personal Estates, 1799–1804"
>
> *Evidence Explained* [publication details], "Filmed or Fiched Manuscripts, Preservation Film vs. Publications"

Regardless of how an author, compiler, editor, or publisher capitalizes a publication's title, researchers crafting citations use headline style (discussed in chapter 4) for publication titles. Readers understand that the capitalization is that of the researcher who crafted the citation, not necessarily the capitalization that appears on a cited book's title page.

Titles of unpublished sources

Researchers typically use headline-style capitalization and no quotation marks for citing titles of individual records and record books. To distinguish unpublished sources from publications, researchers do not italicize titles and subtitles of unpublished sources:

> Deed Record G
>
> Town Records 2 (Land Evidences)

Record books occasionally have titled parts that researchers might cite, especially when the parts are separately numbered or paginated. Volumes of vital or sacramental records, for example, might have sections titled "Births," "Marriages," and "Deaths," or "Baptisms" and "Burials," each beginning with page 1. In these cases, placing the part's title after the record book's title can be helpful. This placement clarifies that the page number is that of the section, not of the entire book:

> Probate Records 3, part 2, p. 78
>
> Register of Baptisms and Burials, for Baptisms, p. 3, no. 18

The word *for* in the latter citation is discretionary. That small addition clarifies that *Baptisms* is a section within the register. Capitalizing *Baptisms* in this context signals that the word is the section's formal title, not the researcher's description.

Researchers usually do not put quotation marks around record titles when they are generic. They do, however, when they have a reason to draw readers' attention to a title or something within it:

> "a Family Bible which Bible was burnt in a School house in Steventown in the state of New York" [title of a record in a pension file]
>
> "A Tax List of Stephen Town District" [archaic spelling of town's name]

Papers in court case files and pension files often have titles that researchers can cite. Printed forms, for example, might have titles or numbers identifying them. In addition, clerks usually wrote titles on papers shown in court and then filed. Researchers often find these titles on the paper's back side:

> Admin—On the Assets of Jehosaphat Starr Late of New Port
>
> Levy on Personal Property
>
> Return of Sale by Sheriff

Researchers conventionally place quotation marks around titles of unpublished narratives—a manuscript family history, for example. Because of that quoting, the citation uses the original author's capitalization:

> "Snell families in New England and descendants"

Titles of online publications

Electronic publications, including websites, have titles. Some also have subtitles. Using headline-style capitalization and italics, researchers cite these titles and subtitles like those of print publications. A colon and semi-colons separate subtitles.

A website's title usually appears at the top of its home page, but it could be at the bottom. Also, what initially appears to be a home page might be below that level. Researchers might have to click links or study the site's structure to determine which page shows the official website title.

Web pages typically are a website's parts. Other parts—for example, databases, links, and search engines—often are tied to specific pages. A web page can have an obvious title, a hard-to-find title, or no title. Citing a web page's title is not mandatory. When citing it is helpful, researchers place it within quotation marks—the standard format for a cited part of a publication. If the page has no title, researchers need not note its absence, just as they would not mention the absence from a book of chapter or section titles.

Researchers punctuate and capitalize cited titles of websites and web pages like cited titles of other kinds of publications and their parts:

> "Connecticut, Church Record Abstracts, 1630–1920," *Ancestry*
>
> "Essex County, MA: Probate File Papers, 1638–1881," *American Ancestors*

Titles of microfilm and CD-ROM publications

Titles of published microfilms and CD-ROMs typically appear on their containers. They also can appear on the CD-ROMs themselves and at the beginning of each roll in microfilm publications.

Microfilm and CD-ROM publications, like other kinds of publications, can have titles with subtitles, and they also can have parts with titles. Researchers conventionally cite these titles, subtitles, and titles of parts with the same formatting and punctuation that they use for citing other kinds of publications:

> "The Southern Claims Commission: A Source for African American Roots," *Ancestry Magazine: 1994–1999*
>
> *Passengers Lists of Vessels Arriving at New York, 1820–97*

Most microfilm publications contain more than one roll, and the rolls within each publication are numbered, typically starting with roll 1. Each roll might also have its own title. If so, that title can be cited as a publication part. The roll number, however, is not a title. It usually is cited to help answer the *Wherein* citation question, not the *What* question.

Descriptions besides titles

At a glance, readers can see from a citation's formatting and content whether it refers to a book, journal, newspaper, or website. Citations to less common publications—for example, blogs, newsletters, and CD-ROM and microfilm publications—have formats like those for books and websites. Without added descriptions, readers might assume that a citation refers to a book, rather than the source's true form. To avoid that miscommunication, researchers place descriptive words after a comma and the title that the words describe:

> *Ancestry Magazine: 1994–1999,* CD-ROM publication
>
> "Blown away with DNA," posting, *The Legal Genealogist,* blog
>
> *Southern Echoes,* monthly newsletter of the Augusta Genealogical Society
>
> *World War I Selective Service System Draft Registration Cards,* microfilm publication

Researchers also add descriptive words to identify source characteristics that help themselves and their readers understand a source's qualities. Those qualities might indicate reliability—or questionable reliability—of information the source provides. A published source, for example, might be edited or translated. It might be one of several editions—reissues in which a publication's prior content is altered. A collection of records might be abstracted, compiled, or transcribed. In those cases, descriptive words, or their abbreviations, typically follow the title that they describe:

> *The Apriori Foundations of the Civil Law,* trans.
>
> *Black's Law Dictionary,* 4th ed. rev.
>
> *Early Church Records: St. John Lutheran Church; Red Bud, Illinois; 1855–1937,* 2 vols., comp. and transl.
>
> "Guckers," typescript report
>
> memorial 73247929, digital image

Descriptions instead of titles

Researchers answer the *What* citation question with their own words in two contexts:

1. The source or a part of a source has no title. Unpublished records, for example, often bear no title—like deeds in deed books and some papers in pension files. Similarly, articles in historic newspapers can be untitled.
2. The source's formal title does not reflect the source's content, is too generic to be meaningful, or creates unnecessary complications for researchers or readers. For example, a title like "Births" could be too broad to be useful, and *Eighth Census of the United States* requires readers to remember the year of the first census and calculate the year of the eighth.

The first context—an absent title—requires a researcher's description to answer the *What* citation question:

account of administration

declaration for pension

Beath to Greenfield, quitclaim deed

membership lists

untitled questionnaire

In the second context—an uninformative title—a researcher description would be more useful than the source's formal title. Researchers place such descriptions in their citation's field for the answer to the *What* question. These descriptions can replace any title the source might show. Because researchers capitalize citations like sentences, they do not capitalize words in their descriptions except proper nouns:

1860 U.S. census [for *Eighth Census of the United States*]

Griffith's valuation [for *General Valuation of Rateable Property in Ireland*]

Researchers also can add or supply descriptions for newspaper articles having no title or an uninformative title. If capitalization does not show that these descriptions are the researcher's words, placing them between square brackets signals that they are researcher additions:

death notice for James Greenfield, *People's Advocate*

"Obituary [of Charles D. McLain]," *Newaygo Republican*

Correcting titles

If a cited work's title contains a typographical error, researchers crafting the citation may correct it silently, or they may leave it unchanged. Leaving the misspelling, however, could create the appearance of researcher error. Pointing out the error, and perhaps embarrassing the original author, would not help the researcher's work or citation. The same is true of unconventional punctuation in a source title. Researchers crafting citations may silently correct such deviations. They should avoid, however, changes that would make a work difficult for readers to find in an electronic catalog.[2]

Conclusion

The answer to the *What* citation question arguably is a genealogy citation's most important component. A clear understanding of that question's answer enables the researcher to craft accurate answers to the other citation questions. The next chapter addresses the first of these, the *Who* citation question.

2. *The Chicago Manual of Style*, 16th ed. (Chicago: University of Chicago Press, 2010), 451–52, for sect. 8.163, "Permissible changes to titles." Also, Elizabeth Shown Mills, *Evidence Explained*, 3rd ed. (Baltimore: Genealogical Publishing, 2015), 75–56, for "Corrections," and 90, for sect. 2.76, "Titles."

Chapter 7 exercises

54. Identify the titles of sources, the titles of source parts, and any subtitles in Greenfield footnote 30.
55. In Greenfield footnote 36, what are the answers to the *What* citation question?
56. In Greenfield footnotes 23 and 43, what is the purpose of the quotation marks?
57. In Greenfield footnote 52, what is the first source cited? Is this a title or description? How do you know?
58. What is the last source cited in Greenfield footnote 52?
59. In Greenfield footnote 7, how are the three citations' answers to the *What* citation question similar?
60. Greenfield footnotes 1 and 2 cite photocopies made for personal use. What might be the reasons for citing them instead of the underlying sources?

Using sources consulted in your own genealogical research, answer the *What* citation question for one or more sources of each of the following types. Include any descriptive words that might be helpful.

61. Published books
62. Print periodicals
63. Online publications
64. CD-ROM publications, microfilm publications, or both
65. Untitled sources

Chapter 8

Authors, Creators, and Informants

> "Who—*the person, agency, business, government, office, or religious body that authored, created, edited, produced, or was responsible for the source; or, if identified, the source's informant*"[1]

Organizations, people working for organizations, and private individuals create the near-infinite variety of sources that genealogists consult. Many of them also provide information for those sources. Answers to the *Who* citation question identify some of those organizations, people, or both.

Determining those answers requires researchers to understand the creation of each source they consult. That information includes the identities of the organizations and people involved, their roles in the source's creation, and aspects of their reliability as informants and recorders. Sources often specify those people, organizations, roles, and reliability. When a source does not name an informant, researchers often can deduce the person's role, identity, or both.

Like answers to other questions about sources, the answer to the *Who* question helps genealogists and their readers understand a cited source's likely reliability. Perhaps in conjunction with descriptive statements, that answer gives information about the care taken in creating the source, including the reliability of the organizations and people providing and recording its information—the raw material that genealogists use as evidence.

Informants and recorders

All kinds of sources provide information that genealogists might use as evidence. Each information item came from someone. A person who gave information—whether identified in the source, deduced by the researcher, or unknown—is the informant for that information.

Informants might recall information about something they witnessed or something they heard or read. Informants who were eyewitnesses give primary information about what they saw. If they report information

1. Board for Certification of Genealogists [BCG], *Genealogy Standards* (Nashville, Tenn.: Ancestry.com, 2014), 7, for standard 5, "Citation elements." Quoted here with permission.

they heard or read, then their information is secondary.[2] One person in one account can provide primary information only, secondary information only, or a combination—often the latter.

When giving primary information, informants remember events, while providers of secondary information remember words. Both kinds of memories are imperfect, but given that events usually create more vivid memories than words, primary information often is more accurate than secondary information. Besides that shortcoming, retelling—the creation of secondary information—often introduces exaggerations, omissions, or errors. When researchers' documentation does not show the kind of information they are citing, they should clarify whether the supporting information is primary or secondary, or whether that determination has not been made.

Sources can—and often do—have multiple informants. A death certificate, for example, might contain separate information items from a county official, family member, physician, and sexton. Signers and designated witnesses and recorders might provide separate information for parts of legal records. In such cases, researchers cite the document as a whole, answering the *Who* citation question with the name of the organization or person who created it. A sentence following the citation identifies the informant who provided information supporting the researcher's statement or conclusion, like this citation and accompanying comment:

> Texas Department of Health, Standard Certificate of Death 30935 (1937), Charlie Peyton Jones; Bureau of Vital Statistics, Austin. The informant was "Mrs. Chas Jones."

The person providing information can be the person writing it down—for example, an autobiographer, diarist, or someone filling out an application. Alternatively, someone else—a recorder—could have written down an informant's information, chiseled it into stone, or recorded it in an audible, digital, or visible medium. Some recorders—census enumerators, for example—record information while an informant tells it. Others—newspaper reporters, for example—make the record later.

Recorders can be informants for some information in records they make. Priests, for example, record burials they conduct on behalf of their employers. Census enumerators—as public officials— identify the town or township where a family lives. In both cases, however, other information comes from other informants—for example, a buried person's birth and parental data and the ages and relationships of people in a census household.

Informant and recorder roles are important to genealogists. Care in recording affects the reliability of information that genealogists use, just as careful informing affects accuracy. Both can affect a genealogist's conclusion.

2. For these technical terms and their definitions, see BCG, *Genealogy Standards*, 24 (for standard 39, "Information preference") and 63–79 (glossary definitions of "information," "informant," "primary information," and "secondary information").

Citations can answer the *Who* question with the informant's name, especially when the supporting information comes from an affidavit, deposition, or other statement recorded while a private person gave the information. Unless the recorder seems to have affected the source's accuracy—pro or con—the recorder's name can be unmentioned. This citation fragment, naming the informant but not the recorder, provides an example:

> Seth Miner, deposition, 15 December 1832, in James Greenfield Pension application file S13192

Like citations to depositions, citations to interviews answer *Who* with the informant's name. Citations to interviews, however, usually also mention the recorder, like this citation fragment:

> Nellie (Wright) Jones, interview by Camille (Jones) Parker, 13 May 1965

Organizations as source creators

Organizations create most records that genealogists consult. They include all kinds of businesses, educational facilities, funeral homes and cemeteries, governments from national to local levels, libraries and archives, membership societies, publishing companies, religious organizations from international to local levels, and website creators.

Those organizations create records for their own purposes. With few exceptions, they do not create them for genealogists. A resource's usefulness for genealogical research is a by-product of its original purpose. That purpose, however, helps genealogists understand the record and the people it mentions.

Specific employees in an organization create records on the organization's behalf. They do this as a routine part of their employment. They usually are trained to create clear and accurate records. Usually as unbiased clerical personnel, they objectively write down information that someone tells them, create official records of events they witness, or both.

An organization's records often name the people who created them. Their names, however, usually are irrelevant to genealogical research. Those recorders created the records as employees representing their employers, not as private individuals reporting personal experiences and observations. When citing records made by an organization, therefore, researchers default to citing the employing government, institution, or organization as the creator. They mention or name the clerk, enumerator, or other official making a record only when that person's individual contribution to the record is noteworthy. This usually appears in a comment that follows the citation:

> The enumerator, Thomas Thorndale, recorded not only the state of birth but also the county.

The opposite can be true of narratives—not records—created within an organization. Professional personnel might write books and articles as part of their employment. When those sources identify them as author, genealogists cite their names as the answer to the *Who* citation question. If, however, the source identifies the organization as its creator, researchers cite the organization name.

Individuals as source creators

Besides organizations, people on their own can create sources that genealogists use. The answer to the *Who* citation question can be the name of the person who recorded an event or authored a narrative or some part of it. The answer also can be the name of a person who provided information—or some of the information—that a source contains. That informant's name might appear on or in the source, or the genealogist could deduce it from the source's content or context.

Individuals create sources describing or recording their personal beliefs, experiences, memories, observations, or research results. Most of those sources are narratives, like biographies, diaries, histories, memoirs, and travelogues. Individuals also create personal records—for example, family Bible records and filled-out forms. Individuals also can abstract, compile, edit, index, or transcribe public or private records. Any of those narratives and records can be published or unpublished.

Besides narratives and personal records, private people can create official records. These include applications for passports, pensions, and land grants, as well as affidavits supporting those applications. The creator of information on an official filled-in form—like a draft registration card, pension questionnaire, or Social Security application—is the person who provided the information, usually not the organization that created the form.

When answering the *Who* citation question with a person's name, researchers show the name that appears on the source. If they add to the name—for example, spelling out an initialized first or middle name or giving the name of a married woman identified under her husband's name, the citation shows the addition between square brackets.

After an author's name, sources might show initialisms signifying the author's certifications, degrees, and honors. Citations default to omitting these postnominals. Researchers may opt to cite them when the initials help readers understand the author's reliability.

Multiple creators of one source

In some cases, people cooperatively create a source, or part of a source. Most often this is a narrative in the form of an article, book, or chapter. The coauthors' contributions can be relatively equal, or some could have more significant roles in the source's creation than others. Researchers answer the *Who* citation question by giving coauthors' names in the order they appear in the source.

Coauthors sometimes have the same surname. Researchers might be tempted to shorten the citation by combining the names:

> Diana and Gary Smith

Conventionally, however, citations give each author's name in full:

> Diana Smith and Gary Smith

When a source has more than three authors, *The Chicago Manual of Style* recommends citing, in reference *notes*, only the first author's name followed by *et al.* (the abbreviation of *et alii*, Latin for *and others*) and with no intervening comma.[3] A fragment of a reference-note citation to a textbook with six authors provides an example:

> John Blum et al., *The National Experience*

A citation in a reference list, however, would name all six authors, with only the first author's name given last-name first.

Besides jointly creating a source, or part of a source, people or organizations can fill different roles in sources. One person or organization might create, edit, or contribute a part of a source for which another was the overall creator or editor. Examples include a receipt created by a private person in a government-created file or an authored chapter in an edited book. In each case, the answer to the *Who* citation question names both creators, like these examples (where the answers to *Who* are bolded for emphasis):

> **Reginald Washington**, "The Southern Claims Commission: A Source for African American Roots," in **Ancestry.com**, *Ancestry Magazine: 1944–1999*, CD-ROM (Provo Utah: MyFamily.com, 2001), July/August 1999.

> **Frederick von Berum**, special master, to S. L. Bryan, judge, report of sale, filed 6 May 1863; in **Monroe Co., Ill.**, Bernum vs. Gross; Foreclosures 1859–1860, box A-4; Circuit Court, Waterloo, Ill.

Typically, creators' names precede the titles of what they created. Sometimes, however, placing book editors' names *after* a book title avoids confusion. In this example, that placement ensures that readers will understand that the editors worked on the entire book, not just the cited chapter:

> Alvy Ray Smith, "Writing Using Word for Genealogy: Utilizing Microsoft Word® in Genealogical Documents in Register, or Modified Register (NGSQ), Format," in *Genealogical Writing in the 21st Century: A Guide to Register Style and More*, ed. Michael J. Leclerc and Henry B. Hoff (Boston: New England Historic Genealogical Society, 2006), 65–107.

---

3. *The Chicago Manual of Style*, 16th ed. (Chicago: University of Chicago Press, 2010), 695–96, for sect. 14.76, "Two or more authors (or editors)."

In that example, the abbreviation *ed.*, after the book title, stands for *edited by*. When the abbreviation follows editors' names, however, it stands for *editors*. In both cases, the abbreviation shows the role of people whose names the abbreviation precedes or follows.

In either case, the placement of the answer to the *Who* citation question follows Elizabeth Mills's "Velcro principle." An organization or person's name is "attached to" an answer to the *What* citation question—the name or description of what an organization or person created. Except for intervening information in parentheses or set off with commas, by default the *Who* answer immediately precedes the *What* answer, but the *Who* answer can follow the *What* answer when the rearrangement improves a citation's clarity.

Answering the *Who* citation question

Most published sources identify their creators. Book title pages and the first pages of articles and chapters usually name them. Newsletters sometimes place author's names at the ends of articles. Websites might prominently name their creators or bury the name in a copyright statement or elsewhere.

Records created by governments—local to national—often name the jurisdiction that created the record, whether it is a file, paper, or volume. If the source does not name the government that created it, researchers usually can deduce the creator from the source's location, context, or archival description.

Answers to the *Who* citation question should give the source creator's name as it was when the source was created, regardless of the creator's present-day name or location. State and county formations and boundary changes after a source's creation might change the source's location and government, but the historic creator's name remains unchanged.

Signers of original documents in files often are those records' creators. They include individual estate administrators, appraisers, and executors; people providing information for affidavits, applications, depositions, and questionnaires; and people submitting invoices and signing receipts. Those creators' names often answer the *Who* citation question.

When an entire file (the answer to the *What* citation question) supports a researcher statement or conclusion, the answer to the *Who* citation question is the organization or person that created the file. When information within a file supports a genealogist's research, the name or description of a document within the file answers the *What* citation question and the name of that document's creator, as well as the file's creator, answers the *Who* question.

Answers to the *Who* citation question help distinguish official copies from originals. People, for example, write and sign their own wills. Then county, district, or other governments copy them into will books. A private person created the original will, and a government's employee created the copy in the will book. When citing the original will, the testator's name answers the *Who* citation question, but when citing the copy in the will book the name of the county or other government answers that question. The names of government officials and employees, however, usually do not answer the *Who* citation question—that answer, instead, is the employing government's name.

Optional omission of author or creator

A source creator's name can also be the source's title or publisher. If a same-name creator is an organization, the citation need not repeat the name. Researchers, instead, omit the answer to the *Who* citation question, leaving the source title or publisher name to provide that answer. Examples include many city directories and websites:

- Citations to city directories created and published by R. L. Polk begin with the directory name, leaving the name in the publisher field to answer the *Who* citation question.
- Because the Find A Grave organization created the *Find A Grave* website, citations to the website omit the field for answering the *Who* citation question. *Find A Grave,* in the field for answering the *What* citation question, answers both questions.

Citations also can omit answers to the *Who* citation question when the source creator's name is unknown. If a source does not name its creator, but researchers can deduce the name, they place it between square brackets at the citation's beginning. Outside the citation, researchers have the option of commenting on the absence of a creator name where it might be expected. Often, however, they omit the answer, beginning the citation with the answer to *What*. Answering the *Who* citation with "Anonymous" usually is unnecessary.[4]

Describing source-creator roles

Source creators fill any of several roles related to the source. Because the usual role is "author," citations usually do not specify that role. When a creator fills another role, however—for example, abstractor, compiler, editor, or translator—understanding the role will aid in understanding the source. Some sources specify these roles, and sometimes researchers determine them. In either situation, researchers can amplify the answer to the

4. *Chicago Manual of Style,* 697, for sect. 14.79, "Anonymous works—unknown authorship."

Who citation question by adding a description of a creator's role, immediately after the name. This description usually is abbreviated in reference-note citations:

> Ida J. Lee, abstr.
>
> J. Reynolds Medart, comp.
>
> Charles Latham Jr., ed.
>
> Shirley A. Harmon and Esther R. Laumbattus, trans. and comp.

Conclusion

Answers to the *Who* citation question say who authored, created, or informed a genealogical source. Those answers, along with answers to the *What* citation question, help researchers and research consumers understand how credible or error-prone a source might be. The next three chapters address, respectively, the three remaining citation components, answers to the *When*, *Whereis*, and *Wherein* citation questions.

Chapter 8 exercises

66. In the Greenfield article in Appendix A, footnote 2, what is the answer to the *Who* citation question for both citations? How do you know what those persons' roles were in creating the cited sources?
67. Greenfield footnote 3, second citation, shows a source within a source. What is the answer to the *Who* citation question for each?
68. In Greenfield footnote 23, what is the answer to the *Who* citation question?
69. In Greenfield footnote 38, who is the informant? How is the informant's identity shown?
70. Greenfield footnote 36 cites an image and describes the source underlying the image. How does the citation answer the *Who* citation question?

Use sources from your own genealogical research to answer the *Who* citation question for the source categories listed in exercises 71–73. Include any descriptive words that might be helpful.

> 71. Sources created by organizations that are not governments
> 72. Sources created by private individuals
> 73. Sources created by governments

74. Under what circumstances could you omit the answer to the *Who* question in a citation you are crafting?

Chapter 9

Citing Absent, Hidden, Obvious, and Perplexing Dates for Sources, Information, and Events

> "When—*the date the source was created, published, last modified, or accessed; in some cases if the source is unpublished, the date of the event it reports*"[1]

A partial or complete date or range of years typically answers the *When* citation question. The date can be the year only, year plus month or season, or full date, depending on the kind of source. Date placement varies in citations to unpublished sources, but it is relatively consistent in citations to publications.

Researchers should avoid citing dates that do not help citations achieve their purposes of communicating information about source qualities and location. Except for easily changed or damaged sources, like websites and gravestones, a viewing, photographing, or photocopying date usually is unimportant. Citations do not include all dates in a record. Instead, they include dates that help with identifying sources and information items, assessing their reliability, and locating them.

Dates of publications

For publications, the answer to *When* could be the copyright or publication year (or range of years for multivolume works), the exact date of publication, the month or season and year of publication, or the year or exact date of access, viewing, or downloading. Varying date content in citations to publications helps readers quickly understand which kind of publication the citation describes. See table 7 for date content and formats for answering *When* in reference-note and reference-list citations to different kinds of publications. That table includes sample citation fragments.

---

1. Board for Certification of Genealogists [BCG], *Genealogy Standards* (Nashville, Tenn.: Ancestry.com, 2014), 7, for standard 5, "Citation elements." Quoted here with permission.

Table 7

Date Forms for Citing Publications, with Examples

PUBLICATION TYPES	REFERENCE-NOTE CITATIONS	REFERENCE-LIST CITATIONS
Books, CD-ROMs, microfilms, microfiche	Copyright year, publication year, or "no date" or "n.d."; in parentheses after publisher information: (. . . , [publisher], 1947), . . . (. . . , [publisher], n.d.), . . .	Same as in reference-note citations or a range of dates; no parentheses: . . . [publisher], 1947.
Journals, magazines, newsletters	Month or season and year of publication as it appears in the publication; between parentheses after the journal's or magazine's number: . . . 17 (Spring 1965): . . . . . . 9 (Fall 2010):	Same as in reference-note citations or a range of dates set off with a comma: . . . , 1865–70.
Newspapers	Exact date after title or place of publication; placed between parentheses or set off with commas: . . . , Fla., 3 July 1910, ... , Ga. (3 July 1910), . . .	Date or date range; no parentheses: . . . , 3 July 1910. . . . , 1890–1910.
Websites	Exact viewing date or item posting date; in parentheses after URL and a colon: ([URL] : viewed on 20 February 2017). ([URL] : accessed on 20 February 2017).	Year of viewing; no parentheses: [URL] : 2017.

Note: Date ranges in reference-list citations reflect the research scope within the respective source.

Print publications

As the examples in table 7 show, different kinds of print publications show dates in different ways, and researchers cite them differently:

- Most published books show copyright years. Researchers cite that year after the place of publication and publisher's identity—two items separated by a colon. In reference-note citations, the publication details and date are enclosed in parentheses, usually followed by a comma. Reference lists omit the parentheses.
- Federal government publications, not copyrighted, give a printing year, which researchers cite like a copyright year.
- Different volumes of published multivolume sets can have different copyright dates. Researchers may cite the date of the volume they consult, or the range of years for an entire set, depending on which will be more helpful to their readers. To show that a series is continuing, they cite the earliest volume's year followed by an en dash—for example, *1967–*.
- Newspapers and some newsletters give exact publication dates. In reference notes, researchers cite those dates after the title or place of publication. That date can be parenthetical or set off with commas. Reference lists show the range of dates a researcher consulted, set off from the title with a comma.
- Journals and magazines bear a date reflecting a publication period. Usually this is month and year or season and year. Researchers cite this date like it appears on the issue they consulted. The date appears parenthetically after the periodical's title in reference notes and reference lists. A colon often follows the closing parenthesis.

Microfilm and CD-ROM publications

Contents of published microfilm and CD-ROMS typically show copyright or publication years. Researchers cite them like book copyright years.

A special case is National Archives non-census microfilm publications, used today mostly as online images. Those images typically do not show the microfilm publication dates, but researchers can find them online on a "descriptive pamphlet" (DP), a National Archives guide to the microfilm publication and its contents. Googling the word *microfilm* and the publication designator (M804, for example) often yields a downloadable PDF of the corresponding DP. If not, researchers can locate it with five or six mouse clicks through the National Archives website:

- Open the web page at https://www.archives.gov/shop/.
- Click "Order Reproductions."
- Click "Microfilm."

- Under "Order Microfilm," type in the publication number (for example, *M804*) and then click "Submit."
- If an error message appears, go back, add the letter *a* after the publication number (for example, *M804a*), and try again.
- Click "View Important Publication Details" to download the DP in PDF format.

Websites

Most websites—the most easily altered sources that genealogists consult—provide no date. Researchers, therefore, cite their exact access date. In effect, this date tells them and their readers, "This is what I saw on that date—I make no warranty that the same information will appear on a later date." An appropriately descriptive word like *accessed, downloaded, searched,* or *viewed* can precede the date, which appears after the URL and a colon, all in parentheses in reference-note citations.

Websites occasionally give a copyright or "last updated" date. Researchers can cite that date as well as their own access date. They set off the website's copyright or "updated" date with a comma after the cited title of the web page or website. The researcher's words identify it as a copyright or "last updated" date.

To avoid repetition in their documentation, researchers can check all their website citations shortly before their work goes to press. Then, preceding the work's first citation, they can specify that date, using a phrase like, "All websites referenced herein were last accessed on. . . ." They then can omit the answer to the *When* citation question in their publication's subsequent website citations.

Dates of unpublished sources

For unpublished sources, the answer to the *When* citation question is the date or year the source was created or recorded, the date of the event it documents, or both. Researchers cite the date or dates they believe will be most helpful and economical in their citation's context. Using Elizabeth Mills's "Velcro principle," they set off the date with commas immediately after the source title or event description that the date refers to.

General considerations

When a source does not answer the *When* citation question directly, the researcher should estimate the date, if possible, using a word—like *about, between, probably,* or *say*—showing that the date is an estimate. The words *no date* (or their abbreviation, *n.d.*) give an uninformative and unhelpful answer to the *When* citation question. Researchers use them only when no estimate is possible.

Studying sources in context or studying about sources sometimes is necessary to determine the best answer to the *When* citation question. Dates of court minutes and court orders, for example, often appear pages before the item of interest to the researcher. A court case's or probate's ending date can help researchers locate a file in a collection sequenced by ending date.

Colonial dual dating[2]

The English government adopted the Gregorian calendar in 1752. In prior years, under the Julian calendar, England and her colonies began each year—officially and religiously—on 25 March. Other governments began the year in January, however, and many English people celebrated the year's beginning in January.

Record keepers dealt with the ambiguity by using two years for dates in January, February, and March. These record keepers represented the two years in various ways, including separating them with a slash and writing one number below the other, like a fraction:

- The first or top number represented the "old style" (O.S.) Julian calendar year.
- The second or bottom number represented the "new style" (N.S.) Gregorian calendar year.

Their notation might resemble one of these examples:

Jany 11 1749/50

Jany 11 1749 O.S.

Jany 11 1750 N.S.

Jany 11 17$\frac{49}{50}$

Researchers might encounter old-style dates that seem wrong to modern eyes. A source might show, for example, that a will dated 12 April 1750 was proved in court on 12 January 1750. From a present-day perspective, someone wrote a will some months after dying, an impossible scenario. Dual dating clarifies the chronology:

Will dated: 12 April 1750

Will proved: 12 January 1750[/1]

Thus, the will was proved in court eight months after the testator wrote it.

2. This section is based on Donald Lines Jacobus, "Dates and the Calendar," in *Genealogy as Pastime and Profession*, 2nd ed. rev. (1968; reprint, Baltimore: Genealogical Publishing, 1986), 109–13.

Where confusion could occur, researchers encountering old-style January, February, and March dates predating 1752 can transform them into dual dates in their citations. Square brackets show their addition:

> 17 February 1748[/9].

Conclusion

Answers to the *When* citation question place sources in time. Those answers show researchers and research consumers the chronological closeness—or distance—of narratives and records to or from the events they describe. That information, like the answers to other citation questions, helps them assess each source's likely reliability. *When* answers also help researchers locate sources and information items that are chronologically arranged.

Chapter 9 exercises

75. Greenfield footnotes 1 (its first citation), 2 (its second citation), and 18 (within the quotation), cite unknown dates in different ways. What are those ways, and why do they differ?
76. Greenfield footnote 18, the last citation, has two answers to the *When* citation question. What does each refer to?
77. Explain the answer to the *When* citation question in Greenfield footnote 44, the second citation.
78. How many answers to the *When* citation question appear in Greenfield footnote 52? What do they tell you?

Using materials from your own research, answer the *When* citation question for the kinds of sources listed in exercises 79–83:

> 79. One or more books
> 80. One or more journals or magazines
> 81. One or more websites
> 82. One or more unpublished sources for which only one answer to *When* is helpful.
> 83. One or more unpublished sources for which more than one answer to *When* is helpful.

84. Under what circumstances is it acceptable to not give a date as the answer to the *When* question in a citation you are crafting?

Chapter 10

Citing Numbered, Grouped, and Subgrouped Offline Sources and Information Items

> "Wherein—*the specific location within the source where the information item can be found, for example, page, image, or sequence number; or—if the source is unpublished—its box number, folder or collection name, or similar identifying information*."[1]

Entire sources rarely document facts, paraphrases, quotations, statements, and other aspects of genealogical research. Typically the documentation comes from specific information within a source. Citations, therefore, not only describe sources, they also point to specific information within sources.

Most citations refer to information by specifying the details that document a fact or statement, that information's location within the source, or both. That specification, location, or both form the answer to the *Wherein* citation question. Researchers answer it with sufficient detail for anyone to turn to the cited information with minimal effort. When the answer to *Wherein* is clear and complete, researchers using their own citations—and readers following a citation—do not need to repeat the original search.

This chapter addresses options and complications for answering the *Wherein* question for offline sources. Many are publications. More often, however, genealogists refer to offline information in unpublished materials.

Page numbers

Answering the *Wherein* citation question is easiest for paginated standalone sources. If the source is published, the answer usually is a page number or range of page numbers. If the source is unpublished, researchers typically add to the citation a brief description of the information found

---

1. Board for Certification of Genealogists, *Genealogy Standards* (Nashville, Tenn.: Ancestry.com, 2014), 7–8, for standard 5, "Citation elements." Quoted here with permission.

on the cited page. These citation segments answer the *Wherein* citation question for three paginated stand-alone unpublished sources and three publications:

> p. 139, Sarah Greenfield birth, 30 March 1742 [unpublished record]
>
> records 1:57, James Greenfield, 5 November 1738 [unpublished record]
>
> "Land Tax list of the South East Quarter of the Manor of Ranselear District in the County of Albany," 1779, pp. 18 (Raymond Greenfield) and 21 (James Greenfield) [unpublished record]
>
> *Families of Early Hartford, Connecticut . . .*, 340 [book]
>
> *Boston Gazette*, 14 November 1720, page 2, col. 2 [newspaper]
>
> *New England Historical and Genealogical Register* 77 (July 1923): 194–213 [journal]

Citations to page numbers can identify them with the initials *p.* (for one page) or *pp.* (for more than one page). Researchers may omit those identifications in citations to publications, where the number typically appears in a default position at or near the end of the citation, like the book example above. Newspaper citations, however, usually identify page numbers, to distinguish them from column numbers. Some researchers spell out the word *page* in newspaper citations, to break up the numbers and make the citation a bit more readable.

Researchers also have options for citing multiple page numbers from a paginated source:

> 107–9
>
> 17, 23, 37
>
> 17, 23, and 37
>
> 123–25, 147–49
>
> 123–25 and 147–49

Those examples show conventionally abridged inclusive numbers joined with en dashes.[2] The inserted *and* is optional, but it breaks up the numbers, helping improve a citation's readability.

Folio numbers

Foliation resembles pagination. Page numbers appear sequentially on both sides of a book's leaves, but folio numbers can appear on just one side of each leaf, or the same number can appear on both sides of a two-page spread. In both cases, a folio number refers to two sides. Citations to folios, therefore, must refer to a specific folio, a specific side, or both. Figure 3 shows two kinds of foliation:

2. *The Chicago Manual of Style*, 16th ed. (Chicago: University of Chicago Press, 2010), 483, for sect. 9.60, "Abbreviating, or condensing, inclusive numbers."

Figure 3

Two Kinds of Foliation

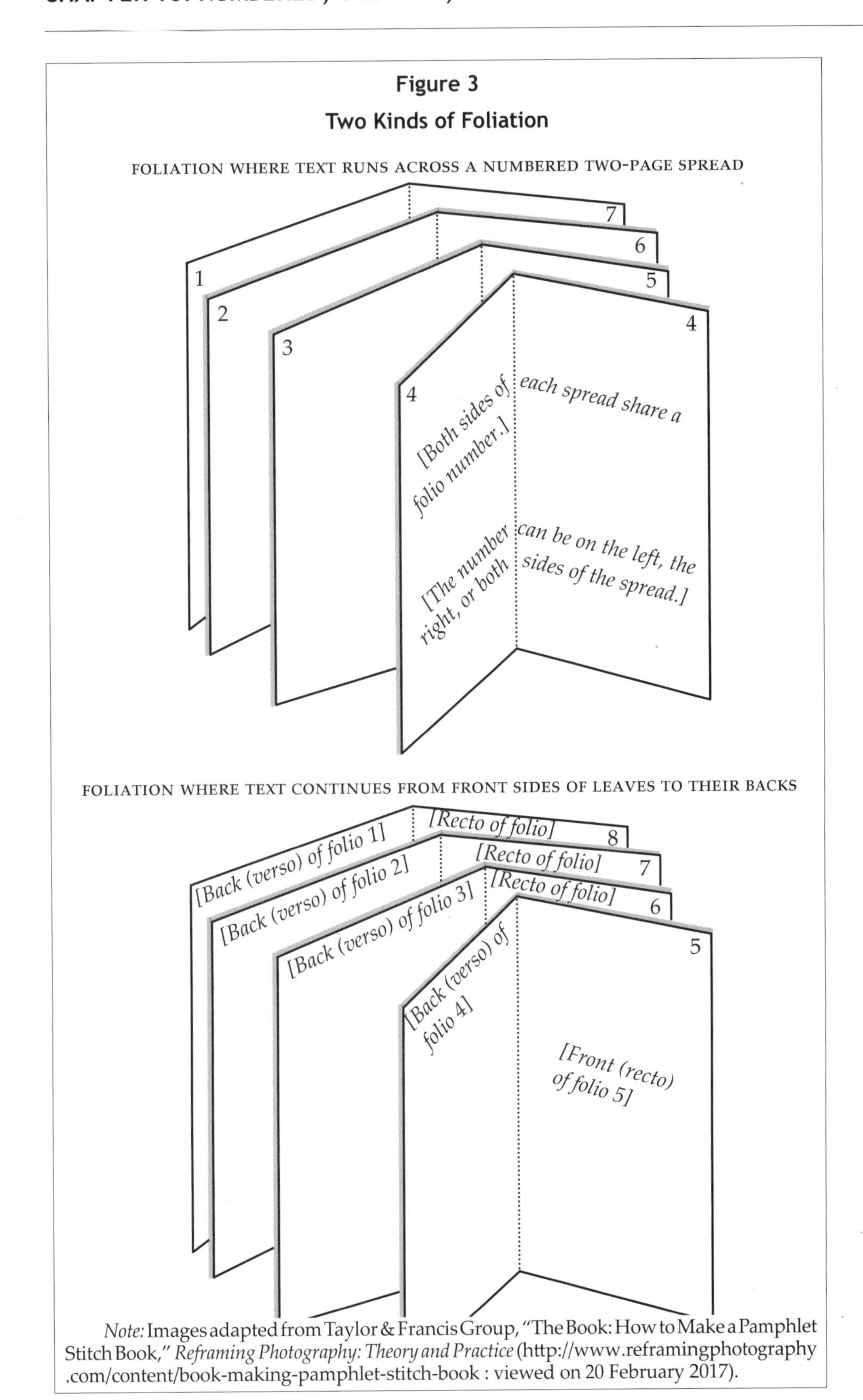

Note: Images adapted from Taylor & Francis Group, "The Book: How to Make a Pamphlet Stitch Book," *Reframing Photography: Theory and Practice* (http://www.reframingphotography.com/content/book-making-pamphlet-stitch-book : viewed on 20 February 2017).

1. Records run in rows from the left side of a two-page spread to the right, like some early censuses or registers of vital records. The folio number, referring to both sides of the spread, can appear on either side of the spread or on both sides. Citations to information on the spread give the folio number, identifying it with the abbreviation *fol.* (when citing records on one folio) or *fols.* (when citing records on more than one folio.) No confusion would occur, however, if a researcher identified this kind of folio number as a page number.
2. Information continues from the fronts of leaves onto their backs. The folio number, typically on the right side of a spread, refers to both the leaf's front (recto) and its unnumbered back (verso). Thus, the left side of a two-page spread is the unnumbered back of a numbered leaf and the right side is the numbered front of the next leaf. Citations to folios where the information is continuous from front to back give the folio number with the letter *r* (for *recto*, the front of the leaf) or *v* (for *verso*, the back of the leaf). Several combinations are possible—fol. 12r, fol. 20v, fols. 27r–v, fols. 32v–33r (a spread), and fols. 42v–53r. By pointing to specific sides of numbered leaves, this convention avoids ambiguity and awkwardness when more than one folio or side is involved. Also, citing the back (verso) of folio 33 as *page 34 left* varies from the original writer's intent, the volume's organization, and longstanding citation practice for folios. That example and other idiosyncratic page designations could confuse readers.[3]

Unnumbered pages

Unnumbered pages, folios, or loose sheets of paper can tempt researchers to count them and then cite them as if they were numbered. This risks doubly confusing readers. When they consult the source and do not see page or folio numbers, they could believe they have not found the researcher's source. In addition, if readers count the pages—especially if the number is high or some pages or their backs are blank—their count could differ from the researcher's count. The researcher might appear to have cited a nonexistent record, compromising the work's credibility.

Understanding how unbound papers or unnumbered pages or folios are organized helps researchers answer the *Wherein* citation question with information, rather than with a page or folio number:

- Sometimes the sequence is alphabetical, or grouped by first letter of surname. In those cases, the citation answers *Wherein* with a word or phrase about the alphabetical arrangement and supplies the name needed to locate the cited information.

3. For more information on citing folio numbers, see *Chicago Manual of Style*, 725, for sect. 14.162, "Folio editions." Also, Elizabeth Shown Mills, *Evidence Explained: Citing History Sources from Artifacts to Cyberspace*, 3rd ed. (Baltimore: Genealogical Publishing, 2015), 260–61, for sect. 6.8, "Citing Page, Folio, or Sheet Numbers."

- Often the sequence is chronological, and a date and the words *chronologically arranged* suffice to show where a specific item is located. Researchers might need to determine the date a clerk used for filing or sequencing a record. Rather than a personal event date, it could be a recording or filing date, a court date several pages away from the information of interest, a case's ending date, or a ship departure or arrival date shown only on the manifest's first page. In any case, the citation should specify the date's basis—for example, "filed under court session July 1854."

Only rarely are sources so disorganized that they offer no way to cite them by describing the location of specific information within them. Describing a source's arrangement is more helpful than citing it as "unpaginated."

Multiple numbers on one page

Unpublished manuscripts can bear one or more sets of numbers. The original creator probably provided one of those sets. Other numbers could be additions by record keepers and archivists long after a manuscript's creation.

Multiple numbers on a page create a dilemma for source citation. The conciseness principle suggests citing only one of the numbers. In conflict, the completeness principle suggests citing all of them. When citing more than one number, the clarity principle requires distinguishing each set of numbers from the others.

Researchers often, however, can achieve clarity and conciseness by citing one number and ignoring the others. This requires the researcher to understand what each number refers to—pointing again to the importance of understanding a source before describing it in a citation. Researchers who understand a record's numbering usually do not need to describe cited numbers as "stamped," "penned," and the like.

When different numbers appear on a page, they likely enumerate different elements within the source. Folio numbers, for example, count each side of a bound leaf, while page numbers count both sides. In a census, one set of numbers might refer to pages or folios within an enumeration district (ED), and another set could refer to pages or folios of a county, township, city, ward, or other civil subdivision or to a bound census volume. Citing the number as a page number or folio number and attaching it to what it counts—for example the ED or township—identifies the number that is cited. "Attached" page numbers usually follow what they count., like these examples:

> 1850 U.S. census, New London Co., Conn., fol. 397r [Refers to the recto (back) side of the 397th sheet for New London County]
>
> 1860 U.S. census, New London Co., Conn., Old Lyme, p. 12 [Refers to the twelfth page of Old Lyme]

Nested levels

Complications in answering the *Wherein* citation question arise when an offline published or unpublished source is part of a group, a common situation. These groups typically are series of three or more levels, each nested in a larger level—like Russian dolls. A page in a numbered volume, for example, is the smallest of three nested levels: page, volume, and multivolume set. Researchers can cite the levels from largest to smallest:

> *The Acts and Resolves, Public and Private, of the Province of the Massachusetts Bay*, vol. 15 ([publication data]), 280.

In that example, the largest level is the titled twenty-one-volume set, the middle level is a numbered volume, and the smallest level is page 280.

Periodicals like journals, newsletters, and newspapers also contain nested levels, which their citations reflect:

> *National Genealogical Society Quarterly* 104 (December 2016): 283–93.
>
> "Death of David Mitchell," *Litchfield Independent* (Litchfield, Minn.), 28 December 1910, page 1, col. 7.

In the first citation, the levels—from general to specific—are the journal, its 104th volume, and pages within that volume. In the second citation, those levels are the conventionally sequenced titles of the article and newspaper, a specific issue of that paper, a page within that issue, and a column on that page.

Unpublished sources also nest in levels. Beside pages in a volume in a set of volumes, nested levels of unpublished sources can include record groups, collections, series, boxes, and files. The three segments of the following citation identify *(a)* an untitled paper in *(b)* a titled file in *(c)* a titled and numbered box of files:

> Report of sale, filed 6 May 1863; in Bernum vs. Gross file; Monroe Co., Foreclosures 1859–1860, box A-4. . . .

In that example, the citation is sequenced from specific to general. Semicolons group information about each nested level and separate each level from other levels. The smallest level is a dated report. It is nested in a file with other papers concerning a court suit. That file is nested in a box with files of other cases opened during the same two-year period.

The uniqueness of unpublished sources adds three more levels to the previous example: the repository holding the box, its city, and its state:

> Report of sale, filed 6 May 1863; in Bernum vs. Gross file; Monroe Co., Foreclosures 1859–1860, box A-4; Circuit Court, Waterloo, Ill.

The full range of six nested levels in that example gives answers to both the *Wherein* citation question (discussed in this chapter and chapter 11) and the *Whereis* citation question (addressed in chapter 12).

Records in archives and historical societies can be located within nested levels, like this example, which cites levels from a page to an archive and its location:

> "Land Tax list of the South East Quarter of the Manor of Ranselear District in the County of Albany," 1779, p. 18, Raymond Greenfield; document 43, box 2; New York Treasurer's Office Account and Tax Assessment Lists, series A3210; New York State Archives, Albany.

Tables 8 and 9 provide further examples of citations to published and unpublished sources in nested levels.

Identifying nested levels

Citing a source in nested levels requires noting and understanding the levels. This can come from studying the source, its context, and source guides. Library catalogs and archival finding aids often are helpful. Archival request forms can identify levels for which information is required to retrieve—and, therefore, to cite—the source. As is often the case, even without nested levels, citing a source clearly and completely requires more than simply looking at one item of interest within the source.

Papers and containers in nested levels can bear numbers, letters, or number-letter combinations, besides titles. See table 10 for examples. Identifiers (like *page*, *box*, and *record group*) show what the number counts. The identifier and number precede or follow the item's title or description. In these citation segments the numbers and their identifiers are bolded for emphasis:

> **box 6**, [of the] Van Rensselaer Manor Land Survey and Maps
>
> **collection SC7079**, [of the] Van Rensselaer (Rensselaerwyck) Manor Records
>
> **box A-4**: Foreclosures 1859–1860
>
> **Record Group 15**: Department of Veterans Affairs

A number preceding a container's title can imply it numbers an item within the container, like the first two examples above. When a colon sets off the title, like the second two examples, it implies that the number, as well as the title, designates the container. Researchers choose the sequence and punctuation that best answers the *Wherein* citation question for each source with nested levels that they cite. Subsequent citations, shortened, can use the container designation and number, omitting its title, in other words just the bolded information in the above examples.

Table 8

**Answering the *Wherein* Citation Question:
Parts of Citations to Four Publications with Nested Levels**

. . . *Pennsylvania Archives*, 2nd ser., 13:114.

The citation segment contains four nested levels, cited from general to specific:

1. The title of the publication (*Pennsylvania Archives*)
2. The number of the series (2) under that title
3. The number of a volume (13) within that series
4. The number of a page (114) within that volume containing the cited information

---

. . . *William and Mary Quarterly*, 3rd ser., 58 (. . .): 373–402.

The citation segment contains four nested levels, cited from general to specific:

1. The title of the periodical publication (*William and Mary Quarterly*)
2. The number of the series (3) under that title
3. The number of a volume (58) within that series
4. Page numbers (373–402) within that volume containing a cited article

---

. . . *State Papers of Vermont*, vol. 3, *Journals and Proceedings of the General Assembly of the State of Vermont, 1778–1781* . . ., part 1, p. 17.

The citation segment contains four nested levels, cited from general to specific:

1. The title of a set of books numbered as 13 volumes of one title (*State Papers of Vermont*)
2. The single volume number (3—given by the publisher) and title (*Journals and Proceedings* . . .) of a set of four separately bound and paginated books together considered to be volume 3 of the set's thirteen numbered volumes
3. The number (1—given by the publisher) of one of the four books (identified by the publisher as "parts") in the set's volume 3
4. The number of a page (17) within that part containing the cited information

---

. . . *Passenger and Crew Lists of Vessels Arriving at New York, New York, 1897–1957* . . . roll 870 . . . 17 April 1907, SS *Carmania*, list 1, line 22.

The citation segment contains six nested levels, cited from general to specific:

1. The title of the microfilm publication (*Passenger and Crew Lists* . . .)
2. The number of one microfilm roll among 8,892 rolls in that publication
3. A specific arrival date, among many arrival dates on that microfilm roll
4. The name of one ship (SS *Carmania*), among several arriving on that date
5. The number (1) of one of that ship's several manifests
6. The number (22) of a line on that manifest naming a person of interest

Table 9

Answering the *Wherein* Citation Question: Parts of Citations to Two Unpublished Sources with Nested Levels

Survey book, fol. 2, Archibald Greenfield leasehold, 9 April 1793; folder 2, Stephentown Survey Book, 1788–1796; box 6, Van Rensselaer Manor Land Surveys and Maps, ca. 1785–1840; collection SC7079, Van Rensselaer (Rensselaerwyck) Manor Records, 1630–1899; New York State Archives, Albany.

That citation contains six nested levels, grouped and separated with semicolons, and cited from the specific item to the most general level:

1. The specific item of interest (a survey on a specific folio [2] in a specific bound book)
2. The folder containing that book and its label (Stephentown Survey Book . . .)
3. The box containing that folder and the title of the series of boxes (Van Rensselaer Manor Land Surveys and Maps, ca. 1785–1840)
4. The number and name of the collection (collection SC7079, Van Rensselaer [Rensselaerwyck] Manor Records, 1630–1899) containing that series of boxes
5. The name of the archive (New York State Archives) housing that collection
6. The city (Albany) where the archive is located
7. (The state is omitted in this example, because the archive name implies it.)

Robert S. Whitney, deposition, 23 April 1855; in bounty land warrant file, act of [18]50 — 80 W.T. 93906, for service of Thomas Greenfield (Sgt., Capt. Lemuel Potter's Regt., N.Y. militia, War of 1812); Case Files of Bounty-Land Warrant Applications Based on Service Between 1812 and 1855; Record Group 15: Department of Veterans Affairs; National Archives, Washington, D.C.

That citation contains six nested levels, grouped and separated with semicolons, and cited from the specific item to the most general level:

1. The specific document (untitled, but described as "deposition"), with its informant (Robert Whitney) and date (23 April 1855)
2. The label on the envelope holding the paper ("bounty land warrant file, act of [18]50 — 80 W.T. 93906")
3. The official title of the series containing that file (Case Files of Bounty-Land Warrant Applications Based on Service Between 1812 and 1855)
4. The number of the record group (15) and its title ([Records of the] Department of Veterans Affairs), of which the series is a part
5. The name of the building (National Archives) housing that record group
6. The place (Washington, D.C.) where that building is located

Table 10

Examples of Numbers on Documents and Containers in Nested Levels

TYPICAL OF PUBLICATIONS	
series 2	2nd series
volume 4 [changed from iv]	page 192
Spring 2017 [issue]	part 3
TYPICAL OF UNPUBLISHED MATERIALS	
folder 3, box 29	ward 6
form 3—409	bundle 73
exhibit 19	dwell./fam. 22
series 14A	ref. HO107/786/11
item 12	dwelling 20, family 24
line 7	County Records collection 3
ED 72	local no. 23, state no. 1407

Citing sources in nested levels

Through formatting, descriptive wording, or both, citations show how levels are nested. When cited, the sequence creates a path for researchers to efficiently retrieve and examine a specific item.

Researchers have three options for sequencing nested levels in citations:

1. Start with the largest, most general level and follow a declining sequence to end with *(a)* a specific page or sheet, *(b)* description of a specific information item on that page, or *(c)* both. This sequence is common in citations to publications with nested levels, which usually end with a page number. Refer back to table 8 for examples.
2. Start with the specific item and follow an increasing sequence to end with the largest, most general level—the reverse of option 1, above. This sequence is common in citations to unpublished sources in nested levels, which usually begin with a document title or description and end with a province, state, or country. Refer back to table 9 for examples.
3. Mix the levels, rather than follow a rigid specific-to-general or general-to-specific sequence. This sequence risks confusion, except for publications with widely used and understood formats, like those shown in table 11.

Table 12 shows a summary of these options and suggested defaults. Researchers should deviate from the defaults, however, when the deviation adds clarity to a citation's answer to the *Wherein* question.

Table 11

Two Citations with Properly Out-of-Sequence Nested Levels

"Died," *People's Advocate*, New London, Conn., 13 December 1843, page 3, col. 3.

That citation contains six nested levels, but the standard format cited above lists them in neither a strict general-to-specific nor a strict specific-to-general order. Citing them in either order would be unconventional. These are the six levels, shown for comparison in the general-to-specific sequence often used for citing publications but not recommended for citing newspapers:

1. The state (Conn.)
2. The city (New London)
3. The newspaper issue (*People's Advocate*, 13 December 1843)
4. The page (3) within that issue
5. The column (3) on that page
6. The title of the article ("Died") in that column

---

1 John 4:16 (King James Version)

That citation implies six nested levels, but the standard format cited just above lists them in neither a strict general-to-specific not a strict specific-to-general order. Citing them in either order would be unconventional. These are the six levels, shown for comparison in the general-to-specific sequence often used for citing publications but not recommended for citing Bible verses:

1. Any version of the Bible (implied but not cited)
2. Of those versions, the King James version
3. That version's four books titled John (one gospel and three epistles)
4. The first epistle of John
5. That book's chapter 4
6. Verse 16 within that book

Table 12

Suggested Sequences for Citing Sources in Nested Levels

SEQUENCE	SUGGESTED CITATION USE
General to specific	Publications
Specific to general	Unpublished sources ("American" style; can be different elsewhere)
Mixed	Publications and unpublished sources with widely understood citation formats

Serials, also known as periodicals

Publications produced serially (periodically) on a regular schedule are called serials or periodicals. They can be scheduled or issued daily, weekly, monthly, seasonally, biannually, or annually. Sequential issues bear the same title; however, periodical titles occasionally change while maintaining the periodical's identity. In those cases, researchers may cite either the title on the issue they consulted or the present-day title. If only the latter appears in library catalogs, it is the better title to cite.

Familiar examples of periodicals include journals, magazines, and newspapers. Less familiar examples include proceedings and reports of conferences, organizations, and societies. Library cataloging, which distinguishes serials from other kinds of publications, will show whether a particular publication is a periodical or not.

Publishers of journals identify each issue with a year and a month or season—for example, *June 2016* or *Summer 2015*. Anticipating that libraries will bind each year's issues into a volume, publishers also assign a volume number. Instead of starting each periodical issue with page 1, most journal publishers number pages sequentially throughout each annual volume.

Volume and page numbers usually answer the *Wherein* citation question for most serials except newspapers. Newspaper citations typically omit a volume number and add a column number, answering the *Wherein* question with only page and column numbers.

Volume-page designations

Many published and unpublished sources are numbered or lettered volumes in a titled set. Each volume typically has its own pagination beginning with page one. Researchers may answer the *Wherein* citation question with the volume designation (letters, numbers, or a combination) and page number (or numbers). They may identify numbers or letters with words or the abbreviations for *page, pages, volume,* and *volumes* (*p., pp., vol.,* and *vols.)* This is common when the numbers do not appear in a default position or other citation information separates the volume and page designations.

When the volume designation and page number would appear together in a default position, researchers can omit the identifiers and separate the volume designation and page number with a colon. The number or letter preceding the colon is the volume number, and the number or numbers after the colon are the page number or numbers. These citation fragments give volume and page numbers of one published and four unpublished volumes:

> *The Acts and Resolves, Public and Private, of the Province of the Massachusetts Bay*, 15:280

Marriages 7:49

Will Book 5:431–33

Deed Book BB:206–10

Land Records M2:73–77

Citations to articles and pages in bound periodicals follow a similar practice. There the periodical issue descriptor—month or season plus year—appears in parentheses after the volume number. For aesthetic reasons, a space can follow the colon when parenthetic information, rather than a number or letter immediately precedes it:

National Genealogical Society Quarterly 104 (June 2016): 99

A few journal publishers do not identify a periodical with a month or season designation. Citations in that case give only the year in parentheses, and the issue number follows the volume number:

Newport Historical Magazine 4, no. 3 (1883): 243.

Multivolume sets and series

Multivolume sets, collections of volumes created simultaneously or sequentially, are the top level of up to four nested levels: set, series, volume, and page. The sets can be published (like library books) or unpublished (like will and deed books). Publishers and record keepers identify some sequentially created multivolume sets as series and give them series titles, series numbers, or both. Volumes within a set can have any combination of volume number, volume letter, and volume title.

Each volume in a set usually begins with new pagination, rather than continued page numbers from one volume to the next. When the pagination does continue across volumes, citing the volume number helps researchers and readers by telling them which volume to consult.

Researchers regularly use and cite multivolume sets, each with its own combination of titles, no titles, numbers, and no numbers for *(a)* the entire set, *(b)* any series of or within the set, and *(c)* volumes within the set or series. Table 13 shows combinations of titles and numbers for four commonly encountered kinds of multivolume sets, and table 14 gives examples.

In order to cite information in a multivolume set—to answer the *Wherein* question clearly and completely—researchers must identify the sets's nested levels, besides the page. They check for set, series, and volume titles and numbers. Table 14 gives a sample citation for each of four kinds of multivolume sets, showing the information necessary for complete answers to *Wherein*.

Table 13

Four Kinds of Multivolume Sets

TYPE OF SET	SET CHARACTERISTICS	SERIES CHARACTERISTICS	VOLUME CHARACTERISTICS
Titled set comprising untitled volumes	Titled set	No series title	Numbered* and not titled
Titled set comprising titled volumes	Titled set	No series title	Numbered and titled
Numbered series	Titled set	Numbered, perhaps also with a series title	Numbered and all or most not separately titled
Titled series comprising titled volumes	Set not titled separately from series	Titled series	Titled, perhaps numbered

*In this context, volume numbering includes the designation of individual volumes with numbers, letters, or letter-number combinations—for example, vol. 7, F, 4C, or D2.

Libraries typically catalog published multivolume sets by either its series title (if it has one) or its volume title, but not both. Because readers use library catalogs to locate cited books, citations to multivolume sets should include cataloged titles. Researchers may additionally cite an uncataloged series title or volume title. They take that option when the information helps them or their readers understand the relevance of the volume or series to a work's documentation. The second and fourth citations in table 14 reflect the option of including an uncataloged series or volume title.

Table 15 summarizes the set, series, and volume information needed and optional for answering *Wherein* when citing four kinds of multivolume sets.

Conclusion

In citations to offline materials, answers to the *Wherein* question typically refer to a page, folio, or information item on a sheet of paper within a source. Sometimes the source's sheets are numbered; sometimes they are not. Sometimes the sheet is the smallest and most specific of a series of nested levels that vary among sources, whether they are published or not.

Clearly and completely answering the *Wherein* citation requires researchers to go beyond looking only at information of interest. They must understand that information's context, including the source's arrangement, the levels in which the information can be nested, and what any numbering refers to. Armed with that understanding, they can precisely describe where specific information is to be found.

Table 14

Answering the *Wherein* Citation Question for Four Kinds of Multivolume Sets

TITLED SET COMPRISING UNTITLED VOLUMES

[Compiler], *Descendants of Thomas Durfee of Portsmouth, R.I.*, vol. 2 ([publication details]), 416.

Set title: *Descendants of Thomas Durfee of Portsmouth, R.I.*

Volume number: 2

Page number: 416

Comment: This type of multivolume set is not serialized. It has no series title, no series number, and no volume titles. It is cataloged—thus located and cited—by the title of the set.

TITLED SET COMPRISING TITLED VOLUMES

Mayflower Families Through Five Generations, vol. 15, *James Chilton – Richard More* ([publication details]), 5–7.

Set title: *Mayflower Families Through Five Generations*

Volume number and title: vol. 15, *James Chilton – Richard More*

Pages: 5–7

Comment: The volume title is italicized because it is a publication title. The volume is not cataloged and, thus, not required for a citation. It is cited when it helps show the volume's relevance to a researcher's work. The volume number, which is not part of the title, is not italicized.

NUMBERED SERIES

[Article title], *Pennsylvania Archives*, 2nd ser., vol. 13 ([publication details]), 114

Series title and number: *Pennsylvania Archives*, series 2

Volume number within that series: vol. 13

Page number: 114

Comment: Some volumes in this series have titles.

TITLED SERIES COMPRISING TITLED VOLUMES

[Authors], *Genealogy and the Law : A Guide to Legal Sources for the Family Historian*, National Genealogical Society Special Topics Series ([publication details]), 87.

Volume title and subtitle: *Genealogy and the Law : A Guide to Legal Sources for the Family Historian*

Series title: National Genealogical Society Special Topics Series

Page number: 87

Comment: This multivolume set, a titled series, has no series number. The volume number, 114, though cataloged, would not add to a citation. Citing the series title (uncataloged) is optional. If cited, it is not italicized, showing that the source is cataloged—thus located and cited—by the volume title.

Table 15

Citation Essentials and Options for Four Kinds of Multivolume Sets

KIND OF SET	CITATION **ESSENTIALS** FOR ANSWERING *WHEREIN*	CITATION **OPTIONS** FOR ANSWERING *WHEREIN*
Titled set of untitled volumes	Title of set (italicized), number of volume,* page number(s)	
Titled set of titled volumes	Title of set (italicized), number of volume,* page number(s)	Volume title (italicized), if cataloged†
Numbered series	Any series title (italicized), number of series, number of volume, page number(s)	
Titled series and volumes	Title of volume (italicized),* page number(s)	Series title (not italicized), if helpful or cataloged†

*Volume numbering includes the designation of individual volumes with letters or letter-number combinations—for example, vol. 7, F, 4C, or D2.

†Library cataloging typically uses either the series title or volume title. The cataloged title should be cited. The uncataloged title is optional.

Chapter 10 exercises

85. In Greenfield footnote 3, second citation, what are the source's nested levels? How are they sequenced in the citation? What are the citation's answers to the *What* and *Wherein* citation questions?
86. In Greenfield footnote 4, first citation, what are the source's nested levels? How are they sequenced in the citation? What are the citation's answers to the *What* and *Wherein* citation questions?
87. In Greenfield footnote 24, what are the source's nested levels? How are they sequenced in the citation?
88. In Greenfield footnote 30, first citation, what are the source's nested levels? How are they sequenced in the citation?

89. Greenfield footnote 39 uses nested levels to cite two unpublished sources. What are each source's levels, and how are they sequenced in the citation?

90. Greenfield footnote 61, second citation, references an unpublished image of an unpublished archival record. What are the nested levels in this source? How are they arranged in the citation? How does the citation answer the *What* and *Wherein* citation questions?

91. Arrange these source levels for a citation to a publication:

    p. 92

    The Great Migration: Immigrants to New England, 1634–1635

    Alice Ashby [item]

    vol. 1

92. Arrange these source levels for a citation to a publication:

    vol. 22

    Administrative Papers of Governors Richard Nicolls and Francis Lovelace, 1664–1673 [volume title]

    p. 76

    New York Historical Manuscripts: English [series title]

93. Arrange these sources levels for a citation to an unpublished source:

    New York State Archives

    box 2

    Albany

    "1779 Land Tax list of the South East Quarter of the Manor of Ranselear District in the County of Albany"

    folder 7

    New York Treasurer's Office Account and Tax Assessment Lists, series A3210

94. Arrange these source levels for a citation to an unpublished source:

    D.C.

    Record Group 217: Records of the Accounting Officers of the Department of the Treasury

    National Archives

    Final Payment Vouchers, 1818–1864

    Claim no. 283, pension for Enos Greenfield

    Washington

95. Arrange these parts of a multivolume set into a citation:

    in *Records and Papers of the New London County Historical Society*

    "The Story of the Vessels Built in Connecticut for the Continental Navy: II, The Confederacy"

    p. 61

    vol. 1

96. Sequence an answer to the *Wherein* citation question for books used in your own genealogical research. Include at least one example of each of the following:

    Titled multivolume set with volume numbers and no volume titles

    Titled multivolume set with volume numbers and titles

    A multivolume set with numbered series and volume number (could be a book series or a journal series)

    A multivolume set with volume titles and a series title

97. Sequence an answer to the *Wherein* citation question for at least one offline unpublished source with nested levels used in your own genealogical research.

98. Sequence the answer to the *Wherein* citation question for serials used in your own genealogical research. Include at least one example of each of the following:

    - Journal
    - Newspaper

Chapter 11

Answering the *Wherein* and *Whereis* Citation Questions for Online Sources

> *"A web-based reference work must take into account the fact that readers will typically consult smaller pieces of content and will expect to be able to click through many parts of a work in a very short period of time."* [1]

Specific online information, like specific offline information, documents a researcher's paraphrases, quotations, statements, and other material that originated with another person. Genealogy standard 5 requires citations to describe where that information can be found by answering the *Wherein* citation question.

Regardless of whether the information is online or offline, the answer to the *Wherein* citation question concisely tells researchers and readers where to turn to the information. Using a clear and complete citation, they avoid repeating the prior research. With answers to other citation questions, the *Wherein* answer helps readers and researchers understand qualities that might contribute to—or detract from—an information item's reliability.

Online sources are publications

As described in chapter 6, virtually all online sources are publications, viewable at home, at work, in a library, or elsewhere.[2] Therefore, accepted formats for citing publications apply to online materials.

Online publication, however, adds complications to citing sources and the information items they contain. Online sources differ from offline sources in their variations of format and organization. Genealogists routinely encounter online sources from any of three origins:

---

1. *The Chicago Manual of Style*, 16th ed. (Chicago: University of Chicago Press, 2010), 49, for sect. 1.113, "Navigation as the primary organizing principle for web-based publications."

2. Ibid., 658, for sect. 14.9, "Authority and permanence [of electronic resources]." Also, Elizabeth Shown Mills, *QuickSheet: Citing Online Historical Resources Evidence! Style*, laminated folder (Baltimore: Genealogical Publishing, 2005). Also, Elizabeth Shown Mills, *Evidence Explained*, 3rd. ed. (Baltimore: Genealogical Publishing, 2015), 50–51, for sect. 2.18, "Citing Published vs. Unpublished Materials."

1. *A source created specifically for the online environment.* Before its online publication, the source did not exist in a form that researchers could access. Examples include *Find A Grave* searchable databases and memorial web pages.

2. *Material originally published offline and subsequently digitized for online publication.* Before—and since—the material's online publication researchers could purchase it for use at home or office or they could access it in libraries. Examples include online images made from published books, CD-ROMs, journals, microfilms, and newspapers.

3. *Unpublished offline material subsequently digitized for online publication.* Before—and since—the material's online publication researchers could access the unpublished material only in the repository holding it. In some cases, they could access the material as images on unpublished microfilm at specified locations. Examples include online images made from archival manuscripts or from unpublished research and preservation microfilms.

Each of those three origins has its own implications for citation content and structure within the broad format for publications. For example, online content showing new materials or previously unpublished images (origins 1 and 3 above) constitute new publications. In contrast, online images of previously published sources (origin 2) show them via a medium.[3] Chapters 13 to 16 discuss in depth the implications of imaging.

The present chapter discusses only the broad options for answering the *Wherein* citation question for online sources in general. The issues are similar, whether the online publication is a new publication or an electronic version of a prior publication.

Answering the *Wherein* citation question for online sources usually is harder than answering it for offline sources. Most offline sources comprise discrete numbered pages or are arranged in describable sequences enabling readers to turn to specific pages. Websites, on the other hand, might have no pages, or long numbered pages with content in no meaningful or describable sequence. Publishers of image collections might or might not number the images. Online publishers might or might not provide links, search forms, image-specific URLs, paths, or other devices to help researchers turn to specific information and describe its location to others. These devices, which apply only to the online environment, could be unfamiliar to offline researchers.

Options for answering *Wherein* with online sources

Given the issues, researchers use at least six options, of varying validity and usability, for answering the *Wherein* citation question for online

3. For principles underlying new publication–new edition distinctions, see *Chicago Manual of Style*, 14, for sect. 1.26, "What constitutes a new edition?"

information items. Each has strengths and weaknesses, none is optimal for all online contexts, and two options do not meet genealogy standards.

Researchers first must understand the source's online context and its offline context, if it has one. Then they can select the option that will most clearly and completely answer the *Wherein* question. That answer should enable them and others to turn to the information as quickly as possible—more efficiently than repeating the original search—and to evaluate its provenance.

Option 1: Copy the online publisher's citation (rarely useful)

Some online publishers provide citations to their images or other information, like these examples, each attached to an online record image:

> Ancestry.com. *Georgia, Property Tax Digests, 1793-1892* (database on-line). Provo, UT, USA: Ancestry.com Operations, Inc., 2011. Original data: *Georgia Tax Digests (1890)*. 140 volumes. Morrow, Georgia: Georgia Archives.[4]
>
> "New York Probate Records, 1629-1971." Images. *FamilySearch*. http://FamilySearch.org : 14 June 2016. County courthouses, New York.[5]

Those citations, in reference-*list* format, are too general for answering *Wherein* in reference-*note* citations, which should point to specific locations or information items. The first example also shows two unconventional uses of italics. First, it italicizes a part of a publication as if it were an entire stand-alone publication, and then it italicizes the title of manuscript material.

The copying option's advantage is its ease of use. Researchers need not know or generate anything. They can simply copy the citation from the website and paste it in a reference note or source list or label. The shortcomings, however, are major:

- Copying and pasting a citation bypasses understanding the source. It prevents researchers from learning as much as they can about the people they are researching and about the source itself.
- Reference-list citations are too broad to document specific statements, but online publishers rarely provide separate citations for each image or information item on their websites.
- When a publisher-generated citation does not convey information about where to locate a specific information item, it fails to answer the *Wherein* question. When it refers to a broad category of sources, like the examples, it fails to meet a genealogy citation's purpose showing qualities of the information. Broad reference-list citations do not show the informant or date of the information the researcher has used.

4. "Georgia, Property Tax Digests, 1793–1892," *Ancestry* (http://search.ancestry.com/search/db.aspx?dbid=1729 : viewed 20 February 2017).
5. "New York Probate Records, 1629–1971," *FamilySearch* (https://familysearch.org/search/collection/1920234 : viewed 20 February 2017).

- Simple copying bypasses information about the sources underlying the images, details needed to assess their likely accuracy and vulnerability to error. Adding that information requires an analytical approach, not mere copying.

In most cases, using a publisher-generated citation to document a specific statement or fact is unwise. This format rarely meets genealogy standard 5 for reference-note citations.[6]

Recommendation: Researchers should choose option 1 only when the publisher's citation meets the field's standards and their citation's purposes.

Option 2: Describe links to the information (rarely useful)

Citations can describe the links to specific information:

> "New York Probate Records, 1629–1971," *FamilySearch* (https://familysearch.org/search/collection/1920234 : accessed 20 February 2017), link for Cayuga, then link for Estate papers 1799–1904 box 4, then change image 1 successively to image 426 and image 427, for Raymond Greenfield, will, 10 October 1821.

This option offers advantages:

- In the absence of a searchable database, this approach points unambiguously to a specific page or image in a specific location.
- As long as the URL and links, based on the source's offline context, remain stable, the citation provides a reliable path from the website's home page to the image. This is likely when the path reflects the arrangement of the underlying collection.
- By taking researchers and readers through a path to the information, option 2 can show much of the information's online context. If that context is based on the underlying source—like the example—readers can see both the underlying source's context and the published image's context.
- If the citation contains a typo, readers can bypass it to turn to the source.
- The format resembles the familiar format for citing publications, with the *Wherein* answer and information specifics last.
- Information about source quality is easily integrated at the end of the citation as a description of what the image shows, rather than as an added citation appendage.

The option also offers disadvantages:

- It requires a stable URL and stable links along the path to the information.
- Researchers using this citation option must generate more wording than other citation options require.

6. Board for Certification of Genealogists, *Genealogy Standards* (Nashville, Tenn.: Ancestry.com, 2014), 7, for standard 5, "Citation elements."

Advantages of describing links outweigh that option's disadvantages, but other options offer similar advantages with fewer disadvantages.

Recommendation: Choose option 2 only when it is the clearest and most concise format for the source and information. In those cases, include information showing source and information qualities, including the creator's and database or collection's name.

Option 3: Cite the search terms

Researchers sometimes cite a search that will lead to the information or image:

> "Search," *Ancestry* (search.ancestry.com : searched on 20 February 2017), exact search for "Fryk Higele."
>
> "Search Historical Records," *FamilySearch* (https://familysearch.org/search : searched on 20 February 2017), search for John Jones who died in Tennessee in 1849.

The search-terms option has advantages:

- It is direct when the target is unique, like example 1, or with enough search terms to yield only the cited item, like example 2.
- The search-term approach works best when each web page or item has a unique identifier for a search term, like a *Find A Grave* memorial number.
- This approach does not depend on the stability of links and URLs within the website.
- The format resembles the familiar format for citing publications, with the *Wherein* answer and information specifics at the end.

This option also has disadvantages:

- It applies only to websites and image collections where each image is linked individually to an item in a searchable database.
- It does not apply to websites and image collections with no options for searching for certain kinds of data—dates or places, for example.
- In many cases, the number and specificity of search terms required to "hit" the target makes the citation long and unwieldy.
- Citing a search engine to locate information online resembles citing an index to locate information in a book. Citations direct readers to the documenting information, not the place where it is indexed.
- Search terms can require researchers to cite an indexer's misreadings or a record keeper's misunderstanding (like "Fryk Higele" when searching for "Fritz Huegle").
- Search terms might not reveal the source's relevance to the research it documents.

- The approach requires precision in the search terms. For example, a search for someone in "St. Louis" will reveal no hits if the database identifies the town or county as "Saint Louis" or vice versa. Troubleshooting accidental errors by an indexer or researcher can be difficult.
- Simply copying search terms omits information about the sources underlying the images, details needed to assess their likely accuracy and vulnerability to error.

This approach could meet standard 5 only when the citation appends information about what a cited image shows.

Recommendation: Use this option when simple search terms lead directly to the information of interest. Include information showing source and information qualities, including the creator's and database or collection's names.

Option 4: Create a URL-based citation

Some researchers cite URLs pointing to specific web pages or online images,:

> "New York Probate Records, 1629-1971," *FamilySearch* (https://familysearch.org/ark:/61903/3:1:3QS7-99HY-1RW?i=425&cc=1920234 : accessed 20 February 2017), Cayuga Co., N.Y., estate papers box 4, Raymond Greenfield, will, 10 October 1821.

The URL option offers advantages:

- Absent a searchable database, this approach can take readers directly to a cited web page or image.
- The citation format resembles the familiar format for citing publications, with the *Wherein* answer and information specifics at the end.
- This approach works well in contexts with short stable URLs tied to specific web pages, images, indexes, or alphabetically arranged entries; or where website structure makes cited information easy to locate.
- Information about source quality is easily integrated at the end of the citation as a description of what the page shows, rather than as an add-on citation segment.

The option also has disadvantages:

- Many URLs are long, cryptic, unwieldy, and unstable.
- Typos in URLs are difficult to troubleshoot.
- Some websites do not provide a structure that makes cited information items easy to locate.

This option meets genealogy standard 5 in many circumstances, especially if the URL is reasonably short and the website's structure makes cited information items easy to find. If the URL is long, uninformative, and difficult to troubleshoot, however, another option would be better.

Recommendation: Use this option for citing websites where information and images are expected to have stable URLs. Include or append information showing source and information qualities, including the creator's and database or collection's names.

Option 5: Cite the underlying source first

Many researchers opt to cite a source underlying an image, whether the source is published or not, through the underlying source's answer to the *Wherein* citation question. Then they append information about the online publication:

> Cayuga Co., N.Y., Estate Records, box 4; Raymond Greenfield file; Raymond Greenfield, will, 10 October 1821; digital image, *FamilySearch* (https://familysearch.org/search/collection/1920234 : accessed 20 February 2017), images 426–27.

This underlying-source option offers two advantages:

- It resembles the citation approach for unpublished offline sources familiar to experienced researchers.
- Information about the qualities of the source underlying the image appear first in the citation.

Like other options, the underlying-source approach has disadvantages:

- It risks misleading readers by implying the researcher examined a source in its original context. Only at the citation's end do readers see that the citation references a publication, which could be confusing.
- Focusing on the underlying source complicates the citation with an added segment atypical of traditional citations to publications.
- The underlying-source approach does not tie image numbers directly to a specific collection or part of a collection, requiring readers to repeat part of the researcher's work rather than following the citation directly to the information of interest.

Despite its shortcomings, this approach meets standard 5. It shows a source's qualities in its offline context but shortchanges the online context that the researcher used and that readers are likely to use. Another option (below) can take readers more directly to the information of interest via a one-part citation.

Recommendation: Use this option for indexed or unindexed collections showing numbered images in titled or numbered collections without publisher-provided paths (waypoints) leading from the website's home page to a numbered image. Append information showing online publication details, including the database or collection title.

Option 6: Cite the publisher's waypoints

Waypoints (sometimes called "bread crumbs") are location titles and numbers connected by greater-than signs (>). A series of waypoints forms a path from an online collection's title to a record's image. Publishers provide them to help researchers clearly and unambiguously answer the *Wherein* citation question, like this example:

> "New York Probate Records, 1629–1971," *FamilySearch* (https://familysearch.org/search/collection/1920234 : accessed 20 February 2017) > Cayuga > Estate papers 1799–1904 box 4 > images 426–27, Raymond Greenfield, will, 10 October 1821.

See appendix B for two examples of creating a citation using a publisher's waypoints to a numbered image.

Waypoints, though relatively new in citations, offer several advantages:

- They are precise and clear.
- They follow the standard format for citing publications, with item specifics at the citation's end.
- They often use publisher-provided information based on the collection's physical structure to help researchers turn to information within the publication.
- Information about source quality is easily integrated at the end of the citation as a description of what the image shows, rather than as an added citation segment.
- When waypoints are based on the physical groups and subgroups of underlying sources, they can be more stable than URLs and links that are not waypoints.
- Typos in a researcher's waypoints are easy to troubleshoot, because the waypoints are tied to a website's menus or listings.
- Waypoints, using "nested levels" principles, lead directly to the information of interest; no searching is needed.

Waypoints also have disadvantages:

- Many online publishers do not number images or do not provide waypoints to specific images or information.
- Some publishers, lacking information about a collection's structure, might provide waypoints that change or mislead researchers about the source's qualities and prior context.
- Waypoint citations can be longer than other citation options.
- They can include more redundancy than other citation options.
- As with any online source, website revisions can invalidate a waypoint-based citation's answer to the *Wherein* citation question.

Recommendation: Use waypoints for unindexed collections showing numbered images in titled or numbered collections. If they do not include information showing source and information qualities, it should be added.

Selecting the best option for the online-source context

None of the six options consistently is best for answering the *Wherein* citation question for all online sources. Researchers should use the two substandard options only with great caution. Four options are viable, depending on the respective characteristics of the online source. See table 16 for a comparison and summary of the recommendations.

The *Whereis* citation answer for online sources

A URL, found in web browsing software's "address" area, answers the *Whereis* question for citations to websites. Researchers may cite the URL for the site's home page, or the URL for the page containing the information of interest. They choose the home-page option when citing waypoints, links, or another way to navigate to an image or information of interest. (They choose the internal-page option when it provides a clear, efficient, and stable way to answer the *Wherein* citation question.)

For website citations that will appear in print, researchers often can shorten a URL by deleting *http://*, *www.*, or both. In some cases, they also can delete characters between an internal question mark and the end of the URL. To ensure the truncated URL's functionality, they test it in a web browser different from the one used for their prior visit to the web page. Not recommended is removing *http://* and *www.* when publishing in electronic environments, including PDFs, Microsoft Word files, and other electronic files. In those contexts, the deletion could impair a URL's "hot link" functionality.

Conclusion

In the twenty-first century, the widespread availability of online sources has added complexity to genealogical source citation. Chapter 11 has compared options for describing the location of specific information within an online source, and it recommends some more than others. It also discussed the answer to the *Whereis* citation question for online sources. Chapters 13–16 will address other issues for clearly and completely describing online sources. In the meantime, chapter 12 will address the answer to the *Whereis* question for offline sources.

Table 16

Comparison of Options for Answering the *Wherein* Citation Question for Information from Online Sources

OPTION	RECOMMENDATION	RATIONALE
1. Copy the publisher's citation.	Use rarely and then only with great caution.	Most publishers' citations contain insufficient information to answer the *Wherein* citation question. Researchers should apply an analytical approach to crafting citations.
2. Describe links.	Use only when no better option applies.	Options 4–6 show the same information in more concise and less idiosyncratic formats.
3. Cite the search terms.	Use when simple search terms lead directly to the information of interest. Include information showing source and information qualities.	Except when a simple search term leads directly to the cited information, this option requires long, complex citations. It can also require readers to repeat prior research rather than turn to the information of interest.
4. Cite the URL and describe the *Wherein* answer, if it is not evident.	Use for websites where images have stable URLs and the website's structure makes cited information items easy to find. Include or append information showing source and information qualities.	Option 4 cites what the researcher used and what readers are likely to use. It is most useful when the URL is reasonably short and the cited information's location is easy to find within the website. Citing a URL can be unhelpful when the URL is unstable, unwieldy, long, or problematic to troubleshoot.
5. Cite the underlying source plus digital image information.	Use for indexed or unindexed collections showing numbered images in titled or numbered collections without waypoints. Append information showing online publication details.	Option 5 implies waypoints but does not specify them, requiring readers to repeat part of a prior search. It uses an unconventional 2-part format for citing publications. Besides complicating the citation's structure, the appended publication details could confuse readers about what the researcher saw and where.
6. Cite waypoints.	Use for unindexed collections showing numbered images in titled or numbered collections. Include information showing source and information qualities.	Option 6 cites what the researcher used and what the reader is likely to use. Formatted like a standard one-part citation for a publication, it enables readers to turn directly to cited information. Waypoints are more stable than links and URLs.

Chapter 11 exercises

99. In Greenfield footnote 4, second citation, what is the answer to the *Wherein* citation question? What information does the citation imply but does not state? Is that information necessary to cite? Why or why not?

100. In Greenfield footnote 5, second citation, what is the answer to the *Wherein* citation question? Which of the six options in table 16 does the citation use? Why do you think the author chose that option and not one of the others?

101. In Greenfield footnote 5, second citation, is the cited source an original record, derivative record, or authored narrative? How do you know? What information does this citation document? Who provided that information? How do you know? Is that information primary or secondary?[7] How do you know? What is that citation's answer to the *Whereis* question

102. The first citation in Greenfield footnote 7 (1855 census) and the citation in footnote 10 refer to different information in the same source. How would you describe the difference between these two citations' formats? Is the absence of an image number in footnote 10 a problem? Why or why not? What else is intentionally omitted from the citation in footnote 10?

103. In Greenfield footnote 7, which of the six options for answering the *Wherein* citation question for an online information item does the citation show? What answer does the citation give?

104. The second citation in Greenfield footnote 7 (1865 census) documents a negative online search. How does this citation differ from one that documents a specific information item (like the first citation, to the 1855 census, in footnote 7)?

105. In Greenfield footnote 18, the third citation (*Google Maps*), what is the answer to the *Wherein* question? Is further information needed? Why or why not? If yes, what could be added to the citation? What is that citation's answer to the *Whereis* question?

106. The author used an online image for the source cited in Greenfield footnote 24, but the published citation does not acknowledge it. What might be his rationale? Where is this source online? The citation appears differently in the author's working notes. What differences would you expect?

107. In Greenfield footnote 28, first citation, what is the answer to the *Wherein* citation question? Referring to table 16, identify the option the

---

7. See this book's glossary for definitions of original record, derivative record, narrative, primary information, and secondary information.

author used for answering the *Wherein* question about online information. What is that citation's answer to the *Whereis* question?

108. Greenfield footnote 30, first citation, includes a sentence after the citation. Does it help answer the *Wherein* citation question, even though it is separate from the citation? Why or why not?

109. Answer the *Wherein* citation question for online sources from your own genealogical research with each of the following sets of characteristics:

    - Simple search terms lead directly to the information of interest.
    - Digital images or cited information items have stable URLs, and the website structure makes cited information easy to find.
    - An indexed or unindexed collection shows titled or numbered collections without waypoints.
    - An indexed or unindexed collection shows numbered images in titled or numbered collections with waypoints.

Chapter 12

Identifying Offline Publishers and Repositories

> "Where[is]—*if unpublished, the source's physical location; if a published book,* CD-ROM, *microfilm, or newspaper, its place of publication; if an online resource, a stable* URL"[1]

Citations to published and unpublished sources differ in how they answer the *Whereis* citation question. For publications, the answer is a publisher and its location. That information allows researchers and readers to choose among many places that make publications available to the public. For unpublished materials, the answer is a repository and its location, directing readers to one or more designated offline places where the material can be viewed.

Citing publishers

All publications have publishers. Ranging from private individuals to megacorporations, publishers make quantities of a written or imaged work available to the public. Some publishers distribute their publications at no cost, but most distribute them by purchase or subscription.

Publications, by definition, are distributed to the public. Thus, readers of documented genealogical works have options for consulting publications a researcher has cited. One reader could consult an offline publication in a different library from the researcher, and another reader might purchase the publication and receive or keep it at home. All three see the print publication in different buildings, but they all will see the same information in the same context within the publication. The location where a researcher or any reader viewed a publication is unimportant.

What *is* important is each specific publication's unambiguous identification. The citation must describe the publication so clearly that readers will not confuse it with any other publication, including others with the same title. That clear description is the answer to the *What* citation question.

1. Board for Certification of Genealogists [BCG], *Genealogy Standards* (Nashville, Tenn.: Ancestry.com, 2014), 7, for standard 5, "Citation elements." Quoted here with permission.

Researchers using the citation expect to see exactly what the researcher saw within the cited publication and in the place within that publication that the citation's *Wherein* answer specifies. Combined with a citation's answers to *What* and *When*, its answer to *Whereis* helps make a publication unique. For most publications, that answer is the publisher's identification and location.

Citations to nearly all publications identify their publisher. That identification's format varies with the kind of publication. These variations help readers understand, at a glance, the kind of publication that a researcher has cited. See table 17 for a summary of these differences and an example of each with the answer to *Whereis*—the publisher information—bolded.

As the examples show, publisher details in citations usually appear in parentheses. When citing newspapers, researchers may use either parentheses or commas to set off the place of publication.

The examples also show that the same information can answer more than one citation question. In the journal and newspaper examples, the publication title helps answer both *What* and *Whereis.* Similarly, when citing offline materials in nested levels, the same information will help answer the *Wherein* and *Whereis* citation questions.

Issues in citing publishers

The location of publisher information varies with the kind of publication:

- For books, it most often appears on the book's copyright page—the back of the title page. It could, however, appear elsewhere, including the title page or a page following the title page. In rare cases, the publisher's name appears only on the book's spine.
- For CD-ROM publications, the publisher's name typically appears on the packaging and the CD-ROM itself.
- For microfilm publications, the publisher's name appears on the microfilm's original container, an image near the beginning of the microfilm roll, or both.
- A journal's or newsletter's title serves to answer the *Whereis* question. That title typically appears outside or inside the publication's front cover, the page with the table of contents, or a dedicated display page near the publication's front. The place of publication, if shown, is not cited.
- Citations to newspapers typically answer the *Whereis* question with the title and place of publication. Both typically appear on the paper's first page or a masthead near the top of the paper's second or third page. If the publisher's location is obvious from the newspaper title—for example, *Boston Globe* or *Los Angeles Times*—researchers may cite only the newspaper title.

Table 17

Publisher Citation Information by Publication Types

TYPE OF PUBLICATION	PUBLISHER INFORMATION TO CITE
Book, CD-ROM, or microfilm	Publisher name and location
Journal or magazine	Title only; no further publisher information
Newspaper	Title and location

Reference-note Citation Examples with *Whereis* Answers Bolded

BOOK

1. "Biographical," in *Portrait and Biographical Record of Randolph, Jackson, Perry, and Monroe Counties, Illinois* (**Chicago: Biographical Publishing**, 1894), 313–14.

CD-ROM

2. *Paths to Your Past*, CD-ROM (**Arlington, Va.: National Genealogical Society**, 2009).

MICROFILM

3. *Passenger Lists of Vessels Arriving at New York, 1820–97*, microfilm publication M237, 95 rolls (**Washington, D.C.: National Archives,** 1962), roll 74, chronologically arranged, 15 July 1848, ship *Bowditch* manifest, nos. 173–75.

JOURNAL

4. "Ship Registers for the Port of Philadelphia, 1726–1775," ***Pennsylvania Magazine of History and Biography*** 23, no. 4 (1899): 502.

NEWSPAPER

5. "Jacob Gross and Wife Wed Half Century," ***Belleville News-Democrat* (Belleville, Ill.)**, 1 August 1921, page 3, col. 1.

When print publications provide varying publisher names, researchers check library cataloging and cite the cataloged name. Universities as publishers should be distinguished from university presses. For example, the University of Virginia, departments within the university, and the University of Virginia Press are different publishers.

When a work shows more than one place of publication, researchers cite the first one listed. If the publication is a publisher's imprint, citing the imprint, not the company, is conventional.[2] For example, the Turner Publishing Company, which lists offices in Nashville, Tennessee, and New York City, publishes *Genealogy Standards*. The book's copyright page says "Published by Ancestry.com, an imprint of Turner Publishing Company." Following conventional practice, researchers would answer the *Whereis* question with the first city listed and the publisher's imprint:

> Nashville, Tenn.: Ancestry.com

Researchers cite the publisher name and location that appear in the work they consulted, even when they know a publisher has changed its name or moved its office. Citing a new name or location will confuse readers using library catalogs to find a cited book. If the place of publication is not shown and researchers can make a reasonable guess, they cite their guess between square brackets. If they cannot guess the place, they cite it as *no place* or with the abbreviation *n.p.*[3]

Researchers take care to cite publishers, not printers. A printer's name could appear on a title page or copyright page, especially if an author or a government or other organization published the work. If an author published a work, the answer to *Whereis* is cited with words like *privately published* or *privately printed*. If a work names no publisher and apparently was not privately published, researchers can cite only the place of publication.[4] They may comment on the absence of a publisher name when the information will be helpful to readers or other researchers.

Governments publish. If a title or copyright page identifies a printer as a government printer (for example, *State Printer* or *[Federal] Government Printing Office*), those designations are cited because they refer to the government that published the work.

Researchers may omit the state, province, or country when readers will understand the city's location. Chicago and New York, for example, do not need state names, but Portland does. London, Paris, and Rome likely refer to national capitals with publishing houses. If the publisher were in Ontario's London, Kentucky's Paris, or New York's Rome, the citation would specify more than a city name.

Researchers also may abridge publisher names in citations. They omit an initial *The* and generic words like *Incorporated, Press, Printer, Publishing Company,* and their abbreviations.[5] Only enough words from the publisher's name need to be cited for the description to make sense and to

2. *The Chicago Manual of Style*, 16th ed. (Chicago: University of Chicago Press, 2010), 719–20, for sect. 14.144, "Parent companies, imprints, and such."

3. Ibid., 718, for sect. 14.138, "No place."

4. Ibid., 718, for sect. 14.143, "Publisher unknown or work privately published."

5. Ibid., 718–19, for sect. 14.140, "Abbreviations and omissible parts of a publisher's name."

differentiate one publisher from others with a similar name. For example, citing *Genealogical* for *Genealogical Publishing Company* seems too general or incomplete, but citing *Genealogical Publishing* is unique to one Baltimore publisher and seems complete.

Newspaper citations in reference notes have at least nine options for placing or omitting the place of publication when the city or state name appears in a newspaper's title:

1. *Bradenton Herald* (Bradenton, Fla.)
2. *Bradenton Herald,* Bradenton, Fla.
3. *Bradenton Herald*[6]
4. *Bradenton (Fla.) Herald*[7]
5. *Bradenton Herald,* Fla.
6. *Bradenton Herald* (Fla.)
7. *Bradenton, Fla., Herald*
8. *Bradenton [Fla.] Herald*
9. *Herald*, Bradenton, Fla.

Any of the options is clear and complete, thus acceptable, if the researcher applies it consistently throughout the same genealogical work. All the options except the first two avoid repeating the city name. This book recommends both those options, however, because they maintain the newspaper title's integrity and identify the place of publication. Of those, this book prefers option 1 for newspapers because the place of publication for other publications typically appears within parentheses. Few researchers or readers would object to options 1, 2, or 9, which reflect traditional practices.

If an overseas publisher is in a city or country with a well-known English-language name, the citation in English-language contexts can show the publisher's city or country name or names in English—for example *Rome* and *Vienna,* rather than *Roma* and *Wien*. Otherwise, researchers cite the foreign city and country as they appear on the publication.

Researchers in English-language contexts need not translate foreign publisher names into English. They may translate, however, when they believe the information will help or interest consumers of their research. In those instances, they place the translation, capitalized sentence-style, in square brackets immediately after the publisher's foreign name.

---

6. For a recommendation of this option, see ibid., 739–40, for sect. 14.203, "Newspaper citations—basic elements." All *Chicago*'s examples refer to well-known city newspapers.

7. For this option with the state name spelled out, see Elizabeth Shown Mills, *Evidence Explained*, 3rd. ed. (Baltimore: Genealogical Publishing, 2015), 807.

Citing repositories

Unpublished materials are unique, or nearly so. Researchers have limited options for accessing them, usually just one repository. For this reason, citations to unpublished sources direct readers to the place (or designated places) where they can examine the source. Answers to the *Whereis* citation name the repository holding the source and give its location.

Public repositories holding unpublished sources range in complexity, purpose, and size. They include local, state or provincial, and federal agencies, archives, courthouses, and offices. They also include historical societies of varying focuses, scopes, and sizes. Nearly all make their records available—in varying degrees—to researchers.

Private repositories range from large business archives and offices to private homes. They include membership societies and religious organizations. Most have no obligation to make their records available to researchers or the public, though many do.

In citations to unpublished sources, the answer to the *Whereis* citation question usually contains at least three elements. They begin with the repository name—usually the name of an agency or office. The *Whereis* answer concludes with the repository's city and state or province. If the repository lies in a foreign country, the answer names the country.

The answer to *Whereis* typically appears at the end of a citation to an unpublished source. Commas separate the answer's parts and a semicolon separates the entire answer from the citation's other elements.

Issues in citing repositories

Some repositories use initialisms—like LVA for Library of Virginia. After spelling out the repository name in its first citation and announcing its initialism in parentheses after the spelled-out repository name, researchers can cite only the initialism thereafter. Works where a repository is cited only once need not announce an initialism, unless it adds clarification for readers.

Researchers also can invent and announce initialisms for repositories they cite frequently, even if the repository does not use one:

> Red Bud Area Museum (RBAM), Red Bud., Ill.

If a work cites many invented initialisms, a master list will help readers understand what they represent.

Occasionally the repository is unknown. For example, the researcher may have an image of a source that was lost after imaging or one from an unknown repository. A researcher also might have a partial memory of a source's content or private conversation. When the researcher records the memory, all these sources would have a repository—the researcher's files. The answer to the *Whereis* question is the researcher's collection:

> . . . ; files of Thomas W. Jones, Monroe, N.Y.

For the material's greater accessibility, genealogists should publish their unique records or place them in a repository that will preserve them for other researchers. Citing a permanent public repository is more helpful, especially for future generations, than citing a private home or record.

Answering the *Whereis* citation question with a repository that once allowed access to the source, and then closed it, might seem pointless. Citing that repository, however, could help future researchers, should access be reopened. At the same time, researchers should cite their privately held image or notes, answering the *Whereis* citation question with the location of an accessible source for the benefit of contemporary researchers:

> . . . ; held by Public Record Office of Northern Ireland, Belfast, but now restricted; photocopy in author's collection, Monroe, N.Y.

Researchers sometimes withhold repository information at the request of a source owner, usually when the source is in a private home or on private property. In such cases, researchers can answer the *Whereis* citation question with a phrase like *location withheld at Bible owner's request*. In both sets of circumstances, sentences explaining the situation, in the same footnote as the citation, can help other researchers understand the source.

Options for foreign places of publication, addressed above, similarly apply to repository locations.

Provenance

Provenance refers to a source's history of custody, its chain of title. In effect, provenance is an answer to a *Where-was* question.

When provenance is relevant, genealogists note it. This is especially helpful for online materials, items in personal custody, and sources far from their origin. Features of the source's origin and the intervening provenance can help with genealogical assessment and authenticating the source's information. Usually this appears in a comment after a citation:

> Gaddis family Bible record. . . . The author inherited the Bible from his granduncle William Lanahan, who received it from his mother, Anna (Gaddis) Lanahan, daughter of the Bible's original owners, John and Allenah (Boyd) Gaddis.

Including provenance in the citation would make the citation overly long and hard to parse or digest.

Researchers most often use provenance to locate an earlier, more authoritative version of a source. Once they find it, they use and cite the more authoritative version. In other cases, supplementary information about provenance helps researchers and readers understand the source's strengths and shortcomings as a container of genealogical information.

Conclusion

Citations to published and unpublished offline materials provide different kinds of answers to the *Whereis* question, each appropriate for the source. These answers appear near or at the end of most citations. Thus, *Whereis* is the fifth of five citation questions that genealogy standard 5 addresses.

Chapter 12 exercises

110. The two citations in Greenfield footnote 2 give a cryptic answer to the *Whereis* citation question. Why are no repository, city, and state cited in this context? Also, why is the *Wherein* citation question not answered?

111. In Greenfield footnote 3, what is the answer to the *Whereis* citation question?

112. In Greenfield footnote 6, second citation (the questionnaire), what locations does the cryptic answer to the *Whereis* citation question refer to? Where is this short initialism announced? Why does it differ from the more familiar intialism NARA?

113. In Greenfield footnote 17, what is the answer to *Whereis?*

114. In Greenfield footnote 18, second citation (the atlas), who was the publisher? How do you know?

115. In Greenfield footnote 22, first citation, decode the information in parentheses.

116. In Greenfield footnote 37, first citation, citing the book as "privately published" or "privately printed" could mislead readers. Why?

117. In Greenfield footnote 39, first citation, explain the capitalization in the answer to the *Whereis* citation question.

118. What answer does Greenfield footnote 43 give to the *Whereis* citation question? What does that answer tell you about the creator? Why is that answer omitted from the citation in footnote 46?

119. Greenfield footnote 52, first citation, gives a fifteen-word answer to the *Whereis* citation question. Why is it so long?

120. The second citation in Greenfield footnote 61, like many other citations to GSU/FamilySearch microfilm, includes a repository. Because the source was viewed on microfilm elsewhere, why does this kind of citation include the repository?
121. In Greenfield footnote 84, last citation (the finding aid), why does the answer to the *Whereis* citation question omit the state?
122. In Greenfield footnote 87, last citation (the newspaper), what is the answer to the *Whereis* citation question?
123. Why does the citation in Greenfield footnote 88 not answer the *Whereis* citation question?
124. From your own research, answer the *Whereis* citation questions for one or more published sources in each of six categories:
    - Book
    - CD-ROM
    - Microfilm
    - Journal
    - Newspaper
125. From your own research, answer the *Whereis* citation question for one or more unpublished sources in each of six kinds of repositories:
    - Archive
    - County, state, or provincial government building or office
    - Local government building or office
    - National government building or office
    - Religious organization location or office
    - Anyone's personal files
126. Describe the provenance of one or more privately held or online sources used in your own genealogical research.

Chapter 13

Citing Original Online Content

> *"T'is true, there's magicke in the web. . . ."*
>
> *—William Shakespeare, Othello, act 3, scene 4.*[1]

Genealogists often use online images, transcriptions, indexes, and other material based on offline material. A large body of genealogical material, however, was created only for the online environment. These sources include content on archive and library websites, blogs, discussion forums, *EvidenceExplained.com, Find A Grave,* websites showing land plats, much web content by genealogy societies, genetic genealogy websites, family trees on many sites, and much, much more.

Large genealogical websites provide mixtures of original content and images of previously unpublished and already published material. Original content at *FamilySearch,* for example, includes "Family Tree" (https://familysearch.org/tree/#view=find&tab=name), "Family History Research Wiki" (https://familysearch.org/wiki/), and "FamilySearch Catalog" (https://familysearch.org/catalog/search).

Comparison of citation elements

Citing original online information is uncomplicated. The standard format is nearly identical to the familiar format for citing published books. Guidelines for citing online genealogy resources since 2005 have defined online sources as publications with "the same core elements as printed publications."[2] Table 18 compares a citation to a book with a citation to original online material. It shows how original online content answers

---

1. The author thanks his second cousin William Wright Arnold for drawing his attention to this seemingly anachronistic out-of-context quotation.

2. Elizabeth Shown Mills, *QuickSheet: Citing Online Historical Resources Evidence! Style,* laminated folder (Baltimore: Genealogical Publishing, 2005); also rev. ed., 2007. All editions of *Evidence Explained* (Baltimore: Genealogical Publishing Company) reflect the 2005 recommendations. Its first edition was published in 2007, the second in 2009, a revised second edition in 2012, and the third edition in 2015. For a different recommendation, see *The Chicago Manual of Style* (Chicago: University of Chicago Press, 2010), 16th ed., 752–54, secs. 14.244–14.246, under "Websites and Blogs."

Table 18

Comparison of Citations to an Offline Book and Original Online Material

CITATION QUESTIONS	CITATION TO AN OFFLINE PUBLISHED BOOK	CITATION TO AN ORIGINAL ONLINE PUBLICATION
Who?	1. Margaret D. Falley,	2. ThosJones,
What?	"Ireland," in *Genealogical Research: Methods and Sources,* vol. 1, ed. Milton Rubincam	"Jones Family Tree," *Ancestry*
Whereis?	(Washington, D.C.: American Society of Genealogists,	(http://trees.ancestry.com /tree/4280476/family :
When?	1960),	viewed 20 February 2017),
Wherein?	344–74.	Henry Lanahan.

THE CONNECTED CITATIONS

1. Margaret D. Falley, "Ireland," in *Genealogical Research: Methods and Sources,* vol. 1, ed. Milton Rubincam (Washington, D.C.: American Society of Genealogists, 1960), 344–74.

2. ThosJones, "Jones Family Tree," *Ancestry* (http://trees.ancestry.com /tree/4280476/family : viewed 20 February 2017), Henry Lanahan.

the five citation questions and illustrates the format similarities between citations to books and to original online sources. Some answers, however, are more similar than others:

Who—When books and websites identify authors or creators, researchers cite them. When such publications do not identify the author or creator, researchers omit the answer to the *Who* citation question. When a title and its creator's name are the same—a frequent situation with websites and occasionally with books—researchers avoid repetition by omitting the answer to the *Who* citation question.

What—Nearly all books and websites have titles. They often have parts with titles. Researchers cite these. They also might add descriptors that enhance clarity about the source's characteristics.

When—When citing a published book, researchers give its copyright or publication year. When citing websites, they give their most recent access, downloading, or viewing date. If the website has a copyright year or "last revision" date, researchers can cite those dates after the website or web page title.

Wherein—Researchers citing books usually give only page numbers to answer the *Wherein* citation question. Web pages, however, usually are not broken into numbered pages or parts. Researchers use one of three options for pointing to original online information. (See below.)

Whereis—Researchers citing published books answer the *Whereis* citation question with the publisher name and its city and state or province. Citations to original online information answer that question with the URL of a website or web page.

Options for pointing to original online text

Citations to published books, journals and other paginated sources answer the *Wherein* citation question with page numbers. Researchers do not have that option with unnumbered web pages. An online article, blog, discussion, wiki, or other original online content can be longer than several printed pages. Without numbered content to cite, researchers have three options for answering *Wherein* when citing original online material:

1. Cite the page's URL and leave readers to find the information for themselves:

   Judy G. Russell, "Mayhap a different mayhem," posting, 26 May 2016, *The Legal Genealogist*, blog (http://legalgenealogist.com/blog/2016/05/26/mayhap-a-different-mayhem/ : viewed 20 February 2017).

2. Describe the information's location on the page:

   Judy G. Russell, "Mayhap a different mayhem," posting, 26 May 2016, *The Legal Genealogist*, blog (http://legalgenealogist.com/blog/2016/05/26/mayhap-a-different-mayhem/ : viewed 20 February 2017), ninth paragraph.

3. Give a unique phrase to search for:

   Judy G. Russell, "Mayhap a different mayhem," posting, 26 May 2016, *The Legal Genealogist*, blog (http://legalgenealogist.com/blog/2016/05/26/mayhap-a-different-mayhem/ : viewed 20 February 2017), search for "slit the nose."

If the cited information's location on a web page is not obvious, the first two options place a burden on readers. They must either find the information with no direction or count unnumbered paragraphs, hoping they count like the researcher who created the citation. The third option, however, can direct readers to a specific information item. Typing control-F or command-F when using most web browsers opens a search area where readers can type a cited search term. The software also can highlight occurrences of the term on the page.

Example cases

Find A Grave and online database searches demonstrate the issues and principles of citing original online content.

Find A Grave

Since 1995 Find A Grave, an organization of more than one million contributors, has offered original online content on the *Find A Grave* website.[3] Each entry, a numbered web page called a *memorial*, provides one of three combinations of potentially useful information for genealogists:

1. A narrative or data (usually based on a gravestone transcription) with one or more images, all by the same contributor
2. A narrative or data by one contributor, with one or more images from another contributor or contributors
3. A narrative or data with no images

Depending on what researchers are using and documenting, they will cite a written narrative or data, an image, or both, each with its respective contributor.

Some *Find A Grave* contributors, like those on other websites, use pen names with unconventional capitalization, spacing, or content. Citations typically show names as they appear in the source, regardless of any idiosyncrasies.[4] Researchers can, however, put unconventional names between quotation marks—for example, "GeekyGraveGirl" and "Jean." The quotation marks assure readers that the name does not reflect a researcher error or omission.

The most efficient way to cite a *Find A Grave* page is with *(a)* a truncated URL for the *Find A Grave* search form and *(b)* the memorial number, like this citation segment:

> *Find A Grave* (https://www.findagrave.com/cgi-bin/fg.cgi : viewed on 20 February 2017), memorial 81653095.

Like most citations to original online content, that example resembles a book citation. The *Find A Grave* memorial number occupies the field where a book's page number would be cited. It at least partially answers all five citation questions. (The answer to *What* also answers the *Who* citation question.)

Missing is information about the information the researcher has used. Also, courtesy and convention suggest the citation should credit the contributor

3. "Who is behind Find A Grave," *Find A Grave* (https://findagrave.com/cgi-bin/fg.cgi?page=whois : viewed 20 February 2017).

4. *Chicago Manual of Style*, 388, at sec. 8.4, "Capitalization of personal names," says "Unconventional spellings strongly preferred by the bearer of the name or pen name (e.g., bell hooks) should usually be respected." Also, ibid., 447, sec. 8.153, "Names like eBay and iPod."

of the image, narrative, transcription, other data, or some combination. It also should include the cited information's dates. Citations to the image should specify both the cemetery and the marker—like any citation to a grave-marker reading or photograph. Those citations might include information about the cemetery's location and the marker's location within the cemetery.

Regardless of what information is and is not included in a *Find A Grave* citation, sequencing should minimize wordiness and repetition. It also should avoid confusion—among, for example, who was buried, who wrote the narrative, and who made the image. Several sequencing options meet standards when the researcher uses them consistently for the same kind of information in the same kind of source throughout a documented work.

Citing a memorial page with no image is straightforward:

> *Find A Grave* (https://www.findagrave.com/cgi-bin/fg.cgi : viewed on 20 February 2017), memorial 81653095, "Calista Jane Greenfield Tucker," 7 December 2011, by Ralph Edwards; no gravestone image.

Following Elizabeth Mills's "Velcro principle," that citation attaches the memorial page title to its number. The memorial page's date follows the title, a conventional placement for a title's date, also reflecting the "Velcro principle." The preposition *by* shows the memorial creator's role.

Conventional citations to grave markers credit the cemetery as creator by placing the cemetery name before identifying the grave marker. Citations to *Find A Grave* images can do the same:

> *Find A Grave* (https://www.findagrave.com/cgi-bin/fg.cgi : viewed on 20 February 2017), memorial 40735875, for Southern Cemetery (Central Lake, Mich.), G. M. D. Tucker gravestone; digital image, 16 August 2009, by "drbuck."

A similar sequence could be used to cite a narrative and image by the same contributor and by different contributors:

> *Find A Grave* (https://www.findagrave.com/cgi-bin/fg.cgi : viewed on 20 February 2017), memorial 40735875, "George Moore Davis Tucker"; also image from Southern Cemetery (Central Lake, Mich.), G. M. D. Tucker gravestone; both on 16 August 2009 by "drbuck."

> *Find A Grave* (https://www.findagrave.com/cgi-bin/fg.cgi : viewed on 20 February 2017), memorial 122232362, "Andrew Clark," 26 December 2013, by "This Side of the Grave"; also, Bellefontaine Cemetery (St. Louis, Mo.), Andrew Clark gravestone, digital image, 28 November 2014, by Connie Nisinger.

Both examples attach the date of the page, image, or both to the respective information.

Placing the cemetery name parenthetically after the marker's identification adds clarity:

Find A Grave (https://www.findagrave.com/cgi-bin/fg.cgi: viewed on 20 February 2017), memorial 40735875, "George Moore Davis Tucker," and G. M. D. Tucker gravestone (Southern Cemetery, Central Lake, Mich.), digital image; both on 16 August 2009 by "drbuck."

Find A Grave (https://www.findagrave.com/cgi-bin/fg.cgi : viewed on 20 February 2017), memorial 122232362, "Andrew Clark," 26 December 2013, by "This Side of the Grave," and Andrew Clark gravestone (Bellefontaine Cemetery, St. Louis, Mo.), digital image, 28 November 2014, by Connie Nisinger.

All those citations, except the first, provide clear and complete information about memorial essays, images, or both. They answer the *Who-What-When-Wherein-Whereis* citation questions for the online publication and the specific memorials and images that it provides. The principles that the *Find A Grave* examples demonstrate can be applied to citations to original online content on other websites.

Online database searches

Many online image collections are tied to searchable online images or indexes. The images themselves typically are not original online content—instead they are facsimiles of previously published or unpublished offline material. The manually keyboarded or machine-created databases, indexes, and abstracts, however, often are original online content. Their purpose is to help genealogists locate images of interest, which they would cite. Instead of an image, however, genealogists would cite a searchable database in at least three contexts:

1. Their research plans, to describe databases they plan to search
2. Their research notes, to document searches they have undertaken
3. Their works in progress and final polished written products, to document negative searches, negative evidence, and incorrect database entries—for example, a misread date or badly mangled name. (For successful searches and sources providing direct or indirect evidence, researchers would cite in finished products the found images, not the database search.)

Like citations to most original online content, citations to database searches resemble the familiar format for citing a chapter in a book. See table 19.

Citations to online database searches answer the five citation questions with similar content, regardless of the website:

Who—The answer would be the database creator, if different from the website title. If the answers are the same, researchers have—and usually take—the option of not providing a separate answer to the *Who* citation question.

What—The answer often has two parts—database title and website title. As the title of part of a publication, the database title appears within quotation

Table 19

Comparison of Citations to an Offline Book and a Database Search

CITATION QUESTIONS	CITATION TO AN OFFLINE PUBLISHED BOOK	CITATION TO A DATABASE SEARCH
Who?	1. Margaret D. Falley,	[Omitted in this example because the source creator and title are the same]
What?	"Ireland," in *Genealogical Research: Methods and Sources*, vol. 1, ed. Milton Rubincam	2. "1880 United States Federal Census," *Ancestry*
Whereis?	(Washington, D.C.: American Society of Genealogists,	(http://ancestry.com/search /db.aspx?dbid=6742 :
When?	1960),	accessed 20 February 2017),
Wherein?	344–74.	searches for Jac* Gros* in Illinois and Missouri.

THE CONNECTED CITATIONS

1. Margaret D. Falley, "Ireland," in *Genealogical Research: Methods and Sources*, vol. 1, ed. Milton Rubincam (Washington, D.C.: American Society of Genealogists, 1960), 344–74.

2. "1880 United States Federal Census," *Ancestry* (http://ancestry.com /search/db.aspx?dbid=6742 : accessed 20 February 2017), searches for Jac* Gros* in Illinois and Missouri.

marks. As the title of a publication, the website name is italicized. Traditionally, the part—the database title—appears first in the citation. Researchers can, however, place the database title after the information parenthetical to the website title.

When—The answer is the search date.

Wherein—In citations to searchable databases the answer to the *Wherein* citation question is a description of the search, like the example in table 19. As succinctly as possible, that answer provides enough information to serve two purposes: *(a)* to show researchers what they searched for (and, by implication for future reference, what they did not search); and *(b)* to enable others to replicate and verify the failed search. Like the format for citing books, the answer to *Wherein* appears at the end of the citation.

Whereis—The answer is the URL for the database search page, which includes the website URL.

Except for the way online-search citations answer the *Wherein* citation question, they resemble citations to other original online material and offline books, CD-ROMs, and microfilm publications.

Conclusion

Original online content is one of three kinds of genealogical information published on the Internet. The others are images of previous publications and images of previously unpublished material. Chapters 14 and 15, respectively, will address issues in citing both kinds of images, including some that are offline.

Chapter 13 exercises

127. What is the first example in the Greenfield article of a citation to original online content? How does that citation answer the *Wherein* citation question? What statement or information does the cited source document?

128. Greenfield footnote 18, last citation, describes original online information. Referring to pages 136–37, devise two different ways for that citation to point precisely to specific information of interest.

129. Does Greenfield footnote 54, last five lines, cite original online content? Why or why not?

130. Create a free account online at https://familysearch.org/register/1, sign in, and then cite the original online information at this URL:

    https://familysearch.org/wiki/en/Genealogical_Society_of_Utah

131. Create a free account at https://www.gedmatch.com/. Then, using *GEDMatch*'s default settings, run a "'One-to-one' compare" analysis on kits T829710 and T316184. Finally, cite the resulting report.

132. Cite a negative "Descendants" search at this URL:

    http://services.dar.org/Public/DAR_Research/search/

133. From your own research, cite at least three *Find A Grave* resources:
    - A memorial essay only
    - A grave-marker image only
    - An entry with both a memorial essay and a grave-marker image

134. From your own research, cite negative searches on the *Ancestry* or *FamilySearch* website or both.

Chapter 14

Citing Images of Previously Published Material

> *"As history researchers, we are justified in treating image copies as originals so long as (a) the images are legible; and (b) their information does not conflict with other evidence."*[1]

Businesses, governments, libraries, religious organizations, and commercial and nonprofit archives have imaged countless reels and volumes of previously published material. Through websites and other media, they make images available to researchers in their homes and at libraries. These images show all kinds of previously published media—including books, CD-ROMs, journals, microfilms, other microforms, and newspapers.[2]

Most of the imaged versions, however, are exact facsimiles of the prior publications with little or no human additions, editing, or revision. (Optical character recognition [OCR] technology, which makes digital images of text searchable, usually neither adds much human intervention nor affects what researchers see.)

What is (and is not) a facsimile?

Genealogy Standards defines *facsimile:*

> An image showing a source with no sign of cropping, blurring, or other alteration, including color or shading changes that mask information; an exact copy.[3]

For research purposes, an image is a facsimile when it shows researchers no less information and context than they would see when examining the

---

1. Elizabeth Shown Mills, *Evidence Explained: Citing History Sources from Artifacts to Cyberspace*, 1st ed. (Baltimore: Genealogical Publishing, 2005), 30, for sect. 1.26, "Image Copies."Also, ibid., 3rd ed. (2015).

2. Many online images of prior print publications can be found via *Google* (https://www.google.com/). For extensive listings and links, see Cyndi Ingle, *Cyndi's List of Genealogy Sites on the Internet*, for "Books » eBooks – Online Books" (http://www.cyndislist.com/books/ebooks/), "Maps and Geography" (http://www.cyndislist.com/maps/), and "Newspapers » General Resources" (http://www.cyndislist.com/newspapers/general/), all viewed on 20 February 2017.

3. Board for Certification of Genealogists [BCG], *Genealogy Standards* (Nashville, Tenn.: Ancestry.com, 2014), 68 (glossary definition of the term "facsimile").

source underlying the image. This includes, for example, the same handwriting or typeset font in the identical place and context as the underlying source. A page or paper's context can include surrounding pages in a bound source and other papers in a folder or collection. If the image is a facsimile, the imaging process has not removed or rearranged information, changed its form, or altered its content or context in any way.

Researchers create, use, and cite images via various online and offline media. Photocopies, photographs, and scans made from publications are common for personal use. In the mid-twentieth century, images on microfilm and other microforms started becoming popular for research and preservation. In the twenty-first century, online digital images are a staple of genealogical research. Digital scanning, photography, printing, and other processes have created all those images. Regardless of the process or medium used to create an image, it can be a facsimile—or not.

When a process creates an image that is not a facsimile, it has created a derivative of the underlying source. The image shows less of the underlying source's information. Genealogists reason from the most accurate, complete, and authoritative sources available.[4] Whenever they suspect an image could be a derivative, they pursue the original from which the image was made.[5]

Some image alterations are obvious. Blurring, cropping, and masking, for example, are noticeable because they have covered or removed information or made it unreadable. Intentional alterations of information, digitally or with a copying machine, can be visible. When sequential images do not show sequential pages, rearrangement or omission is likely.

In other cases, the removal or alteration of information is invisible. Only researchers with knowledge of the source and what it should show could suspect alteration. In some military and tax records, for example, varying ink colors—undetectable in a grayscale image—can convey useful information.

Context sometimes alerts researchers to the possibility of an invisible removal or alteration of information. For example, an image of interest might differ from surrounding images in an illogical way. Or a cross-reference within the image or surrounding images will mention something the image does not show.

Provenance also can trigger suspicion of alteration. Images produced privately are vulnerable to alteration, especially if the holder could benefit by changing or removing information. Reputable organizations might enhance images, perhaps making information more readable, but they are unlikely to remove information or change its content or context.

4. BCG, *Genealogy Standards*, 23–24, for standard 38, "Source preference."
5. Ibid., 14, for standard 17, "Extent."

With even the smallest suspicion of an image's alteration, researchers will consult the underlying source. If that source does not exist, their citation to the image or discussion about the image will note the possibility of alteration and the reasons for the suspicion. Readers will understand that the source was derived from an original that no longer exists. Fortunately, digitally altered images of genealogical sources are rare.[6]

Image collections

Genealogists most often consult image collections. They typically are arranged in linear sequences with beginning and end points. Each image precedes and follows other images in juxtapositions that rarely change. Examples include the sequence of images on a microfilm roll and the linear arrangement of online images through which researchers can scroll.

Genealogists access online images by clicking a link. They should, however, go beyond the image—whether linked or not—to examine its context. Information in a preceding or following image, or in images at the beginning or end of a series, can help genealogists' research. The surroundings of an image of interest within a collection—whether online, on microfilm, or elsewhere—are that image's context. Looking at one image takes it out of context, and arranging images differently from the corresponding material's arrangement removes the primary context.

An image collection's sequencing implies that it reflects sequencing within the underlying source, but that is not always the case. Pages can accidentally be turned together while filming, photocopying, or scanning, for example, so that an internal page or spread is not filmed. Publishers of digital images can rearrange them, removing them from their prior context.[7] Although individual images might be facsimiles in these cases, they appear in a derivative context, diminishing their usefulness to researchers.

Citing derivative images

Citations to suspected derivative images show that the researcher consulted a derivative. Those citations usually exist only for a conscientious researcher's private benefit. They serve as reminders to examine the material from which an image was derived. A genealogist's

6. For discussion of a visibly altered source (not by imaging), see Melinda Daffin Henningfield, "Determining Linnie Leigh Gray's Birth Date," *National Genealogical Society Quarterly* 98 (December 2010): 245–50 at p. 246. For an invisible alteration (also not by imaging), see Thomas W. Jones, "A Name Switch and a Double Dose of Joneses: Weighing Evidence to Identify Charles R. Jones," *National Genealogical Society Quarterly* 84 (March 1996): 5–16 at p. 14.

7. A notable example is "Missouri, Marriage Records, 1805–2002," *Ancestry* (http://search.ancestry.com/search/db.aspx?dbid=1171 : viewed on 20 February 2017). Within counties, some sets of images are arranged chronologically regardless of the volume or page in the underlying sources.

finished product typically cites a derivative only when the underlying source is destroyed, missing, or closed to researchers:

> Family Record of James and Margaret (Sweet) Greenfield, typescript transcription in Alice G. Pease to Mrs. Edward W. Cooch (Registrar General, National Society Daughters of the American Revolution [NSDAR]), letter, 4 September 1942; in file for Alice G. Pease, membership application, national no. 336220, on James Greenfield (1753–1812, New York), approved 30 October 1942, NSDAR.

Image publisher and library functions

Publisher and library roles are distinct. Publishers create publications and various editions of those publications. They also distribute publications, usually through sales or subscriptions. Libraries, on the other hand, purchase publications and subscriptions and provide the public with access to them, sometimes for a fee. Publishers might house a library, though it might not be available to the public. Similarly, libraries might publish and sell books or distribute periodicals by subscription.

The genealogical-research context, with its heavy use of online images, blurs publisher and library roles. Commercial, governmental, religious, and other organizations provide collections of record images, typically microfilmed or online, besides original content like searchable databases or family trees. Those image-providers function as publishers for some image collections and as libraries for others:

Publisher. When image-providers publish images of previously unpublished material, they function as publishers. They create publications of previously unpublished material or new editions of previously published material, and they distribute them through sales (like commercial microfilm and other microforms) and subscriptions (such as online image collections). Examples include images made from archival materials, governmental records (at any level of government), gravestones, and research or preservation microforms, including most Genealogical Society of Utah/FamilySearch microfilm. Chapter 15 discusses images of previously unpublished material.

Library. When image-providers show exact paginated facsimile images of many complete publications in their original sequence and context with no material added or modified, they make those publications available for public use, like a library does. Two points reinforce this view—the images show no changes in pagination or any feature of the publication, except its medium; human involvement in the image-production process is minimal.

The view is not universal that image providers fill library and publisher functions for different image collections. Some genealogists view image providers solely as publishers, whether they distribute new material (a publisher function) or make others' published material available to the public (a library function).[8] Some genealogists believe that online or microfilm or microfiche images are "digital editions" or "microform editions" of publications. The image providers, however, usually do not annotate the images as new editions of prior publications.

This book's view is that facsimile images—whether published or not—show researchers neither more nor less than the underlying source. Functionally, images online and on microfilm or other microform seem little different from photocopies, photographs, and scans that researchers make from publications for personal use. Consistent with the longstanding quotation from *Evidence Explained* at this chapter's beginning, researchers viewing online and microform facsimiles of publications in print and other media are justified in citing only the underlying publication.

Options for citing images of previously published material

Given varying viewpoints concerning publisher and library roles and digital and microform "editions," genealogists have at least five options for citing facsimiles of previously published material. The choices reflect different understandings as well as any suspicion that an image or collection is not a facsimile of the prior publication. The options answer the *Who-What-When-Wherein-Whereis* citation questions, but some of them omit critical information and risk misleading readers about what a researcher actually saw. The options vary in the content they provide for describing the previously published pages and the images made from them.

The examples of each option use a published paginated book viewed in an online collection of unnumbered images. The same points apply, however, to images of journals, newspapers, and other publications, whether paginated or not. Similar issues also apply to publications imaged on microfilm, other microforms, or for private use, whether the images are numbered or not.

Option 1: Cite only the online publication (not recommended)

For at least their working notes, researchers might ignore the underlying publication and cite the online image solely as an online publication:

> "New York in the Revolution as Colony and State," digital images, *Archive.org* (https://archive.org/details/newyorkrevolution02statrich : accessed 20 February 2017), pp. 104–5.

8. This might seem to be the view of *Evidence Explained*, which could not have foreseen the proliferation of online repositories like *Archive.org*'s *Digital Library* and *Internet Archive*, *HathiTrust*, *Project Gutenberg*, and *FamilySearch*'s digital images of family histories in the Family History Library. Chapter 2 says "Rule 3: A website is a publication, not a repository." The ensuing explanation, however, focuses on citation differences between websites and repositories holding unpublished material, not libraries, which make publications available to researchers. See Mills, *Evidence Explained*, 57–58, for sect. 2.32, "Basic Elements to Cite."

Option 1 uses a simple straightforward citation following the book-citation format. It serves to remind a researcher where a source was viewed and shows where to turn for the information of interest. (Although the images are unnumbered, they show paginated material, enabling readers to turn to a specific image.) Ignoring the original publication, the citation might reflect a view that the image is a new edition or reprint. Cited titles of new and previous editions, however, usually are the same, and citations to reprints mention the original publication date.

More important, by ignoring the original publication, this option could mislead readers by implying that the researcher consulted original online material created in 2017, rather than a book published in 1898. The citation also does not identify the original work's author or credit the publisher of the printed pages that the researcher viewed via a medium. Finally, this citation implies that the page numbers are part of the website, like image numbers, and it cites a book's title as if it were part of a website. That misinformation makes this option substandard.

Option 2: Cite the image and acknowledge the underlying publication

Other researchers might cite the image and acknowledge the prior print publication:

> "New York in the Revolution as Colony and State," digital images, *Archive.org* (https://archive.org/details/newyorkrevolution02statrich : accessed 20 February 2017), for pp. 104–5; images of James A. Roberts, comp. (Albany, N.Y.: Brandow, 1898).

Option 2 conveys answers the five citation questions, and readers can use it to view the source. It breaks up information about the book, however, making another option a better choice for working notes. It also is longer than it needs to be for citing in a context where paper and postage costs are important.

Beginning an option-2 citation with information about an image (like the above example) presents an avoidable risk. Researchers could be tempted to use the word *citing* to bridge the citation to the part about the underlying source. *Images* is a better word, especially when the image provider did not cite the underlying source clearly and completely.

The word *citing* in a citation usually means a researcher copied someone else's citation referencing a source the researcher did not view. This is acceptable if the citation helps readers understand the source the researcher did view and cite, or if the cited source no longer is accessible to researchers. Otherwise, using a prior researcher's citation to document a later researcher's statement could connote a lazy researcher, slipshod research, or both. In academic venues, silently using a prior researcher's citation to document later research is considered a form of theft and is unethical.

Option 3: Cite only the underlying publication

Researchers can choose to cite an image of a publication as if they had viewed the underlying publication in a library:

> James A. Roberts, comp., *New York in the Revolution as Colony and State: A Compilation of Documents and Records from the Office of the State Comptroller*, 2nd ed. (Albany, N.Y.: Brandow, 1898), 104–5.

This approach is cohesive, concise, simple, and traditional. It credits the work's original author and publisher. Like all citations to publications, it does not tell readers where the researcher viewed the publication. Instead, it allows them to choose—from many online and offline venues—a convenient place to consult the material. This option is suitable for finished products.

Option 4: Cite the underlying publication and acknowledge the image

Many researchers would choose to expand option 3 by including information about the image:

> James A. Roberts, comp., *New York in the Revolution as Colony and State: A Compilation of Documents and Records from the Office of the State Comptroller*, 2nd ed. (Albany, N.Y.: Brandow, 1898), 104–5; digital images, *Archive.org* (https://archive.org/details/newyorkrevolution02statrich : accessed 20 February 2017).

This option is desirable for working notes, if not also finished products where space is not a concern. The citation identifies the original author and publisher, gives the information's correct date, and connects the page numbers to the book rather than to the website. It shows one place the source can be viewed, although other options exist both online and off. The citation is longer than option 3. Considering paper and postage costs, producers of print products might cut the citation's digital-image details, reverting to option 3.

Option 5: Cite in full both the underlying publication and its image

A semicolon both joins and separates two complete citations, one citing the image, and the other citing the underlying publication. Either citation can appear first, depending on which one the researcher wants to emphasize. Thus, two versions of option 5 are possible:

> "New York in the Revolution as Colony and State," *Archive.org* (https://archive.org/details/newyorkrevolution02statrich : accessed 20 February 2017); digital images showing James A. Roberts, comp., *New York in the Revolution as Colony and State: A Compilation of Documents and Records from the Office of the State Comptroller*, 2nd ed. (Albany: Brandow, 1898), 104–5.

> James A. Roberts, comp., *New York in the Revolution as Colony and State: A Compilation of Documents and Records from the Office of the State Comptroller*, 2nd ed. (Albany: Brandow, 1898), 104–5; digital images, "New York in the Revolution as Colony and State," *Archive.org* (https://archive.org/details/newyorkrevolution02statrich : accessed 20 February 2017).

Both examples contain the same information, but the second reverses the order of the first example's two parts. Researchers could choose the first format to emphasize the digital image; they could choose the second to emphasize the 1898 book. Both options are useful for working notes because they contain information that might be needed about both the prior publication and the image publication. They credit the original compiler and publisher as well as the modern image provider. Both citations are double the length of example 3. That length limits their viability for printed works.

See table 20 for a summary of recommendations for using these five options for citing publications viewed as facsimile images. Researchers choose options for their notes, works in progress, and finished products. When they submit those products for publication, however, house styles and policies will affect their choices.

Conclusion

Images of publications, discussed in this chapter, include microfilm, other microforms, photocopies, photographs, and scans. Images of publications also form one of three kinds of genealogical information published online. The others are original online content, discussed in the previous chapter, and previously unpublished material, to be discussed in the next chapter.

Chapter 14 exercises

135. Which of the five options listed in table 20 would you use for your working notes or works in progress? Why is that your choice?

136. Which of the five options listed in table 20 would you use for your portfolio for the Board for Certification of Genealogists (BCG), material for The International Commission for the Accreditation of Professional Genealogists (ICAPGen), journal submission, or family history book? Why is that your choice?

137. In Greenfield footnote 18, the first two citations refer to books that were viewed online. The citations do not acknowledge that online viewing. In this article's context, is that a problem? Why or why not? If it is not a problem in this context, in what context might it be a problem? Why or why not?

Table 20

Comparison of Options for Citing Images of Previously Published Material

OPTION	RECOMMENDATION	RATIONALE
1. Cite only the image.	DO NOT USE.	Omitting information about the original publication, this option can mislead the original researcher and any readers. That shortcoming outweighs the option's conventional and concise format.
2. Cite the image and acknowledge the underlying publication.	Usable in working notes.	This format, the opposite of option 4, breaks up information about the prior publication. Otherwise, it resembles option 3.
3. Cite only the underlying publication.	Ideal for print products. Usable in working notes, but options 4 and 5 could be more useful in working notes.	This option is simple, concise, and traditional. When using it in working notes, researchers must decide where to view the image, a minor issue.
4. Cite the underlying publication and acknowledge the image.	Useful for working notes, and usable in finished products, especially digital media.	The citation provides complete information about the publication. It also shows one place the source can be viewed, although other options exist both online and off. Its length can limit its usefulness for the print medium.
5. Cite in full both the underlying publication and its image.	Ideal for working notes, but option 3 is more concise and almost as useful.	This format provides complete information about both the prior publication and the online images. Researchers choose the order they want. The citations' length limits their usefulness for the print medium.

138. Greenfield footnote 22, first citation, references a source with a page number viewed but not cited as image 305 of an *Ancestry* collection with title similar to the title of of the cited microfilm publication. That collection's URL is http://ancestry.com/search/db.aspx?dbid=1198. The waypoints forming a path from the collection to the image are > 1835–1839 > A–Z >. Suppose you want to cite this source in your working notes. Select an option from table 20 and craft the citation. Explain why you chose the option you used.

139. Using links at https://memory.loc.gov/ammem/amlaw/lwsllink.html, locate the publication cited in Greenfield footnote 24. Using option 5 in table 20 and noting that you will need to gather information beyond that one image, cite this online resource.

140. What strategies might you use to locate the book cited in Greenfield footnote 38? Once you found it, how would you cite it? Why would you cite it that way?

141. Using options 3, 4, and 5 from table 20 and noting that you will need to gather information beyond one image, cite each of the following in a full reference-note format:

    a. Point your Internet browser to https://archive.org and search for "History of the Starr Family of New England." Select the first hit and cite the information about Hannah Greenfield on page 6. (*Hint:* You might find that taking the option to download the book as a PDF is easier than searching and navigating through the book online.)

    b. Point your Internet browser to https://memory.loc.gov/ammem/amlaw/, navigate to "Statutes at Large," then "Browse Statutes at Large." Go to volume 9 and click on "Title Page." Turn to image 428 and cite the law authorizing the 1850 census.

    c. Point your Internet browser to http://chroniclingamerica.loc.gov/, search for "Edmund Cartlidge." Then enlarge and cite the resulting item about Revolutionary War soldiers.

    d. Point your Internet browser to https://davidrumsey.com, search the collection (not the site) for *Cayuga*, and cite the map by David H. Burr.

    e. Log into https://familysearch.org, click "Search" and then "Books." Search for "Early Starrs in Kent and New England." The result will download to your computer as a 146-page PDF. Cite the information about Archibald Greenfield on the book's page 137 (not image 137).

f. Point your Internet browser to https://news.google.com/newspapers, scroll down to "Boston Evening Transcript," search by date for "Feb 26, 1906," turn to its page 14, and cite the first genealogy query on the page.

g. Point your Internet browser to https://www.hathitrust.org/, search for "Records of the First Church in Huntington, Long Island, 1723–1779," select the "Full view" option, and cite the Greenfield marriage entry on page 75.

h. If you are a member of the National Genealogical Society, visit the society's website at http://ngsgenealogy.org, click "Members Only," and login with your e-mail address and password. Then go to the "NGSQ Archives" (http://ngsgenealogy.org/cs/ngsq_archives), find a *National Genealogical Society Quarterly* article of use to you, and cite it.

i. Point your Internet browser to https://digitalcollections.nypl.org, search for "New Topographical Atlas of Saratoga Co., New York," sort by "Sequence," and cite the map for Galway Township.

Chapter 15

Citing Online Images of Previously Unpublished Material

> *"Online sources are publications, with the same basic elements as print publications."*[1]

Besides creating original online content (discussed in chapter 13) and images of previous publications (chapter 14), organizations have digitized countless volumes of unpublished material. Archives, businesses, governmental, and religious organizations image this material, sometimes with little or no human intervention. Much of it has come from unpublished Genealogical Society of Utah/FamilySearch microfilm mechanically run through scanners. Increasingly, however, humans operating cameras and scanners are capturing images of unpublished pages in archival repositories. Organizations creating these images make them available online for researchers using personal computers in their homes and at libraries.

In all these cases, as discussed in chapter 6, organizations creating online images function as publishers. They provide something that did not previously exist—publications of previously unpublished material. They widely distribute their online collections, usually by subscription or at no cost to users.[2] Thus, online images of previously unpublished pages are publications. Researchers should cite them as publications.

Nonviable and viable citation options

Researchers have exercised four options for citing online images of previously unpublished materials. Two options are clear and concise, but they do not answer all applicable citation questions. Thus, they are incomplete

---

1. Elizabeth Shown Mills, *Evidence Explained: Citing History Sources from Artifacts to Cyberspace*, 1st ed. (Baltimore: Genealogical Publishing, 2005), 57, for sec. 2.32, "Basic Elements to Cite." Also, ibid., 3rd ed. (2015).

2. For extensive listings of these providers and link to their websites, see Michael Hait, *Online State Resources for Genealogy*, PDF, version 3.0. (http://haitfamilyresearch.com/onlineStates.htm). Also Cyndi Ingle, *Cyndi's List of Genealogy Sites on the Internet* (http://cyndislist.com). Also, *Linkpendium* (http://www.linkpendium.com). All three sites were viewed on 20 February 2017.

and do not meet genealogy standard 5. Two other options are longer, enabling them to answer the citation questions that genealogy standard 5 specifies. Therefore, the last two options meet the standard.

Four sample citations demonstrating the respective options are based on a previously unpublished probate file that has been imaged and published in an online image collection.

Option 1: Cite only the online publication (not recommended)

Cite the image as if it were an original online publication, without adding details showing the qualities of the source and information:

> New England Historic Genealogical Society, "Essex County, MA: Probate File Papers, 1638–1881," *American Ancestors*, members-only website (https://americanancestors.org/databases/essex-county-ma-probate-file-papers-1638-1881/about/ : viewed 20 February 2017), images 11717:20–22.

Option 1 is economical, but some readers might not understand that the source was a historical record, not a modern creation. That sample citation is substandard because it does not identify, beyond image numbers, the specific record that documents the researcher's work. The citation's answer to the *Who* and *What* questions refer only to a twenty-first-century database linked to images. Its answers to the *When* citation question (*1638–1881* and *20 February 2017*) do not accurately date the source that provides documentation.

Option 2: Cite only the underlying material (not recommended)

Cite only the unpublished material, ignoring the online publication:

> Archibald Greenfield, will, 1 November 1767, proved on 4 September 1769; in Essex Co., Mass., probate files, case no. 11717 (1769), Archibald Greenfield; Registry of Probate, Salem, Mass.

That option is clear and concise, but its answer to the *Whereis* citation question misleads by implying the researcher examined the original record in its primary context. It omits information about the publication that the researcher used for viewing the record, a publication that readers could access more easily than traveling to Salem. The omission makes the citation incomplete. Thus it does not meet genealogy standard 5. Also, this option omits information about a numbered published image instead of specifying its location. The omission requires readers to hunt for the cited document.

Option 3: Cite the published image with added details

Cite the image as an original publication, including any information needed to show the qualities of the source and information:

> New England Historic Genealogical Society, "Essex County, MA: Probate File Papers, 1638–1881," *American Ancestors*, members-only website (https://americanancestors.org/databases/essex-county-ma-probate-file-papers-1638-1881/about/ : viewed 20 February 2017), images 11717:20–22, Archibald Greenfield, will, 1 November 1767, proved on 4 September 1769.

This option combines information from options 1 and 2. Although the example is 25 percent longer than those options, it answers all five citation questions clearly and completely. The format uses a traditional book-citation format with information-item details at the end, showing that the researcher used an original record created in 1767 and eyewitness information. The citation's front part shows that the researcher viewed that historic will as a published image. The phrase *digital images* is not needed to identify the source because the citation already specifies that the researcher viewed numbered images and the URL shows they are online, thus digitized.

This option has long-standing precedent. In 1941 the National Archives began a program of microfilming its records, and its publication program was "firmly established" in 1948.[3] Libraries began purchasing the microfilms, and genealogists and other researchers began using and citing them. They understood they were not using textual records at the National Archives, which were in a different medium and in collections with titles different from the microfilm publications that they handled and read. They also understood that, had they consulted the textual records they might find information that had not been microfilmed clearly or at all. These understandings led to the practice of citing the microfilm publication, not the textual records. In 1980 the genealogy field's first citation manual made that practice explicit:

> The repository holding the original record should be given *if it was seen there by the researcher*. If not, *the form used by the researcher* should be stated.[4]

Consequently, genealogists have long cited published images of original records as publications. For decades they have used that format, with publication information at the citation's front, and item specifics at its end. This example—one among many—has endured from the first edition of *Evidence Explained* to the present:

3. "The National Archives Microfilm Publication Program," *Genealogical and Biographical Research: A Select Catalog of National Archives Microfilm Publications* (Washington, D.C.: National Archives Trust Fund Board, 1983), v. Also H. G. Jones, *The Records of a Nation: Their Management, Preservation, and Use* (New York: Atheneum, 1969), 90–93 and 117–26. At p. 90, Jones says "Microfilm was used in the National Archives as a means of reproduction as early as 1936."

4. Richard S. Lackey, *Cite Your Sources: A Manual for Documenting Family Histories and Genealogical Records* (New Orleans: Polyanthos, 1980), 76 and 79 (same quotation). For amplification of the quoted statement and a sample citation, see ibid., pp. 57–58. For a similar discussion, see ibid., 62. For emphasis, the present author added italics to Lackey's words.

> *Southern Women and Their Families in the 19th Century: Papers and Diaries;* Part 6, *Virginia,* Anne Firor Scott, editor, microfilm publication, 30 rolls (Bethesda, Maryland: University Publications of America, 1992), roll 1, frame 123, and document 2.[5]

Option 3 for citing published facsimiles of previously unpublished material uses a similar format. The context—published facsimiles of previously unpublished material—is identical.

A variation of option 3 is common. The researcher begins the citation with answers to the *Who, What, When,* and *Wherein* citation questions about the underlying source. Those answers show its qualities. The citation does not, however, answer the *Whereis* question for the underlying source, because the researcher did not view it in its offline context. The citation, instead, answers *Whereis* with information about the online publication that the researcher used and that readers are likely to consult, like this example:

> Georgia State Board of Health, Standard Certificate of Death no. 16678 (1923), John Thomas Wright; PDF, "Georgia Death Certificates," *Georgia Archives: University System of Georgia* (http://vault.georgiaarchives.org/cdm/landingpage/collection/gadeaths : 20 February 2017).

That is nearly the opposite format of the two preceding citation examples, which begin with information about the publication and conclude by identifying a specific image and describing its contents.

Option 4: Cite underlying material and online image in full

Cite the offline material and the online publication both in full, using a double citation:

> Archibald Greenfield, will, 1 November 1767, proved on 4 September 1769, in Essex Co., Mass., probate files, case no. 11717 (1769), Archibald Greenfield, Registry of Probate, Salem, Mass.; digital images, New England Historic Genealogical Society, "Essex County, MA: Probate File Papers, 1638–1881," *American Ancestors,* members-only website (https://americanancestors.org/databases/essex-county-ma-probate-file-papers-1638-1881/about/ : 20 February 2017), images 11717:20–22.

That option combines options 1 and 2, enabling each option to correct the other's deficiencies. Thus, option 4 answers all five citation questions. The semicolon and the words *digital images* separate the citation's two divisions. Either division could be cited first. In less complex citations, a semicolon would set off the repository. In double citations, the semicolon serves the more important role of separating two groups of phrases with commas between them.

5. Mills, *Evidence Explained,* 1st ed., 129, for sec. 3.18, "Filmed or Fiched Manuscripts, Commercial Publications." Also, ibid., 3rd ed. (2015). For similar examples, see ibid., 562–68, sec. 11.8, "Basic Formats: Microfilm Records," and elsewhere.

This example is the opposite of the preceding citation:

> New England Historic Genealogical Society, "Essex County, Mass.: Probate File Papers, 1638–1881," *American Ancestors*, members-only website (https://americanancestors.org/databases/essex-county-ma-probate-file-papers-1638-1881/about/ : viewed 20 February 2017), images 11717:20–22; Archibald Greenfield, will, 1 November 1767, proved on 4 September 1769, in Essex Co., Mass., probate files, case no. 11717 (1769), Archibald Greenfield, Registry of Probate, Salem, Mass.

Combining options 1 and 2 makes option 4 long. In this example, it is 58 percent longer than option 3, which meets standards equally well.

The only information that this option provides that option 3 does not is the repository of the underlying file and will. That information is irrelevant, however, because the researcher did not view the file or the will at that repository and readers are unlikely to go there. Consequently, this book recommends option 3 over option 4. Researchers would use option 4 only when readers would benefit from knowing where an underlying source is, even though the researcher citing it did not view it there.

Table 21 summarizes the recommendations for these four options.

Conclusion

This chapter describes how to cite images of previously unpublished material, one of three forms of online sources that genealogists use. The chapter discusses four options for citing those sources and shows that two of them do not contain enough information to meet genealogy standard 5. It recommends option 3 over option 4, which contains added information that most researchers and readers would not need.

Chapters 13–15 have discussed citation logic and options for three forms of online sources that genealogists consult: original online material, images of prior publications, and images of previously unpublished material. Those chapters have provided citation options for each of those three scenarios. Some of those options include appending information about an underlying source, appending information about the medium through which an underlying source is viewed, and crafting a two-part citation that fully cites both the underlying source and its published online image. Structuring those citations is the subject of chapter 16.

Chapter 15 exercises

142. Which option in table 21 did the Greenfield article's author choose for footnote 4, the last citation (to a death certificate)? How does this citation answer the *Whereis* citation question? What might you add to the citation to answer that question more explicitly?

Table 21

Nonviable and Viable Options for Citing Published Images of Previously Unpublished Material

OPTION	RECOMMENDATION	RATIONALE
1. Cite the image as if it were an original online publication.	Do not use.	Omitting information about the original publication, this option can mislead the original researcher and any readers. That shortcoming outweighs the option's conventional and concise format.
2. Cite only the underlying unpublished material, ignoring the online publication.	Do not use.	This option omits information about where the researcher viewed the record and where readers are most likely to access it. Its answer to the *Whereis* citation question is incomplete.
3. Cite the image as an original publication, including any details needed to show the source and information-item qualities.	Ideal for working notes and finished products.	Merging information from options 1 and 2, option 3 answers all five citation questions and communicates qualities of the source underlying the image.
4. Using a double citation, cite in full to the offline material and online publication.	Use in working notes and finished products when information about an underlying source's location aids in understanding it.	Combining options 1 and 2, option 4 is long but complete. It provides information about an unpublished source's repository, which usually is not necessary. Although unconventional, including that detail is not wrong.

143. Greenfield footnotes 5 (second citation, to the probate record) and 7 (first and third citations, to the 1855 census and 1870 mortality schedule) use similar formats for citing previously unpublished material. How are they the same?

144. In Greenfield footnote 8, what is the purpose of the information in square brackets? Which option in table 21 does this citation use?

145. Which option in table 21 does the citation in Greenfield footnote 13 use? Re-craft this citation using another option.

146. Why does the citation in Greenfield footnote 36 omit the URL? Would you do this in your working notes? Why or why not?

147. Which of the four options listed in table 21 would you use for your working notes or works in progress? Why is that your choice?

148. Which of the four options listed in table 21 would you use for your portfolio for the Board for Certification of Genealogists (BCG), materials for The International Commission for the Accreditation of Professional Genealogists (ICAPGen), journal submission, or family history book? Why is that your choice?

149. Remembering that you will need to gather citation information from places other than an image you are viewing, cite sources a–g, listed below. Use table 21's option 3 (both variants described on pages 156–58) and its option 4 (both variants described on pages 158–59) to create three full reference-note citations. Then identify which version you prefer, and explain your choice.

    a. Point your Internet browser to https://familysearch.org/ark:/61903/1:1:KMCQ-M24, click on the image that appears on the screen, and cite the record in the image's top right section.

    b. Point your Internet browser to https://familysearch.org/search/collection/1388122, click *Browse,* and navigate through St. Clair (County), Paderborn, and its only parish. Open the 1861–1898 volume, turn to image 38, and cite the last record on the image that appears.

    c. Point your Internet browser to http://s1.sos.mo.gov/records/archives/archivesdb/deathcertificates/Default.aspx, and search for *Cordelia Ziegler*. Then click the *View Image* link, and cite the record on the PDF that downloads.

    d. Create a free account at mdlandrec.net, log in, and select *Queen Anne's County*. In the form that appears, enter clerk *RT*, book *B*, and page *53*. Click *Go!* and cite the record that *begins* near the middle of the PDF that appears. (*Hint:* That record continues onto another page or pages.)

    e. Point your Internet browser to http://www.virginiamemory.com/collections/petitions. For Keyword, enter *1785-12-01*, for Locality, select *Stafford County*, and click *Search*. Study the online context of the image that appears in a new window, and cite the three-page document, which you can download as a PDF.

    f. Point your Internet browser to http://vault.georgiaarchives.org/cdm/landingpage/collection/TestApps. Search for *Simon Overton,* click the thumbnail that appears, and cite the document in the envelope.

g. Point your Internet browser to http://www.archivesindex.sc.gov/onlinearchives/search.aspx and search Record group *All* for Individual *Collier, Abialbion*. Then examine the page that appears, click *Online images available*, and cite the source, containing three images, that this leads you to.

Chapter 16

Multipart Options for Citing Images

> *"Image[:] A film, photocopy, photograph, scan, video, or other replication of a physical source"*[1]

Chapters 14–15 address citing two kinds of images: *(a)* those showing previously published material, and *(b)* those showing previously unpublished material. The present chapter takes those discussions a step further by explaining content and structure options for citing facsimile images—both online and off—and the rationales for choosing suitable options.

When researchers determine or suspect an image is not a facsimile, they consult the underlying version. In that rare case, they do not cite the image. They cite just the underlying version they examined.

The opposite scenario is common. Because nearly all images are facsimiles, researchers rarely need to consult an underlying version. Thus, they cite facsimiles often.

Images and the sources they show

In a genealogical research context, the presence of an *image* implies that at least two versions of a source exist (or once existed):

1. The image that a researcher consulted
2. The underlying source from which the image was created

Images can be either published or unpublished. Likewise, the underlying sources can be either published or unpublished. Any image and its underlying source form a pair. Five pairings are possible:

Unpublished + published. An unpublished image shows a published underlying source. Examples include a photocopy (unpublished) of a journal article (published), and a GSU/FamilySearch microfilm (unpublished) of a family history book or a city directory (published).

Published + published. Both the image and the underlying source are published. Examples include a commercial microfilm (published) showing images

---

1. Board for Certification of Genealogists [BCG], *Genealogy Standards* (Nashville, Tenn.: Ancestry.com, 2014), 69, (glossary definition of "image").

of a book (published), and online images (published) showing journal or newspaper articles (published). Image versions of sources also can be repeatedly published—for example, a census microfilm (published) imaged on multiple websites (publications).

Published + unpublished. A published image shows an unpublished underlying source. Examples include online images (published) of court papers, tax rolls, or vital records (unpublished), and microfilm publications (published) showing censuses, military records, or pension files (unpublished).

Unpublished + unpublished. Both an image and the underlying source it shows are unpublished. Examples include GSU/FamilySearch microfilm (unpublished) showing county records (unpublished), and print photographs (unpublished) showing gravestones (unpublished).

Published or unpublished + unknown. A published or unpublished image shows a source that disappeared after it was imaged. Examples include town records microfilmed decades ago by GSU and then moved to a now-unknown repository, county records subsequently destroyed in courthouse fires, and personal photocopies of forgotten sources.

Per this book's chapter 1, to cite a source clearly and completely, researchers must understand its characteristics and history. Per chapter 6, one of the first questions they ask to acquire that understanding is, *Is this source published or not?* When viewing an image, they ask that question about both the image and its underlying source. Part of understanding sources comes from determining where an image-source pairing fits into the five categories described above.

Citation choices vary for each category. Understanding the category narrows the options, helping researchers make optimal choices for each citation's content and structure.

Choices for citation content

When citing a facsimile, researchers have five options of varying suitability about the content to include in the citation and to exclude from it. They decide which citation questions to answer and not answer about the image, its underlying source, or both. Some of the options appear with examples in chapter 14, focused on citing images of previously published material, and chapter 15, focused on citing online images of previously unpublished material.

The present chapter builds on those prior chapters' focused discussions. It extends them to all combinations of images and underlying versions, each of which can be published or not. This chapter also compares the rationales, and it combines them into an overarching framework. Although researchers might choose any option, suitability varies with each image-source pairing. A land record on GSU microfilm (unpublished) and examined as an online digital image (published) illustrates the five content options:

1. The researcher cites the image and ignores the underlying source. The citation's content fully describes the image only:

   "Massachusetts Land Records, 1620–1986," *FamilySearch* (https://familysearch.org/search/collection/2106411 : viewed 20 February 2017) > Worcester > Deeds 1733-1735 vol 4-5 > image 479.

2. The researcher cites the image and adds information about the underlying source that would help readers understand its qualities. The citation's content fully describes the image and partially describes the underlying source:

   "Massachusetts Land Records, 1620–1986," *FamilySearch* (https://familysearch.org/search/collection/2106411 : viewed 20 February 2017) > Worcester > Deeds 1733-1735 vol 4-5 > image 479, Worcester Co., Deeds 5:327, Greenfield to Starr, quitclaim, 12 November 1733.

3. The researcher ignores the image and cites the underlying source in full, using information given by the image provider. The citation's content fully describes the underlying source only:

   Worcester Co., Mass., Deeds 5:327, Greenfield to Starr, quitclaim, 12 November 1733; Register of Deeds, Worcester, Mass.

4. The researcher cites the underlying source and adds information about the image. The citation's content fully describes the underlying source but incompletely describes the image:

   Worcester Co., Mass., Deeds 5:327, Greenfield to Starr, quitclaim, 12 November 1733; Register of Deeds, Worcester, Mass.; digital image 479, *FamilySearch*.

5. The researcher cites both the image and the underlying source. The citation's content fully describes both versions:

   "Massachusetts Land Records, 1620–1986," *FamilySearch* (https://familysearch.org/search/collection/2106411 : viewed 20 February 2017) > Worcester > Deeds 1733–1735 vol 4–5 > image 479; for Worcester Co., Deeds 5:327, Greenfield to Starr, quitclaim, 12 November 1733, Register of Deeds, Worcester, Mass.

   Worcester Co., Mass., Deeds 5:327, Greenfield to Starr, quitclaim, 12 November 1733, Register of Deeds, Worcester, Mass.; image at "Massachusetts Land Records, 1620–1986," *FamilySearch* (https://familysearch.org/search/collection/2106411 : viewed 20 February 2017) > Worcester > Deeds 1733-1735 vol 4-5 > image 479.

Although semicolons do not set off the repositories in option 5, in all the examples they separate groups of phrases with internal commas.

The respective example of each citation-content choice answers all five citation questions at least once, but some of the examples are more useful than others. Also, options suitable for some pairings of images and underlying sources are not suitable for others.

Citation structures

Each option for citation content has its own implication for the citation's overall architecture. The formats are analogous, respectively, to simple, complex, and compound sentences.

Simple citations

Simple sentences can be long or short. Regardless of length, they form an independent clause with no supporting clauses.

Simple citations resemble simple sentences. They answer the five citation questions once. They describe one version of a source, either the image or the source underlying it. They do not acknowledge the source's other version.

Examples 1 and 3, above, are simple citations. Example 1 cites a published image in full, answering all five citation questions. Example 3 does the same for an unpublished source.

Complex citations

A complex sentence is a simple sentence—one independent clause—that also contains one or more dependent clauses. Those clauses add supporting or supplementary information to the independent clause. The presence of one or more supporting clauses adds complexity to a sentence's structure. A comma, a connecting word (for example, *because* or *when*), or both typically set off supporting clauses from core sentences.

Complex citations resemble complex sentences. They fully cite an image or an underlying source, answering the five citation questions about the image or underlying source. Then they append supporting information about the other component of the image-source pair, answering some of the citation questions about that component. A punctuation mark (often a semicolon) and usually one or more words (for example, *digital image, microfilm* or *showing*) set off the supporting information from the rest of the citation. Some genealogy journals use parentheses or square brackets to set off supplementary information, maintaining the citation's structure as a simple sentence while providing supplementary information.

Examples 2 and 4 above are complex citations. Example 2 cites a published image in full and provides supplementary information about the underlying source. Example 4 cites an underlying source in full and provides supplementary information about the image. In example 2, a comma (after *479*), sets off the supporting information. In Example 4, a semicolon and the words *digital images* set off the supporting information.

Compound citations

Compound sentences are two (or more) independent clauses joined with a punctuation mark (usually a comma) and a connecting word (*and* or *but,* for example). Joined, the independent clauses form one compound sentence containing two complete thoughts.

Compound citations resemble compound sentences. A punctuation mark (usually a comma or semicolon), connecting words, or both join two complete citations. They form a single citation containing two related citations. Both example 5s, above, are compound citations. Each answers the five citation questions about an image and again about the source underlying that image. In the first example 5, a semicolon and the word *for* join the two parts. In the second example 5, a semicolon and the words *image at* join the citation's two components.

The overall picture

Researchers have five options for the content for citing a facsimile image. They use one of three citation structures to arrange their chosen content within the citation. Each content option, however, has only one corresponding structure possibility. The researcher's choice of citation content determines the citation's structure. See table 22.

Table 22

Citation-Content Options and Their Structures

CITATION-CONTENT OPTION	STRUCTURE
1. Cite only the image.	Simple
2. Cite the image, and supplement it with selected information about the underlying source.	Complex
3. Cite only the underlying source.	Simple
4. Cite the underlying source, and supplement it with selected information about the image.	Complex
5. Cite both the image and the underlying source in full. Join the two citations.	Compound

Table 23

Image-Source Pairs, Theoretically Possible Choices for Citation Content, and Implications for Citation Structure

IMAGE-SOURCE PAIR	CONTENT OPTIONS AND STRUCTURE IMPLICATIONS
Unpublished images of underlying publications	1. Cite only the image (applies the simple structure) 2. Cite the image and add supplementary detail (applies the complex structure) 3. Cite the underlying source only (applies a simple structure) 4. Cite the underlying source and add supplementary detail (applies the complex structure) 5. Cite the image and the underlying source (applies the compound structure)
Published images of underlying publications	1. Cite only the image (applies the simple structure) 2. Cite the image and add supplementary detail (applies the complex structure) 3. Cite the underlying source only (applies a simple structure) 4. Cite the underlying source and add supplementary detail (applies the complex structure) 5. Cite the image and the underlying source (applies the compound structure)
Published images of underlying unpublished sources	1. Cite only the image (applies the simple structure) 2. Cite the image and add supplementary detail (applies the complex structure) 3. Cite the underlying source only (applies a simple structure) 4. Cite the underlying source and add supplementary detail (applies the complex structure) 5. Cite the image and the underlying source (applies the compound structure)
Unpublished images of unpublished underlying sources	1. Cite only the image (applies the simple structure) 2. Cite the image and add supplementary detail (applies the complex structure) 3. Cite the underlying source only (applies a simple structure) 4. Cite the underlying source and add supplementary detail (applies the complex structure) 5. Cite the image and the underlying source (applies the compound structure)
Published or unpublished images of missing or destroyed sources	1. Cite only the image (applies the simple structure) 2. Cite the image and add supplementary detail (applies the complex structure) 3. Cite the underlying source only (applies a simple structure) 4. Cite the underlying source and add supplementary detail (applies the complex structure) 5. Cite the image and the underlying source (applies the compound structure)

Thus, researchers have five content options for citing any one of the five pairings of published and unpublished images and underlying sources. Table 23 shows those twenty-five possibilities, but the number is deceptive.

Once researchers determine an image-source pairing, they choose one of the five content options. Some are more complete, straightforward, and suitable than others. Others have significant drawbacks, including too little information, unnecessary complexity, and the risk of misleading readers. A few are impossible to apply.

Each of the next five sections addresses one kind of pairing of a published or unpublished image with a published or unpublished underlying source—a five-part block in table 23. Citations illustrate the five options for each pairing. Narrative discusses each citation option's strengths and weaknesses for the respective pairing. These discussions are intended to guide researchers in making their own decisions about what information to include in and exclude from a citation to a given image.

Unpublished images of publications

Researchers encounter unpublished images of publications, but they are less common than other image-source pairings. They appear mostly in unpublished microfilm and photocopies, photographs, and scans created for personal use. Researchers can cite this pairing, like any image-source combination, in any of five ways with varying acceptability. These examples cite an unpublished image of a published book.

> [*Option 1:* Cite only the image.] Genealogical Society of Utah, 1965, microfilm 348,355, Family History Library, Salt Lake City.

A less detailed example is more common:

> FHL 348,355.

Option 1 cites an unpublished image only. The first version answers the five citation questions, but citations using this option are *substandard* because they do not identify the underlying source, a publication in this pairing. Such citations do not show readers what the publication is, who created it or when, or its wide availability beyond the unpublished image. Such citations give readers only FHL microfilm as an option for viewing the publication, although many others are available. Citing only an unpublished image, even in full, is *not recommended*, especially when the image shows a publication.

> [*Option 2:* Cite the image and add detail.] Genealogical Society of Utah, 1965, microfilm 348,355, Family History Library, Salt Lake City, showing Frederic Beech Pierce and Frederick Clifton Pierce, *Pierce Genealogy* (1882), 151.

Fully citing an unpublished image and appending information about the underlying publication is *acceptable*. It tells readers what the underlying source is, who wrote it, and when. Italics show that the underlying source is a publication, thus widely available, but the citation does not identify the publisher. The citation's biggest shortcoming is its needless emphasis on the unpublished image. It also takes up space with information that does not help readers understand and locate the source or the image. For this reason, this option, though acceptable, is *not recommended* for citing unpublished images of publications.

> [*Option 3:* Cite only the underlying source.] Frederic Beech Pierce and Frederick Clifton Pierce, *Pierce Genealogy, being the Record of the Posterity of Thomas Pierce* (Worcester, Mass.: Chas. Hamilton, 1882), 151.

Ignoring the unpublished image, option 3 cites the underlying publication in full. It also gives credit to the publisher that created the source. Given that the image shows a widely available source, citing information about the image—especially one that is unpublished—is of little value. Option 3 is *recommended*. Using a simple citation structure, it is a likely option for printed work. It also would be useful in working notes.

> [*Option 4:* Cite the underlying source and add detail.] Frederic Beech Pierce and Frederick Clifton Pierce, *Pierce Genealogy, being the Record of the Posterity of Thomas Pierce* (Worcester, Mass.: Chas. Hamilton, 1882), 151; microfilm 348,355, Family History Library, Salt Lake City.

Fully citing the underlying publication and acknowledging the unpublished image is *acceptable*. The information about the unpublished image is marginally useful because it does not enable readers to turn to it. It might, however, remind researchers where they consulted it. Readers are likely to access the publication elsewhere. Although option 4 meets standards, it is *not* recommended.

> [*Option 5:* Fully cite the image and underlying source.] Frederic Beech Pierce and Frederick Clifton Pierce, *Pierce Genealogy, being the Record of the Posterity of Thomas Pierce* (Worcester, Mass.: Chas. Hamilton, 1882), 151; imaged by Genealogical Society of Utah, 1965, on microfilm 348,355, Family History Library, Salt Lake City.

Adding information about the unpublished image to the option-4 citation produces option 5, with a compound structure. Answering all five citation questions about both the image and the underlying source, it is *acceptable*. Detailed information about an unpublished image, however, is unnecessary. Option 5 is *not* recommended for unpublished images of publications.

Published images of publications

Online publication of facsimiles of underlying publications are common. They include digital images from books, journals, and newspapers. *Offline* examples include microfiche and microfilm publications of city directories and newspapers. Researchers can cite this pairing, like any image-source combination, in any of five ways with varying acceptability. These examples cite online images made from a microfilm publication.

> [*Option 1:* Cite only the image.] "New York, Passenger Lists, 1820–1957," *Ancestry* (http://ancestry.com/search/db.aspx?dbid=7488 : viewed on 20 February 2017) > Roll > T715, 1897–1957 > 0001–1000 > Roll 0870 > image 38.

That example indirectly provides information about the underlying source, but its omissions can mislead. Readers who are unfamiliar with the uncited underlying publication could mistake a historical record for a modern online database. The citation is substandard because it omits the date of the information of interest, critical to weighing this source's value for supporting a narrative. Readers would have to repeat part of the prior researcher's work to understand what this source shows. For citing published images of publications, this option is *not recommended*.

> [*Option 2:* Cite the image and add detail.] "New York, Passenger Lists, 1820–1957," *Ancestry* (http://ancestry.com/search/db.aspx?dbid=7488 : viewed on 20 February 2017) > Roll > T715, 1897–1957 > 0001–1000 > Roll 0870 > image 38, for SS *Carmania*, list 1, line 12, Newell D. Welch, 17 April 1907; citing NARA microfilm publication T715, roll 870.

Fully citing an published image and appending information about the underlying publication answers all five citation questions. The example cites the version the researcher used and that readers are likely to consult. It tells readers what the underlying source is and when it was created. It enables readers to turn directly to the image. The citation briefly says the underlying source is a publication and identifies its publisher. This format cites the image as if it were a new edition, while identifying a prior edition. Debatable points are whether that identification is sufficient, and whether its full identification of the published images is necessary. Given varying opinions, this option is *acceptable* for citing published images of publications in working notes. It likely would be acceptable for printed work.

> [*Option 3:* Cite only the underlying source.] *Passenger and Crew Lists of Vessels Arriving at New York, NY, 1897–1957*, microfilm publication T715, 8,892 rolls (Washington, D.C.: National Archives and Records Administration, n.d.), roll 870, SS *Carmania*, list 1, line 12, Newell D. Welch, 17 April 1907.

Ignoring the published image, option 3 cites the underlying publication in full. Thus, it answers all five citation questions. This option also fully identifies the publisher that created that source. Omitting information about the version the researcher used, and that readers are likely to consult, makes little sense, however. Omitting the information needed to turn directly to the image, it is less than ideal for working notes. Print publications, however, might prefer it. Overall, option 3 is *acceptable*.

> [*Option 4:* Cite the underlying source and add detail.] *Passenger and Crew Lists of Vessels Arriving at New York, NY, 1897–1957*, microfilm publication T715, 8,892 rolls (Washington, D.C.: National Archives and Records Administration, n.d.), roll 870, SS *Carmania*, list 1, line 12, Newell D. Welch, 17 April 1907; digital image, *Ancestry* (http://search.ancestry.com/search/db.aspx?dbid=7488 : viewed 20 February 2017).

Fully citing the underlying publication and acknowledging the published image is *acceptable*. The information about the image, however, does not help readers turn to the image, but it does provide the online image collection's URL. Though longer than option 3, which is more economical, option 4 is barely more useful. Thus, it is *not recommended*.

> [*Option 5:* Fully cite the image and underlying source.] *Passenger and Crew Lists of Vessels Arriving at New York, NY, 1897–1957*, microfilm publication T715, 8,892 rolls (Washington, D.C.: National Archives and Records Administration, n.d.), roll 870, SS *Carmania*, list 1, line 12, Newell D. Welch, 17 April 1907; imaged at "New York, Passenger Lists, 1820–1957," *Ancestry* (http://ancestry.com/search/db.aspx?dbid=7488 : viewed on 20 February 2017) > Roll > T715, 1897–1957 > 0001–1000 > Roll 0870 > image 38.

Adding image information to the option-4 citation produces option 5. Answering all five citation questions about the image and the underlying source, it is *acceptable*. Detailed information about the published image enables readers to turn to it. Option 5 can be ideal for working notes, but options 2 and 3 can be more acceptable for printed work.

Published images of unpublished sources

Published images of previously unpublished records are a recent and rapidly growing phenomenon. Hundreds of camera crews digitally photograph records in archives for publication online. *FamilySearch*, for example, has published over 1.22 billion images, mostly digitized from unpublished GSU/FamilySearch microfilm.[2] *Find A Grave* and other websites publish photographs that people had held privately. Microfilm publications, produced through six decades, show images of unique archival records. Published books occasionally show images of manuscripts. Researchers can cite the pairing of published image and unpublished underlying source, like any image-source combination, in any of five ways with varying acceptability. The examples here cite online images made from unpublished microfilm of county court records.

---

2. "FamilySearch.org Facts for January 2017," *FamilySearch* (http://media.familysearch.org/company-facts : accessed 20 February 2017).

> [*Option 1:* Cite only the image.] "New York, Probate Records, 1629–1971," *FamilySearch* (https://familysearch.org/search/collection/1920234 : viewed on 20 February 2017) > Niagara > Probates 1835–1970 box H3 > images 1059–1100.

This example indirectly provides information about the underlying source, but its omissions can mislead. Readers unfamiliar with the uncited underlying source could mistake a historical record for an index. The citation identifies the record creator—a county government—only indirectly. The citation also omits the date of the information of interest, critical to weighing this source's value for supporting a genealogist's work. Thus it is substandard. Also, readers would have to repeat part of the prior researcher's work to understand what this source shows. For citing published images of unpublished material, this option is *not recommended.*

> [*Option 2:* Cite the image and add detail.] "New York, Probate Records, 1629–1971," *FamilySearch* (https://familysearch.org/search/collection/1920234 : viewed on 20 February 2017) > Niagara > Probates 1835–1970 box H3 > images 1059–1100, for Niagara Co., Surrogate Records Box H3, Isaac Huffman file, 1853.

Fully citing a published image and appending information about the underlying source answers all five citation questions. This example cites the version the researcher used and that readers are likely to consult. It tells readers what the underlying source is and when it was created. It enables them to turn directly to it. When citing published images of unpublished sources, this option is *acceptable* for working notes and likely acceptable for many printed work.

> [*Option 3:* Cite only the underlying source.] Niagara Co., Surrogate Records Box H3, Isaac Huffman file, 1853; Surrogate's Court, Lockport, N.Y.

Ignoring the published image, option 3 cites the underlying source in full. Thus, it answers all five citation questions. Omitting information about the version the researcher used, a publication that readers are likely to consult, makes little sense, however. Omitting the information needed to turn directly to the image also is less than ideal for working notes. For citing published images of unpublished sources, option 3 is *not recommended.*

> [*Option 4:* Cite the underlying source and add detail.] Niagara Co., Surrogate Records Box H3, Isaac Huffman file, 1853, Courthouse, Lockport, N.Y.; viewed at *FamilySearch* (https://familysearch.org/search/collection/1920234 : viewed on 20 February 2017), images 1059–1100.

Fully citing the underlying source and acknowledging the published image is *acceptable* but not ideal. The citation gives the online collection's URL and image numbers, but readers must figure out how to navigate from the collection level to the cited images. Option 4 also cites the underlying source in its primary context, where the researcher did not examine the source.

> [*Option 5:* Fully cite the image and underlying source.] "New York, Probate Records, 1629–1971," *FamilySearch* (https://familysearch.org/search/collection/1920234 : viewed on 20 February 2017) > Niagara > Probates 1835–1970 box H3 > images 1059–1100; images from Niagara Co., Surrogate Records Box H3, Isaac Huffman file, 1853, Surrogate's Court, Lockport, N.Y.

Adding image information to the option-4 citation produces option 5. Answering all five citation questions about both the image and the underlying source, it is *acceptable*. Detailed information about the published image enables readers to turn to it. Option 5, with its compound structure, can be ideal for working notes, but options 2 and 4 can be more acceptable for printed work.

Unpublished images of unpublished sources

This pairing exists mostly as collections of unpublished records imaged on unpublished microfilm, and privately held photocopies, photographs, and scans of unpublished materials. Researchers can cite unpublished images of unpublished sources, like any image-source combination, in any of five ways with varying acceptability. The examples here cite unpublished microfilm showing unpublished vital records.

> [*Option 1:* Cite only the image.] Genealogical Society of Utah, 1975, microfilm 980,363, Family History Library, Salt Lake City.

A less detailed example is more common:

> FHL 980,363.

Option 1 cites an unpublished image only. The first version answers the five citation questions, but citations using this option are substandard because they do not identify the underlying source. Citing only an unpublished image, even in full, with no added information is *not* recommended.

> [*Option 2:* Cite the image and add detail.] Genealogical Society of Utah, 1975, microfilm 980,363; Family History Library, Salt Lake City; for Antrim Co., Mich., Record of Deaths 3:69, no. 127, Calista J. Tucker, 8 October 1907.

Fully citing an unpublished image and appending information about the underlying unpublished source is *acceptable*. It shows what the underlying source is, who created it, and when. The citation's biggest shortcoming is its needless emphasis on the unpublished image, which takes up space with information that would not help most readers to understand and locate the source or the image. For this reason, this option, though acceptable, is *not recommended* for citing unpublished images of unpublished sources.

> [*Option 3:* Cite only the underlying source.] Antrim Co., Mich., Record of Deaths 3:69, no. 127, Calista J. Tucker, 8 October 1907; County Clerk, Bellaire, Mich.

Ignoring the unpublished image, option 3 cites the underlying unpublished source in full. This option cites only one place to view the record, when other options could be convenient. Because another options would be more useful for readers and in working notes, option 3 is *not recommended* for citing unpublished images of unpublished sources.

> [*Option 4:* Citing the underlying source and add detail.] Antrim Co., Mich., Record of Deaths 3:69, no. 127, Calista J. Tucker, 8 October 1907; County Clerk, Bellaire, Mich.; FHL microfilm 980,363.

Even though the researcher did not view the unpublished source in its primary context, fully citing the underlying source and acknowledging the unpublished image gives readers options for accessing the source. Semicolons conventionally set off information about the repository and the medium, separating the citation into distinct segments. This book *recommends* option 4 for citing unpublished images of unpublished sources.

> [*Option 5:* Fully cite the image and underlying source.] Antrim Co., Mich., Record of Deaths 3:69, no. 127, Calista J. Tucker, 8 October 1907,County Clerk, Bellaire, Mich.; Genealogical Society of Utah, 1975, microfilm 980,363, Family History Library, Salt Lake City.

Adding information about the image to the option-4 citation produces option 5, with a compound structure. Answering all five citation questions about both the image and the underlying source, it is acceptable. A semicolon separates the citations two equal segments. Detailed information about the unpublished image, however, is unnecessary. Option 5 is *not recommended* for unpublished images of unpublished sources.

Images of missing or destroyed sources

Researchers occasionally encounter images of records that disappeared after imaging. They can cite this pairing, like any image-source combination, in any of several ways of varying acceptability. This example cites unpublished and published images of a will book burned in a courthouse fire.

> [*Option 1:* Cite only the image.] Mann Film Laboratories, 1960, microfilm 222,090, Family History Library, Salt Lake City.

> [*Option 1:* Cite only the image.] "Georgia Probate Records, 1742–1990," *FamilySearch* (https://familysearch.org/search/collection/1999178 : viewed on 20 February 2017) > Hancock > Wills and administration records 1820–1827 vol K–L > images 317–19.

Option 1 cites an image only. The first version answers the five citation questions, but citations using this option are substandard for citing unpublished images because they do not identify the underlying source. Citing the published image does provide, albeit indirectly, information about the source creator, but it does not date the record of interest. Thus both examples are substandard. Citing only an image, even in full, with no added information is *not recommended*.

[*Option 2:* Cite the image and add detail.] Mann Film Laboratories, 1960, microfilm 222,090, Family History Library, Salt Lake City; for Hancock Co., Ga., Records L:209–12, will of Abednego Wright, 9 October 1822, proved on 6 December 1824.

[*Option 2:* Cite the image and add detail.] "Georgia Probate Records, 1742–1990," *FamilySearch* (https://familysearch.org/search/collection/1999178 : viewed 20 February 2017) > Hancock > Wills and administration records 1820–1827 vol K–L > images 317–19, Hancock Co., Ga., Records L:209–12, will of Abednego Wright, 9 October 1822, proved on 6 December 1824.

Fully citing the unpublished image—like the first example above—includes information that does not help researchers and readers understand or locate the image. Another option is more concise. Option 2 is *not recommended* for citing unpublished images of missing or destroyed sources.

The citation to the published image—like the second example just above—omits that unnecessary information. It is *acceptable* for citing published images of missing or destroyed sources.

[*Option 3:* Cite only the underlying source. A complete citation is not feasible when the repository is unknown.].

When researchers know that an underlying source's location is unknown or that it was destroyed, their citation omits the repository information, because citing a previous repository usually is not helpful. A full citation is not feasible. The reference note containing the citation, however, could explain why the citation omits an answer to the *Whereis* citation question.

[*Option 4:* Cite the underlying source and add detail.] Hancock Co., Ga., Records L:209–12, will of Abednego Wright, 9 October 1822, proved on 6 December 1824; FHL microfilm 222,090.

[*Option 4:* Cite the underlying source and add detail.] "Georgia Probate Records, 1742–1990," *FamilySearch* (https://familysearch.org/search/collection/1999178 : viewed 20 February 2017) > Hancock > Wills and administration records 1820–1827 vol K–L > images 317–19, Hancock Co., Ga., Records L:209–12, will of Abednego Wright, 9 October 1822, proved on 6 December 1824.

Both examples are incomplete citations to the underlying source because repository information would not be meaningful to cite. Given that shortcoming, both citations provide all relevant available information for the unpublished and published image. Both are *recommended*.

[*Option 5:* Fully cite the image and underlying source. When a repository is unknown, a complete citation is impossible.]

When researchers know that an underlying source was destroyed, or its location is unknown, their citation omits the repository information. (Citing a former repository is rarely helpful.) Thus, a full citation to the underlying source is impossible. The reference note containing the citation, however, could explain why the citation omits an answer to the *Whereis* citation question.

Table 24 summarizes the recommendations for citing each kind of image-source pair. Most pairs have more than one acceptable option. Using the reasoning that this chapter explains and illustrates, researchers choose the options that best fit their source, their needs, their readership, and the venues where their research will appear.

Table 24

Options and Recommendations for Citing Image-Source Pairs

IMAGE-SOURCE PAIR	RESEARCHER CHOICES FOR A CITATION'S CONTENT	RECOMMENDATION*
Unpublished images of underlying publications	1. Cite only the image.	NOT recommended
	2. Cite the image and add detail.	Acceptable†
	3. Cite underlying source only.	RECOMMENDED
	4. Cite the underlying source and detail.	Acceptable†
	5. Cite the image and underlying source	NOT recommended
Published images of underlying publications	1. Cite only the image.	NOT recommended
	2. Cite the image and add detail.	Acceptable
	3. Cite underlying source only.	RECOMMENDED
	4. Cite the underlying source and detail.	Acceptable
	5. Cite the image and underlying source	Acceptable
Published images of underlying unpublished sources	1. Cite only the image.	NOT recommended
	2. Cite the image and add detail.	RECOMMENDED
	3. Cite underlying source only.	NOT recommended
	4. Cite the underlying source and detail.	Acceptable
	5. Cite the image and underlying source	Acceptable
Unpublished images of unpublished underlying sources	1. Cite only the image.	NOT recommended
	2. Cite the image and add detail.	Acceptable†
	3. Cite underlying source only.	NOT recommended
	4. Cite the underlying source and detail.	RECOMMENDED
	5. Cite the image and underlying source	NOT recommended
Published or unpublished images of missing underlying sources	1. Cite only the image.	NOT recommended
	2. Cite the image and add detail.	Mixed
	3. Cite underlying source only.	Not applicable
	4. Cite the underlying source plus detail.	RECOMMENDED
	5. Cite the image and underlying source	Not applicable

*See chapter 16's narrative for the recommendations' rationales.

†Although these options are acceptable because they meet standards, this book does not recommend them. Other options are better.

Conclusion

This chapter addresses multipart options for citing images of underlying sources. It describes five image-source pairs, five options for citation content, and three options for structuring citations to facsimiles. The chapter also provides rationales for choosing the most suitable option for citing each kind of image-source pair.

Chapter 16 exercises

150. In the Greenfield article in appendix A, find at least two examples of citations demonstrating each of these pairings of an image with an underlying-source:
    - Published image + unpublished underlying source
    - Unpublished image + unpublished underlying source

151. Give a rationale for the absence of examples in the Greenfield article of these pairings of an image with an underlying source:
    - Unpublished image + published underlying source
    - Published image + published underlying source

150. What are some examples from your own research of the following pairings of an image with an underlying source?
    - Unpublished image + published underlying source
    - Published image + published underlying source
    - Published image + unpublished underlying source
    - Unpublished image + unpublished underlying source

153. In the Greenfield article find at least two examples of each of the following varieties of citation content and structures:
    - A citation to an image supplemented with selected information about the underlying source (complex citation structure)
    - A citation to only an underlying source (simple citation structure)
    - A citation to an underlying source supplemented with selected information about the image (complex citation structure)

154. Explain why you find no examples of the following varieties of citation content and structure in the Greenfield article:
    - Citations to an image only with no supplementary information (simple citation structure)
    - Citations that fully cite both the image and the underlying source with both parts connected (compound citation structure)

155. From your own research, provide examples of the following varieties of citation content and structure:
    - A citation to an image supplemented with selected information about the underlying source (complex citation structure)
    - A citation to only an underlying source (simple citation structure)
    - A citation to an underlying source supplemented with selected information about the image (complex citation structure)
    - A citation that fully cites both the image and the underlying source with both parts connected (compound citation structure)

156. Referring to table 24, select a recommended or acceptable option for citing each of the five sources described below.
    - First, locate the source.
    - Then gather information you might need to cite the source. This might require you to use online library cataloging or finding aids.
    - Next, identify the kind of pairing of an image with an underlying source (table 24's first column) that the source represents.
    - Fourth, use the recommendations in the table's third column to help you select a suitable option for citation content and structure from the middle column.
    - Using the option you selected, craft the citation.

    For each citation, give the following information:
    - The name of the pairing of an image with an underlying source that the source and citation represent (from table 24's first column)
    - The option you chose for citation content (from table 24's middle column)
    - The reason you chose that particular option.

    Here are the descriptions of the five sources to cite:

    a. The first volume of Norwich, Windsor County, Vermont, town records, page 264, documents the births of two of Josiah Burton's daughters. *FamilySearch* shows an image of this record in its online records collection "Vermont, Town Clerk, Vital and Town Records, 1732–2005" at image 154 of Norwich's earliest volume. Cite the information documenting the younger daughter's birth.

    b. That image also is available on Family History Library microfilm. Find information about that microfilm and cite it.

    c. *Archive.org* provides online images and downloadable PDFs of many books, including one titled *Descendants of Elijah B. Cook and Charity Lockwood Cook*. To locate it, search the "Internet Archive," not the "WayBackMachine." Cite the information for this family:

"11—Joseph Lockwood Cook."

d. The Cayuga County, New York, probate file for Jonathan Tucker has disappeared from estate papers box 5, located in the courthouse at Auburn, New York. The Genealogical Society of Utah, however, microfilmed the file in 1971. An image of that microfilm now appears in *FamilySearch*'s online "New York Probate Records" collection as box 5's images 1080–83. Cite the only record that the file contains.

e. The Burton genealogy file in the library of this book's author in Monroe, New York, contains a photocopy of a publication titled *The Life of Asa Burton*. Cite page 8.

Chapter 17

Documenting on Your Own

> *"Document* (verb)*[:] The processes of recording and showing the sources of concepts, evidence, images, and words that an author or compiler has used."*[1]

Previous chapters explain how to gather information from and about sources to answer the citation questions that genealogy standard 5 requires. Those chapters also provide guidance for identifying the kinds of sources that images show, the published/unpublished permutations of images and underlying sources, and suitable citation content and structure options. Finally, they teach how to assemble a coherent citation.

Chapter 17 pulls together those chapters. It outlines steps for citing all kinds of sources, including those for which no model exists. The chapter concludes with suggestions for continuing to advance mastery of genealogical documentation's knowledge base and skill set.

Ten steps to cite any source

Whether a source is familiar, unfamiliar, or unique, following ten steps helps ensure that the citation is clear and complete:

1. *Understand the source's context.* Does the source stand alone, or is it part of a larger collection or series of collections? Does it have parts or subparts that provide documenting information? Is it an image of source or the source itself? If it has a history of derivation or imaging, what is that history? Use the answers to help you respond to the *What* citation question.
2. *Determine the source's publication status.* Is the source published, unpublished, or a hybrid? If a hybrid, is it predominantly published or unpublished? If the source is an image, what is the image-source pairing by publication status (shown in table 24 in chapter 16)? Use the answers to help you respond to the *Whereis* citation question.

---

1. Board for Certification of Genealogists, *Genealogy Standards* (Nashville, Tenn.: Ancestry.com, 2014), 67 (glossary definition of "document").

3. *Determine the source's title or describe the source.* If it has a title, what is it? What are the titles of any titled parts that provide documenting information? Are they sufficiently descriptive for readers to understand what the source is and its qualities as a container of genealogical information? If not, what words will help researchers and readers understand the source, any relevant parts, and their qualities? Use the answers also to help you respond to the *What* citation question.
4. *Identify the author or creator.* What person or entity created the source? What words, if any, are needed to clarify that person or entity's role in creating the source? Does the name of the source's author or creator appear in the name of the source's title or publisher? Use the answers to help you respond to the *Who* citation question.
5. *Determine the source date or dates.* When was the source copyrighted, created, recorded, or published? What other dates does the source show that could help readers understand its strengths or weaknesses? If this source is online, what was your viewing date? Use the answers to help you respond to the *When* citation question.
6. *Understand where researchers can examine the source.* If the source is published, what person or entity published it? If the source is unpublished, where can researchers examine it? Use the answers to help you respond to the *Whereis* citation question.
7. *Locate the documenting information for a reference-note citation.* What information within the source provides documentation for quoted or paraphrased words or concepts? What is the shortest or best path to that information? Use the answers to help you respond to the *Wherein* citation question.
8. *Assemble all those answers to the five questions into a citation:*
    a. If the source is an image, choose a suitable citation content-structure option (summarized in table 24 in chapter 16).
    b. If the answer to the *Who* citation question is not redundant, it should appear first in the citation followed by any clarifying descriptors.
    c. Next should be the answer to *What,* including the title of any helpful part and any clarifying descriptors. Information about parts can precede or follow the overall source title or description.
    d. Answers to the *When* citation question should follow the name, title, description, or publisher location that the dates refer to.
    e. Conclude a reference-list citation by answering the *Whereis* citation question. If the source is published, use standard formatting for the specific kind of publication.
    f. If the source is published, end the citation with the answer to the *Wherein* citation question. If the source is unpublished, place the answer to the *Wherein* question before the answer to the *Whereis* question.

g. Depending on the citation content-structure option you chose in step *a*, append supplementary information or a full citation describing the source or its image. If the source is not an image, skip this step.

9. *Check the assembled citation.* Look for conformity to standard English-language capitalization, punctuation, and spelling for a paragraph (reference-list citations) or a sentence (reference-note citations). Deviate where needed to improve clarity.

10. *Compare the citation against models in* Evidence Explained *and venues where your work might appear.* Where they differ, assess where the differences are more apt for your source than the models. If the models contain or omit information or formatting that would make your citation more clear, complete, or concise, modify your citation accordingly. When your citation provides a clear and complete description of your source, you have cited it correctly.

With practice, the steps will become automatic.

Further learning

Knowledge bases and skill sets continuously evolve, especially for activities requiring specialized learning. This is true for genealogical documentation. Today's citation particulars differ in some ways from those of fifteen years ago. Fifteen years from now they likely will differ in other ways.

Given ongoing evolution of knowledge and technology, researchers continue to grow and adapt their knowledge of sources and their documentation skills. The best ways to do this are *(a)* consult and cite sources, *(b)* read citations in reputable publications, *(c)* cite sources often, and *(d)* engage in all three often and thoughtfully.

Like many activities worth doing well, genealogical documentation can feel awkward at first. Frequent consultations with the recommended guidebooks and this textbook might slow down the novice. Knowledge and skills will grow, however, and the time investment will be worthwhile. Researchers gain multiple benefits by habitually citing every source they use, plan to use, or write about:

- Regular citing helps them understand more sources.
- It helps them understand the people they are researching.
- It helps them improve their documentation skills.
- It builds confidence in their documentation skills.
- It helps them produce conclusions that resolve research stalemates.

Researchers desiring to improve documentation skills frequently read documented genealogical writing. Articles in the *National Genealogical Society Quarterly* and similar journals demonstrate a variety of acceptable genealogical citations. Like any reputable research publication, the *National Genealogical Society Quarterly* regularly adapts to the ever-growing variety of sources to cite.

Researchers and consumers of research dissect citations. They look for the answers that they give to the *Who, What, When, Whereis,* and *Wherein* citation questions. This habit helps them understand researchers' sources, the citations, and the underlying documentation principles.

Conclusion

This book provides a foundation in the principles and logic of genealogical documentation. Readers who apply those principles will create citations that meet today's standards. The field's knowledge bases and skill sets will grow, but serious researchers will stay abreast of that growth.

Chapter 17 exercises

157. Imagine you inherited a linen dish towel from your great-grandmother. Embroidered on it is her birth date, the only known source for that information. Imagine the dish towel's appearance, qualities, and location. Then, cite it in a full reference-note citation.

158. Transform that reference-note citation into *(a)* a shortened reference-note citation and *(b)* a reference-list citation.

159. Imagine that you lost the dish towel after you had digitally photographed it and uploaded the image on your (perhaps imaginary) website or blog. Craft another reference-note citation citing that source for your great-grandmother's birth date.

160. Transform that reference-note citation into *(a)* a shortened reference-note citation and *(b)* a reference-list citation.

Appendix A

Greenfield Article

Note: For this article's use in this book, the author has adapted and updated it from the original publication, Thomas W. Jones, "Too Few Sources to Solve a Family Mystery? Some Greenfields in Central and Western New York," *National Genealogical Society Quarterly* 103 (June 2015): 85–103.

Calista Jane Greenfield knew neither her parents' names nor her birthplace. She knew, however, her birth date—19 March 1828.[1] Two of her granddaughters—sisters—related Calista's explanation:

> Calista's mother married despite parental disapproval. The newlyweds soon had two children, first Calista and then Frank or Ralph. Seeking work, the father left the family and never returned. Without support, the mother and children went to a poorhouse, where the mother died. When Calista was five, a Hoffman family took her into their home. After she cried for her brother, the Hoffmans took him also. They raised the children as servants.[2]

 Tom@JonesResearchServices.com. Dr. Jones, one of the NGS *Quarterly*'s editors, works as a genealogical researcher, editor, and educator. Melinde Lutz Byrne, FASG, edited this piece, which—like all NGS *Quarterly* submissions—was double-blind reviewed. The author thanks Blaine Bettinger and Angie Bush for their comments on a presubmission draft of the paper. He is grateful to Greenfield descendants who provided DNA samples for this study and for their permissions to use their names and cite their test results. He also thanks Darla Harrison Stimbert, a descendant of Luther Greenfield, for her research contributions. The author descends from Calista Jane (Greenfield) Tucker. Living people mentioned herein identified their parents; the cited DNA test results support those identifications. Referenced websites were last checked on 20 February 2017.

1. For Calista's birth date, see "The Family Record of George M. D. Tucker," two handwritten pages, probably late 1880s; location unknown; photocopy, 1965, author's files. Calista was the likely informant. For corroboration of the year, see Antrim Co., Mich., Record of Deaths 3:69, no. 127, Calista J. Tucker, 8 October 1907; County Clerk, Bellaire, Mich.; microfilm 980,363, Family History Library (FHL), Salt Lake City. The microfilm's signboard and the library catalog show this as volume 2, but the microfilm's first frame shows volume 3. Also, 1880 U.S. census, Kent Co., Mich., population schedule, Solon Twp., enumeration district (ED) 112, p. 12, dwelling/family 126, George M. D. Tucker household; National Archives and Records Administration (NARA) microfilm T9, roll 587. For corroboration of the month, see 1900 U.S. census, Marion Co., Ind., pop. sch., Center Twp., "City of Indianapolis Suburban Population," ED 16, sheet 3A, dwell. 52, fam. 55, Earl McLain household; NARA microfilm T623, roll 387.

2. Paraphrased from Bernice (Leach) Turner, interview by author, 1 November 1980; notes in author's files. Also, Fern (Leach) Dr'y to Ina L. (McLain) McPeek, letter, probably 1972; photocopy, author's files. Bernice said Calista's brother was Frank; Fern identified him as Ralph.

TESTING THE STORY

On 9 June 1847 Calista, nineteen, married George M. D. Tucker at West Somerset, in Niagara County, New York.[3] In 1850 George and "Melissa"/"Malissa" Tucker appeared together in two Niagara County households. E[benezer]. L. Tucker (George's father) headed one.[4] Isaac "Hofman" (Huffman) in an adjacent town, headed the other.[5]

Besides Calista (twenty-one) and George Tucker (twenty-two), Isaac's 1850 household included himself (forty-two), wife Julia A. (thirty-seven), son George (fourteen), son William (seven), laborer Franklin Greenfield (twenty), and Betsy A. Lyon (forty-seven). All except Betsy, a Connecticut native, were born in New York State. Franklin Greenfield apparently was Calista's brother, Frank, of the family story.

New York state censuses for 1855, 1865, and 1875 usually give birthplaces as a New York county or another state or country but not for Calista and Frank. By 1855 Calista had moved to Michigan.[6] Frank's 1855-census birthplace is blank, he was not enumerated in 1865, and he died in 1869.[7] In 1861, however, when enlisting for military service, Frank reported he was born in Cayuga County, New York.[8]

---

3. For the date, see Tucker, "The Family Record of George M. D. Tucker." For West Somerset, see George M. D. Tucker, questionnaire 3—402, 1 August 1898; in George M. D. Tucker (Pvt., Cos. C and F, 3rd Mich. Cav., Civil War), pension no. S.C. 874,447, Case Files of Approved Pension Applications . . . , 1861–1934; Civil War and Later Pension Files; Record Group (RG) 15: Department of Veterans Affairs; National Archives (NA), Washington, D.C.

4. 1850 U.S. census, Niagara Co., N.Y., pop. sch., Town of Hartland, pp. 626–27, dwell./fam. 93, E. L. Tucker household; NARA microfilm 432, roll 561. For George's father's first name and their relationship, see "Death Records 1897–1920," *Seeking Michigan* (http://seekingmichigan.org/discover/death-records-1897-1920), for Michigan Division of Vital Statistics, Certificate of Death (1908) no. 506, George M. D. Tucker, Antrim County. The informant was George's grandson, Earl McLain.

5. 1850 U.S. census, Niagara Co., N.Y., pop. sch., Town of Somerset, p. 713, dwell. 179, fam. 183, Isaac Hofman household. For the Huffman surname and identifications of Isaac's widow and children, see "New York, Probate Records, 1628–1971," *FamilySearch* (https://www.familysearch.org/search/collection/1920234) > Niagara > Probates 1835–1970 box H3 > images 1059–1100, for image 1087, Schedule C, Showing Amount Paid to Different Heirs on their Respective Shares of the Personal Estate, 3 February 1853.

6. 1860 U.S. census, Van Buren Co., Mich., pop. sch., Arlington Twp., p. 86, dwell 658, fam. 648, George Tucker household, for Norris Tucker, nine, born in New York, and Esther J. Tucker, six, born in Michigan; NARA microfilm M653, roll 562. Also, George M. D. Tucker, questionnaire 3—402, 1 August 1898; in George M. D. Tucker Civil War pension no. S.C. 874,447, RG 15, NA–Washington. George said his son Norris A. was born on 24 April 1851 and his daughter Esther Jane on 3 July 1854.

7. "New York, State Census, 1855," *FamilySearch* (https://familysearch.org/search/collection/1937366) > Niagara > Hartland > image 6, 1855 New York census, Niagara Co., Town of Hartland, unpaginated, dwell. 96, fam. 98, Franklin Greenfield household. Also, "New York, State Census, 1865," *FamilySearch* (https://familysearch.org/search/collection/1491284), database search for "Greenfield" in Niagara County. For Frank's death, see "U.S. Federal Census Mortality Schedules, 1850–1885," *Ancestry* (http://search.ancestry.com/search/db.aspx?dbid=8756) > 1870 > New York > Niagara > image 2, 1870 U.S. census, Niagara Co., N.Y., mortality schedule, "Subdivision No 46 Hartland," p. 1, fam. 387, Frank Greenfield.

8. "New York, Civil War Muster Roll Abstracts, 1861–1900 [compiled by New York Adjutant General]," *Ancestry* (http://search.ancestry.com/search/db.aspx?dbid=1965) > 12th Independent Battery Light Artillery > A–Z > 812 > image 179, B. F. Greenfield.

Isaac Huffman died before 1855, but his sons' birthplaces corroborate Frank's report.[9] The 1855 census says William "Hoofman," thirteen, was born in Cayuga County, but it leaves blank his brother George's birthplace.[10] The 1865 and 1875 enumerations give Cayuga County as the birthplace for George, thirty and forty, and William, twenty-four and thirty-four.[11]

George and William Huffman's births in Cayuga County in 1834–35 and 1840–42, respectively, mean their parents were there by the mid-1830s. Their father, Isaac, in his twenties, lived there in 1830—in the town of Conquest—with a female in her sixties.[12]

The Huffmans' land transactions and census enumerations suggest a prolonged move from central to western New York. On 20 April 1839 Isaac S. Huffman and his wife Juliann, of Conquest, sold two tracts totaling twenty-five acres in Conquest's lot 38.[13] In 1840 Isaac appeared in both Cayuga and Niagara counties. Ages and sexes in both 1840 households agree with those in 1850 of Isaac, his wife Julia, their son George, Franklin Greenfield, and "Melisa" Tucker. The male between fifteen and nineteen in the 1840 Cayuga County household could have been a farmhand. The Niagara County 1840 household also includes a female between five and nine and a man in his fifties employed in agriculture.[14] On 15 November 1842 Isaac and Juliann, "of Conquest" sold twenty-five-acre lot 26 there, in the town of Brutus. They acknowledged both deeds in Cayuga County.[15] Their first Niagara County land purchase was thirty-seven acres on 10 November 1845.[16]

Family tales about Calista Greenfield's early years seem accurate. The Huffmans took Calista and her brother into their Cayuga County household between 1830 and 1840.[17] The children's youth and Frank's enlistment record agree they were

9. For Isaac's death, on 16 March 1853, see "New York, Probate Records, 1628–1971," *FamilySearch* > Niagara > Probates 1835–1970 box H3 > image 1073, Julia Ann Huffman, Proof for Administration, 24 March 1853.

10. 1855 N.Y. census, Niagara Co., Town of Hartland, unpaginated, dwell. 89, fam. 91, William Hoofman; and dwell. 90, fam. 92, George Hoofman.

11. "New York, State Census, 1865," *FamilySearch* > Niagara > Hartland, ED 02 > image 4, 1865 N.Y. census, Town of Hartland, ED 2, p. 6, dwell. 45, fam. 48, George W. Huffman. Also, ibid., image 6, p. 9, dwell. 73, fam. 76, William Huffman. Also, "New York, State Census, 1875," *FamilySearch* > Niagara > Hartland > image 14, 1875 New York census, Town of Hartland, unpaginated, dwell. 253, fam. 250, Wm Huffman. Also, ibid. > image 29, dwell. 530, fam. 532, George Huffman.

12. 1830 U.S. census, Cayuga Co., N.Y., Town of Conquest, p. 404, Isaac Huffman household; NARA microfilm M19, roll 88.

13. Cayuga Co., Deeds 61:152–53, Huffman to Rathbun, recorded 7 June 1839; digital image, "New York, Land Records, 1630–1975," *FamilySearch* (https://familysearch.org/search/collection/2078654) > Cayuga > Deeds 1839–1840 vol 61–62 > image 120.

14. 1840 U.S. census, Cayuga Co., N.Y., Town of Conquest, p. 674, Isaac S. Huffman household; NARA microfilm M704, roll 270. Also, ibid., Niagara Co., N.Y., Town of Somerset, p. 285, Isaac Hoffman household; roll 311. Two people in the household were employed in agriculture.

15. "New York, Land Records, 1630–1975," *FamilySearch* > Cayuga > deeds 1842–1843, vol. 65–66 > image 409, Cayuga Co., Deeds 61:152–53. Also, ibid., 66:80, Huffman to Rooker, recorded 3 December 1842.

16. Ibid. > Niagara, Deeds 1845–1850, vol. 37–38 > image 180, Niagara Co., Deeds 37:334, Sherwood to Huffman, recorded 29 January 1846.

17. New York's 1835 census of Cayuga County does not survive. See "Table 1: New York State Census; Preserved and Lost Records," in *New York Family History Research Guide and Gazetteer* (New York: New York Genealogical and Biographical Society, 2014), 36.

born in Cayuga. The tracts the Huffmans sold in 1839 and 1842 lie about twelve miles from the county poorhouse, erected in 1826. Anecdotal evidence suggests its records do not survive.[18]

THE CHILDREN'S FATHER

If the above reasoning and Calista's granddaughters' tales are correct, a Greenfield household in Cayuga County in 1830 would contain a girl and boy under age five and no other children. Having eloped without parental support, the adults in that household likely would be in their late teens or early twenties.

Thirteen Greenfield households were enumerated in Cayuga County in 1830.[19] Two included a boy and girl under age five. In one, the oldest male was in his fifties and its oldest female in her thirties. Besides two children under age five, it included a boy five to nine and a girl ten to fourteen.[20] This was not likely Calista and Frank's family.

In contrast, Nathaniel Greenfield's 1830 household has the predicted composition—a girl and boy under age five, a male in his twenties, and a female between fifteen and twenty. In the only Greenfield household in the town of Aurelius, they lived apart from other Cayuga County Greenfields, who were enumerated in Locke and Sempronius, adjoining towns that do not abut Aurelius.[21]

Consistent with Calista's memories, Nathaniel left his family. On 14 April 1839, claiming he was twenty-seven, a laborer, and born in Herkimer County, New York, he enlisted in the United States Army at Buffalo, New York, a few days west of Aurelius via the Erie Canal.[22] Seven months later Lieutenant James Duncan charged Nathaniel with "Mutinous Conduct" and "Habitual Drunkenness." At

18. For the poorhouse's establishment, see Elliot Storke, *History of Cayuga County, 1789–1879* (Syracuse: D. Mason, 1879), 73. For locations of the lots and poorhouse, see David H. Burr, *An Atlas of the State of New York* (New York: privately published, 1829), map 40 (Cayuga County in 1829). For the distance, see *Google Maps* (https://www.google.com/maps/), directions from Cayuga County Nursing Home, 7451 County House Road, Auburn, N.Y., to 9900–9958 Oneil Road, Port Byron, N.Y. If its records for the 1830s have survived, their location is unknown: "I was told by my contact [a sheriff's officer] that when the Poor House turned into a nursing home [in the 1940s], several rickety old buildings were torn down. There were 'tons' of scattered papers and records lying all over the place that were thrown away and/or burned." See Christine J. Spengler, "A Report With Some Photo Images From County House Cemetery: Town Of Sennett—Cayuga County, New York," January 2007, at *The USGenWeb Project* (http://www.rootsweb.ancestry.com/~nycayuga/cem/cem197a/index.htm).

19. 1830 U.S. census, Cayuga Co., N.Y., Town of Aurelius, p. 173, Nathaniel Greenfield household. Also, ibid., Town of Locke, p. 236, Stephen Greenfield household; p. 244, Hiram Greenfield household; and p. 249, Archibald Greenfield, James Greenfield, Sherman Greenfield, Star Greenfield, and Stephen Greenfield households. Also, ibid., Town of Sempronius, p. 309, John W. Greenfield household; p. 311, Elizabeth Greenfield household; p. 312, Jeremiah Greenfield household; p. 313, Nathan Greenfield household; and p. 314, David Greenfield household.

20. Ibid., Town of Locke, p. 236, Stephen Greenfield household.

21. Burr, *Atlas of the State of New York*, map 40 (Cayuga County in 1829).

22. *Register of Enlistments in the U.S. Army, 1798–1914*, microfilm publication M233, 81 rolls (Washington, D.C.: NARA, n.d.), roll 20, for Descriptive and Historical Register of Enlisted Soldiers of the Army, p. 77, no. 42, Nathaniel Greenfield. Also, George Rogers Taylor, in *The Transportation Revolution, 1815–1860* (White Plains, N.Y.: M. E. Sharpe, 1951), 142, writes "Regular packets averaged about 3 to 4 miles an hour on the Erie." The distance from Aurelius to Buffalo is about 120 miles.

his court-martial, on 29 January 1840, Nathaniel pleaded innocence. He lost his case, however, and the judge imposed a harsh sentence:

> To forfeit all Pay and allowances up to the execution of the Sentence, — except the amounts due the Sutler [civilian provisioner] and laundress — to be marked indelibly on the back with the word DRUNKARD in large letters;– to have half his head shaved;– to be dressed in parti-colored clothing, and drummed out of Service.[23]

Disgraced, perhaps branded with eight "large letters," and likely alcoholic, Nathaniel soon disappeared under a new name or died.[24] No Nathaniel Greenfield appears in indexes to the 1840 United States census, the 1842 Upper Canada census, and the 1851 Canada census. Two Nathaniel Greenfields appear in the United States 1850 index.[25] Both were younger than the New York man—one born in Maryland in 1814–15, the other in Ohio in 1824–25.[26]

NATHANIEL'S PARENTS

DNA samples from Nathaniel's descendants help identify his parents. His son's line has died out.[27] His daughter's descendants include living adults six generations from Nathaniel's parents—fifth cousins to same-generation descendants of Nathaniel's siblings.

Fifth cousins can inherit copies of an ancestral couple's autosomal DNA on various chromosomes, averaging .0488 percent, or 3.32 centimorgans (cM) of the descendants' DNA.[28] Some fifth cousins inherit less or no autosomal DNA from the same ancestral couple, but others inherit more. About 10–15 percent of fifth cousins share enough DNA for current tests to reveal a relationship.[29]

---

23. "Trial of Private Nathaniel Greenfield of Company A 2nd Artry," pp. 16–21; folder CC 462, sixty-seven unbound paginated folios; Court-Martial Case Files, 1809–1894; RG 153: Records of the Office of the Judge Advocate General (Army); NA–Washington.

24. Military punishment by branding continued until 1872, when a Congressional act abolished it. See United States, *The Statutes at Large*, vol. 17 (Boston: Little, Brown, 1873), 261, chapter 316, section 2, which made it "illegal to brand, mark, or tattoo on the body of any soldier by sentence of court-martial."

25. *Ancestry*, "U.S. Federal Census Collection" (http://search.ancestry.com/search/group/usfedcen) and "Canadian Census Collection" (http://search.ancestry.com/search/group/canadiancensus), searches for Nathaniel Greenfield. Also, "Canada, Upper Canada Census, 1842," *FamilySearch* (https://familysearch.org/search/collection/1834342), search for Nathaniel Greenfield.

26. 1850 U.S. census, Wayne Co., Ohio, pop. sch., Sugar Creek Township, fol. 62r, dwell./fam. 150, Nathaniel Greenfield household, and fol. 64r, dwell./fam. 179, Z[-] Greenfield household; NARA microfilm M432, roll 739.

27. See appendix.

28. International Society of Genetic Genealogy (ISOGG), "Autosomal DNA Statistics," *ISOGG Wiki* (http://www.isogg.org/wiki/Autosomal_DNA_statistics). Matches to cousins in differing generations would alter the numbers slightly. Autosomal DNA is that found on chromosomes that do not determine sex. See ibid., for "Genetics Glossary" (http://isogg.org/wiki/Genetics_Glossary).

29. For 10 percent, see "What is the probability that my relative and I share enough DNA for Family Finder to detect?" *FamilyTreeDNA* (https://www.familytreedna.com/learn/autosomal-ancestry/universal-dna-matching/probability-relative-share-enough-dna-family-finder-detect/). For 15 percent, see "The Probability of Detecting Different Types of Cousins," *23andMe* (https://customercare.23andme.com/hc/en-us/articles/202907230-The-probability-of-detecting-different-types-of-cousins).

Identifying Nathaniel's parents involved four overlapping processes:

1. Supplying DNA testing kits to enough of Nathaniel's descendants to include some of the 10–15 percent with sufficient DNA to link to other fifth cousins
2. Identifying a candidate couple for Nathaniel's parents and finding their living descendants
3. Supplying DNA testing kits to enough of the candidate couple's descendants to include ones with sufficient DNA to link to other fifth cousins
4. Comparing test results of both pools, looking for evidence indicating or contraindicating a parent-child relationship between Nathaniel and the parental candidates

Eleven of Nathaniel's descendants provided samples for autosomal DNA testing and for comparison at *GEDmatch.com*. Figure 1 shows four of their descents.

Those traced lineages agree with DNA-based estimates of the descendants' generations to a common ancestor.[30] Nathaniel's daughter Calista and her husband are the cousins' common ancestors, traced four generations back. Reflecting different amounts of identical DNA segments, the third-cousins' estimated genetic distances to a common ancestor range from 3.4 to 6.9 generations, averaging 3.97.[31] Ida, traced to three generations before Judd and the author, is their common ancestor. Because Judd and the author descend from each of Ida's husbands, they share less DNA than might descendants from a couple, consistent with their estimated genetic distance of 3.8 generations.

Nathaniel's Candidate Parents

Three events provide evidence of Nathaniel's birth year:

- As a Cayuga County household head reported in his twenties in 1830, he was born in 1800–10.
- In mid-1827 Nathaniel married, conceived Calista, and set up house. He likely was at least fifteen, implying birth by mid-1812. If he was a few years over fifteen, as seems probable, he was born a few years before 1812.
- Enlisting in April 1839, Nathaniel gave his age as twenty-seven, indicating birth in 1812–13. He might have lowered his age, perhaps to facilitate enlistment.

30. "GEDmatch Forums," *GEDmatch: Tools for DNA and Genealogy Research* (https://www.gedmatch.com) > DNA Utilities > Interpreting DNA Comp[a]rison Results > Subject: Does MRCA get thrown off when you match on both, message 3, undated, by Jim Bartlett, Project Administrator. He writes: "The GEN [most recent common ancestor] calculation is a mathematical calculation based on the few parameters we have: SNPs [single-nucleotide polymorphisms], cMs [centimorgans]." Both numbers correlate with genetic-relationship distances. For a caveat, see "GEDmatch.com: DNA One-to-One Comparison Entry Form," *GEDmatch*, which says "Estimates of 'generations' are provided as a relative means of comparison, and should not be taken too literally." For definitions, see International Society of Genetic Genealogy, "Category: Glossary," *ISOGG Wiki*.

31. "GEDmatch.Com Autosomal Comparison," on-request reports, *GEDmatch*, "one-to-one" comparisons among kits F202780, F299963, M201030, and M115137. Family Tree DNA supplied kits F202790 (Jones) and F299963 (Mulder), and 23andMe supplied kits M201030 (Descendant X) and M115137 (Judd). Genetic comparisons in this paper use, except where described otherwise, segments greater than 7 cMs and 700 SNPs, statistically indicating they are "identical by descent" (IBD). See International Society of Genetic Genealogy, *ISOGG Wiki* (http://www.isogg.org/wiki/Identical_by_descent), for "Identical By Descent."

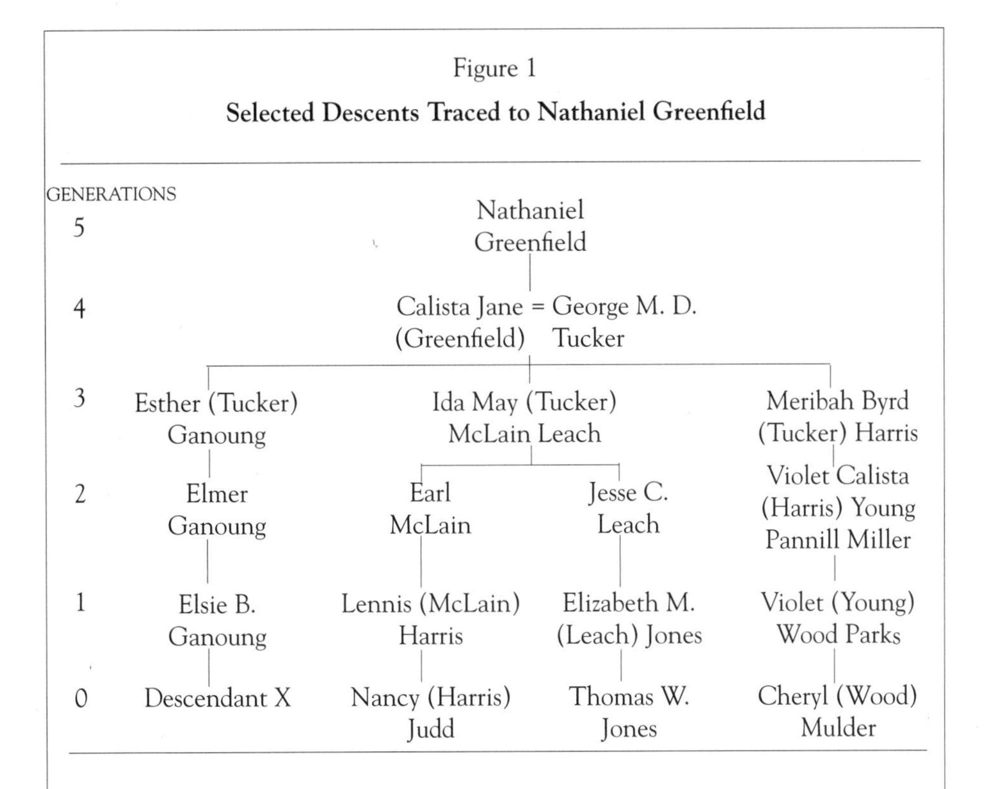

Figure 1

Selected Descents Traced to Nathaniel Greenfield

Sources: For Calista's parentage and husband, see the text.

For Esther, Ida, and Meribah's parents, see George M. D. Tucker, questionnaire 3—402, 1 August 1898; in George M. D. Tucker (Pvt., Cos. C and F, 3rd Mich. Cav., Civil War), pension no. S.C. 874,447, Case Files of Approved Pension Files 1861–1934 . . . , Civil War and Later Pension Files; Record Group 15: Department of Veterans Affairs; National Archives, Washington, D.C.

For Elmer's parents, see "Michigan, Marriages, 1868–1925," *FamilySearch* (https://familysearch.org/search/collection/1452395), digital film 004209154, image 394, Kent Co., Mich., Returns of Marriages in the County of Kent for the Quarter Ending March 30 A.D. 1911, p. 11, Ganoung-Nelson, 25 February 1911. For Elsie's parents, see 1920 U.S. census, Cook Co., Ill., population schedule, Chicago, Ward 24, enumeration district (ED) 1354, sheet 2B, dwelling 31, family 52, Elmer "Ganong" household; National Archives and Records Administration (NARA) microfilm T625, roll 335.

For Earl's parents, see "Michigan, Births, 1867–1902," *FamilySearch* (https://familysearch.org/search/collection/1459684), digital film 004206431, image 424, Van Buren Co., Mich., Return of Births in the County of Van Buren for the Year Ending 31 December 1876, p. 256, no. 890, Earl McLain. For Lennis's parents, see 1920 U.S. census, Sandusky Co., Ohio, pop. sch., Green Creek Twp., Clyde Village, ED 84, sheet 6A, dwell. 161, fam. 167, Earl McLain household; NARA microfilm T625, roll 1428.

For Jesse's parents, see "Michigan, Births, 1867–1902," *FamilySearch*, digital film 004206453, image 22, Allegan Co., Mich., Return of Births in the County of Allegan for the Year Ending 31 December A.D. 1878, p. 7, no. 40, "Jessie D." Leach. For Elizabeth's parents, see 1920 U.S. census, Sandusky Co., Ohio, pop. sch., Green Creek Twp., Clyde Village, ED 84, sheet 11B, dwell. 325, fam. 342, Jesse C. Leach household.

For Violet Harris's parents, see "Michigan, Marriages, 1868–1925," *FamilySearch*, digital film 004210110, image 352, St. Clair Co., Mich., Return of Marriages in the County of St. Clair for the Quarter Ending June 30 A.D. 1922, record 17202, Pannill-Young, 14 June 1922. For Violet Young's mother, see 1920 U.S. census, St. Clair Co., Mich., pop. sch., Port Huron, ward 4, precinct 8, ED 117, sheet 18B, dwell. 408, fam. 572, John Harris household; NARA microfilm T625, roll 795.

If born in 1800–13, Nathaniel was between ages seven and twenty in 1820. He would appear in the 1820 census as a tally mark for a male under twenty-five, likely in a Greenfield household. Nathaniel's enumeration as a young father in Cayuga County in 1830 and his Herkimer County birthplace suggest his parents lived in either place or both. In 1820 fourteen Greenfield households, likely interrelated, were enumerated in those two counties, the counties between them, and those adjoining them. Nearly all include a male under age twenty-five.[32]

Of the fourteen household heads, one—Thomas Greenfield—could have associated with Isaac Huffman. A seemingly inconsequential detail suggests a connection. Isaac's heirs were his remarried widow, Julia Ann Sherwood, and two sons. Although the estate papers do not name Frank or Calista, they mention a fifty-cent debt that Isaac owed "T. Greenfield."[33] If the estate administrator forgot to cross a capital *F*, leaving a *T*, the entry refers to Frank. Otherwise, it inexplicably refers to Thomas, who might have lived in Cayuga County when the Huffmans took Nathaniel Greenfield's children into their home. Beyond Thomas's 1820 household composition and a possible Huffman connection, three considerations make him a candidate for Nathaniel's father:

- In 1810 and 1850 Thomas lived in Cayuga County—Nathaniel's residence in 1830.[34] Thomas lived near Cayuga County in 1840.[35]
- Thomas was in enlistee Nathaniel's birth county—Herkimer—in 1813, when Nathaniel probably was a young child.[36]

---

32. 1820 U.S. census, Cayuga Co., N.Y., Town of Locke, p. 261, James Greenfield household, and p. 267, Archabald, James, and Sherman Greenfield households; NARA microfilm M33, roll 68. Also, ibid., Town of Sempronius, p. 150, Star Greenfield household; p. 155, William Greenfield household; p. 156, William Greenfield Junr. household; and p. 161, Archibald and Raymond Greenfield households. Also, 1820 U.S. census, Herkimer Co., N.Y., Town of Fairfield, p. 3, Bethuel Greenfield household; NARA microfilm M33, roll 67. Also, 1820 U.S. census, Montgomery Co., N.Y., Town of Northampton, p. 403, Michael Greenfield household; NARA microfilm M33, roll 63. Also, 1820 U.S. census, Oneida Co., N.Y., Town of Trenton, p. 244, Thomas Greenfield household, and p. 250, Elijah and Elisha Greenfield households; NARA microfilm M33, roll 73. Omitted are Greenfield households in the New York counties of New York, Rensselaer, Saratoga, and Suffolk. See "U.S. Federal Census Collection," *Ancestry*, search for Greenfield in "New York, USA."

33. "New York, Probate Records, 1628–1971," *FamilySearch* > Niagara > Probates 1835–1970 box H3 > image 1089, for Schedule D, debts, 6 April 1853–28 February 1855, Isaac S. Huffman file, payment to "T Greenfield on a/c," 3 May 1853.

34. 1810 U.S. census, Cayuga Co., N.Y., Town of Sempronius, p. 1128, Thomas Greenfield household; NARA microfilm M252, roll 31. Also, 1850 U.S. census, Cayuga Co., N.Y., pop. sch., Town of Summerhill, folio 4v, dwell. 71, fam. 74, Thomas Greenfield household; NARA microfilm M432, roll 483. Thomas's 1830 location is unknown; a database entry for him points to Sherman Greenfield. See "1830 United States Federal Census," *Ancestry* (http://search.ancestry.com/search/db.aspx?dbid=8058), search for Thomas Greenfield. Also, 1830 U.S. census, Cayuga Co., N.Y., Town of Locke, p. 249, Sherman Greenfield.

35. 1840 U.S. census, Tompkins Co., N.Y., Town of Dryden, p. 98, fol. 197r, Thomas Greenfield household; NARA microfilm M704, roll 345. The town of Groton separates Dryden from Cayuga County. See Burr, *Atlas of New York*, Tompkins County.

36. "New York, Probate Records, 1629–1971," *FamilySearch* > Herkimer > Estate papers 1796–1813 G, no 2869–2905 > images 22–29, Herkimer Co., N.Y., estate papers, file 02871, James Greenfield, 1813. See ibid., images 26–27, for Stephen Greenfield, James Greenfield, and Thomas Greenfield, inventory, recorded 4 May 1813.

- Thomas's wife Mary had a brother Nathaniel Walters, for whom they could have named a son.[37]

Thomas and Mary's youngest child said they had twelve children.[38] Their documented children include no Nathaniel, but identifying Thomas and Mary's children is problematic:

- Thomas's 1850 household shows only children of his wife Lydia. The couple married on 11 January 1837.[39]
- The counties where Thomas lived toward his life's end have no estate record for him that might name his children.[40]
- Thomas never bought land in those counties or show~d evidence of owning land his children would inherit.[41]
- Thomas and Mary lived where counties and towns recorded no marriages before 1847.[42] Their only known church records mention no weddings.[43]

Nonetheless, Thomas and Mary had at least three children whose descendants can be traced to the present:

- Luther Greenfield gave his parents as Thomas Greenfield and Mary Walters.[44]

37. Roger F. Williams, *Cold Brook Methodism* (Russia, N.Y.: Cold Brook Methodist Episcopal Church, 1929), 42. The history includes sketches of several of the church's "old families." The Walters sketch, on pages 41–43, identifies "Mary (Polly) Walters," who "married —— Greenfield." Replete with exact birth, death, and marriage dates spanning 1742 through 1907, the account likely is based on longstanding family records.

38. A. J. Baughman, ed., "Captain Christopher Au," in *Centennial Biographical History of Richland County, Ohio* (Chicago: Lewis, 1901), 425. Au had married Laura Greenfield, Thomas and Mary's daughter. Laura lived in Richfield County in 1901. Probably she provided the information, including her mother's maiden name and date and place of death, from her knowledge and family records.

39. For the parent-child relationships, see "Family record of Thomas Greenfield and Lydia Wattles"; Mather file; Cayuga Co. historian's office, Auburn, N.Y. For the marriage, see Lydia Greenfield, widow's declaration, 2 July 1855; in bounty land warrant file, act of [18]50 — 80 W.T. 93906, for service of Thomas Greenfield (Sgt., Capt. Lemuel Potter's Regt., N.Y. militia, War of 1812); Case Files of Bounty-Land Warrant Applications Based on Service Between 1812 and 1855; RG 15, NA–Washington. Two witnesses confirmed the marriage. See Leonard L. Tompkins and Phebe Connelly, depositions, 5 July 1855; in ibid.

40. "New York, Probate Records, 1629–1910," *FamilySearch* > Cayuga > General index 1799–1919 A–K > image 444, Cayuga Co., N.Y., General Index to Surrogates Records vol. E–K, 1799–1919, p. 322. Also, ibid. > Tompkins > General Index 1818–1910 > image 66, Tompkins Co., General Index to Surrogates Records, p. 111. Also, St. Joseph Co., Mich., Probate Index A–L, Gre– entries; Probate Court, Centreville, Mich.

41. "New York, Land Records, 1630–1875," *FamilySearch* > Cayuga > Grantee index 1808–1916, vol. 1–2 > images 146–47, Cayuga Co., Index to Grantee Deeds 1 (1793–1823): 188–90. Also, ibid. > Tompkins > Grantee index 1817–1860 > image 381, Tompkins Co., Grantee Index A–K, 1817–1860, fol. 176v. Also, ibid. > Grantor index 1817–1860 > image 470, Grantor Index 1817–1860, fol. 204r. Also, St. Joseph Co., Deed Index 1, 1830–1852; Deed Index 2, 1853–1859; Deed Index 3, 1859–1868; and Deed Index 4, 1868–1877; Register of Deeds, Centreville.

42. "Vital Records," in *New York Family History Research Guide and Gazetteer*, 17.

43. Deerfield Baptist Church, "1800 Record Book of Arnold Wells," church records, 1800–1828; First Baptist Church of North Utica, North Utica, N.Y.

44. Certificate of Marriage, no. 794, Greenfield-French, 6 October 1889; New York State Department of Health, Albany. Also, "Pennsylvania, County Marriages, 1885–1950," *FamilySearch* (https://familysearch.org/search/collection/1589502), digital film 004811637, image 211, Bradford Co., Pa., Orphan's Court, Marriage Licenses 7:356, Greenfield-Weaver application, license, and certificate, 9–12 May 1892.

- Caleb Greenfield named his parents as Thomas and Mary Greenfield.[45]
- Lovilla ("Lavilly") Greenfield joined Deerfield Baptist Church, near Utica, New York, in 1824, soon after Thomas and Mary Greenfield transferred their membership there. In 1826 the church gave Thomas and Lovilla letters of recommendation to transfer elsewhere, and Mary received a similar letter in 1827.[46] The juxtapositions suggest Lovilla was Thomas and Mary's daughter.

Figure 2 shows lineages traced from these siblings to descendants who gave DNA samples. Their common ancestors, Thomas and Mary Greenfield, are five generations earlier. Reflecting varying amounts of identical autosomal DNA segments, Bennett's estimated genetic distance from sisters Marx and Hansen is 4.4 generations to their common ancestor, and Greenfield's distance from the sisters is 7.5 generations. His genetic distance from their first-cousin Shawen is 7.1 generations.[47] Bennett and Greenfield did not inherit enough identical DNA to reliably estimate a genetic distance.[48]

DNA Comparisons of Thomas's and Nathaniel's Descendants

At least seven pairs of Greenfield descendants, in varying combinations, inherited identical autosomal-DNA segments greater than 7.0 cM. See table 1. Each pair matches a fifth-generation descendant of Nathaniel, from figure 1, with a fifth-generation descendant of Thomas, from figure 2. One pair shares identical segments on two chromosomes. Two pairs (three donors) have an identical segment on chromosome 3, and three pairs (four donors) have an identical segment on chromosome 18.

Table 1 suggests Nathaniel's and Thomas's descendants have a common ancestor within six generations and thus are fifth cousins or closer:

- Five of the seven pairs' estimated genetic distances are 5.1 generations or less from their common ancestors. These seven average 5.64 generations to their common ancestors. These distances, consistent with fourth cousins, are closer than the six generations traced from Nathaniel's DNA-donor descendants to his parents.
- The paired samples come from four of Nathaniel's eleven descendants with test results on *GEDmatch.com* (36.36 percent) and five of Thomas's seven (71.43 percent)—a combined probability of 25.97 percent.[49] All three percentages exceed the approximately 10–15 percent probability of sharing enough autosomal DNA to detect a fifth cousin.[50]

45. Waushara Co., Wisc., Registration of Marriages 2:19, Greenfield-Baker, 19 September 1870; State Historical Society, Madison; FHL microfilm 1,275,608.

46. Deerfield Baptist Church, "1800 Record Book of Arnold Wells."

47. "GEDmatch.Com Autosomal Comparison," *GEDmatch*, kits A190412 (Shawen), A839038 (Hansen), F329609 (Greenfield), F329613 (Bennett), and M123945 (Young). Ancestry .com supplied kits A190412 and A839038, Family Tree DNA supplied kits F329613 and F329609, and 23andMe supplied kit M123945.

48. The largest segments that Greenfield and Bennett have in common are two 5.0 cM segments of 387 and 230 SNPs, respectively, on chromosomes 2 and 4. Their largest sequence of identical SNPs is 802 on a 1.8-cM segment of chromosome 13.

49. The product of 36.36 percent and 71.43 percent is 25.97 percent.

50. "What is the probability that my relative and I share enough DNA for Family Finder to detect?" *FamilyTreeDNA*. Also, "The Probability of Detecting Different Types of Cousins," *23andMe*.

Figure 2

Selected Descents Traced to Thomas and Mary (Walters) Greenfield

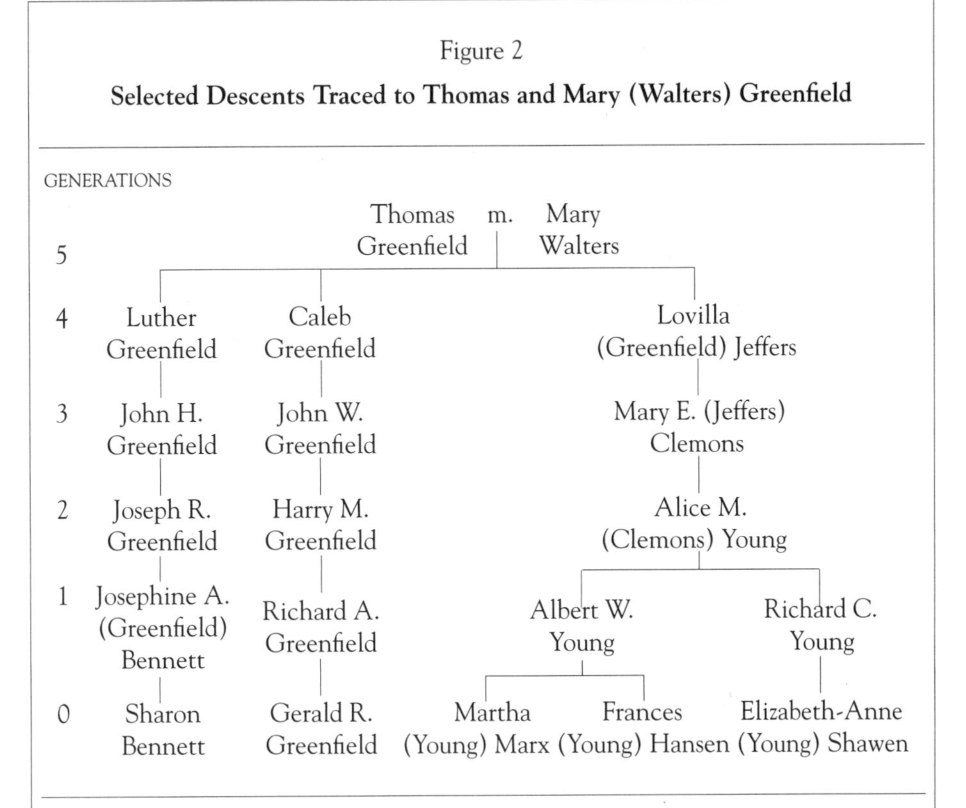

Sources: For Luther, Caleb, and Lovilla's parentage, see the text.

For the parentage of John H., see "New York, Town Clerks' Registers of Men Who Served in the Civil War, ca 1861–1865," *Ancestry.com* (http://search.ancestry.com/search/db.aspx?dbid=1964) > Tompkins > Caroline–Ulysess > image 108 Town of Groton, N.Y., Record of Soldiers and Officers in the Military Service, pp. 55–56, John H. Greenfield. For Joseph's parentage, see Kent Co., Mich., death certificate 59183 (1953), Joseph Reed Greenfield; Circuit Court, Grand Rapids. For Josephine's parentage, see 1920 U.S. census, Kent Co., Mich., population schedule, Grand Rapids, Ward 3, enumeration district (ED) 82, sheet 10A, Joseph R. Greenfield household; National Archives and Records Administration (NARA) microfilm T625, roll 779.

For John W.'s parentage, see "New York, State Census, 1855," *FamilySearch* (https://familysearch.org/search/collection/1937366) > Cortland > Harford > image 8, 1855 N.Y. census, Cortland Co., Harford, unpaginated, dwell. 106, fam. 111, Caleb Greenfield household. For Harry's parentage, see 1880 U.S. census, Waushara Co., Wisc., pop. sch., Plainfield, ED 191, p. 1, dwell./fam. 9, John W. Greenfield household; NARA microfilm T9, roll 1452. For Richard's parentage, see 1920 U.S. census, Winnebago Co., Wisc., pop. sch., Omro Town, ED 161, sheet 2A, dwell. 42, fam. 43, Harry Greenfield household; NARA microfilm T625, roll 2023.

For Mary's parentage, see "Death Records 1897–1920," *Seeking Michigan* (https://seekingmichigan.org) Michigan Division of Vital Statistics, Certificate of Death (1912) no. 8, Mary Elizabeth Clemons, St. Joseph County. For Alice's parents, see "Michigan, Births, 1867–1902," *FamilySearch* (https://familysearch.org/search/collection/1459684) > 004206357 > image 698, Muskegon Co., Return of Births in the County of Muskegon for the Year Ending December 31st A.D. 1875, p. 123, no. 3412, Alice Clemons, 5 November 1875. For Albert and Richard's parents, see 1910 U.S. census, Muskegon Co., Mich., pop. sch., Muskegon City, ward 6, precinct 11, ED 89, sheet 2A, dwell. 26, fam. 27, Joseph Young household; NARA microfilm T624, roll 667.

Table 1

Pairs of Greenfield Autosomal-DNA Test Results

TRACED GREENFIELD ANCESTOR	DNA DONOR	LONGEST COMMON SEGMENT >7, IN CENTIMORGANS	SERIAL SNP COUNT	ESTIMATED GENERATIONS TO COMMON ANCESTORS
Nathaniel Thomas	Cheryl Mulder Elizabeth Shawen, through Lovilla	7.6 (chromosome 1)	717	7.4
Nathaniel Thomas	Descendant X Gerald Greenfield, through Caleb	14.9 (chromosome 2)	1543	5.0
Nathaniel Thomas	Thomas Jones Martha Marx, through Lovilla	12.9 (chromosome 3)	3469	5.1
Nathaniel Thomas	Thomas Jones Frances Hansen, through Lovilla	12.9 (chromosome 3)	3437	4.5
Nathaniel Thomas	Nancy Judd Sharon Bennett, through Luther	14.9 (chromosome 17)	672	5.0
Nathaniel Thomas	Nancy Judd Frances Hansen, through Lovilla	14.3 (chromosome 18)	1500	5.0
Nathaniel Thomas	Thomas Jones Frances Hansen, through Lovilla	14.4 (chromosome 18)	3441	[shown in row 4]
Nathaniel Thomas	Descendant X Frances Hansen, through Lovilla	7.2 (chromosome 18)	1616	7.5

Sources: "GEDmatch.Com Autosomal Comparison," on-request listings, *GEDmatch: Tools for DNA and Genealogy Research* (https://www.gedmatch.com), kits A190412 (Shawen), A839038 (Hansen), M123945 (Marx), F202780 (Jones), F299963 (Mulder), F329609 (Greenfield), F329613 (Bennett), M115137 (Judd), and M201030 (Descendant X). Ancestry.com tested Hansen, Marx, and Shawen; 23AndMe tested Descendant X and Judd; and Family Tree *DNA* tested Bennett, Mulder, Greenfield, and Jones.

Those considerations and table-1's pairings support just one of five relationships between Nathaniel and Thomas:

- *First cousins*. If Thomas and Nathaniel were first cousins, their paternal grandparents would be their common ancestors—two generations older. Thomas's and Nathaniel's fifth-generation descendants would be seven generations from those common ancestors, and identical genetic segments would be infrequent—below 5 percent.[51] Only two of table 1's seven pairs, however, exceed 5.1 generations to their common ancestors. That and the table's average estimated distances—5.64 generations—suggest common ancestors closer than seven generations.
- *Uncle and nephew*. If one of Thomas's siblings were Nathaniel's parent, Thomas and Nathaniel would be uncle and nephew. Thomas's parents—thus, Nathaniel's grandparents—would be their common ancestors. Thomas's fifth-generation descendants would be six generations from his parents, and Nathaniel's fifth-generation descendants would be seven generations from his grandparents. The midpoint would be 6.5 generations. Five of the seven pairings, at 5.1 generations or less, and the 5.64-generation average genetic-distance estimation for all seven suggest a closer relationship.
- *Full Brothers*. Thomas's ten documented siblings, born from 1776 through 1800, include no Nathaniel.[52] No known record suggests the siblings had such a brother.[53] Also, Thomas's mother, born on 28 June 1758, is an unlikely mother of Nathaniel, born about 1812.[54]

51. "What is the probability that my relative and I share enough DNA for Family Finder to detect?" *FamilyTreeDNA*. Also, "The Probability of Detecting Different Types of Cousins," *23andMe*.

52. Membership application, Alice G. Pease, national no. 336220, on James Greenfield (1753–1812, New York), approved 30 October 1942; National Society Daughters of the American Revolution (NSDAR), Office of the Registrar General, Washington, D.C. Pease claimed descent from Thomas's father, James Greenfield, through Thomas's brother, Archibald. Her documentation includes a family record naming Thomas. See James Greenfield family record, transcription by Alice G. Pease, 4 September 1942; in ibid. Pease quoted a letter from Hull Greenfield (Auburn, N.Y.), 21 January 1928, saying "he has an old account book kept by his grandfather, Archibald Greenfield, containing the dates of the births and deaths of many of the Greenfield family." See Alice G. Pease, sworn statement, 2 February 1942, and letter to Mrs. Edward W. Cooch (Registrar General, NSDAR), 4 September 1942; in Pease's membership application file.

53. Two sources corroborate some of Thomas's siblings named in Pease's transcription of Archibald Greenfield's account book. See "New York, Land Records, 1630–1975," *FamilySearch* > Herkimer > Deeds 1833–1835, vol. 29–30 > images 300–301, Herkimer Co., Deed Book 30:68–70, "heirs of Margaret Martin deceased the former wife and relict of James Greenfield of the Town of Russia deceased," to Phelps, 16 January 1834. Also, Herkimer Co., estate papers, file 02871, James Greenfield, 1813.

54. Membership application, Alice G. Pease, national no. 336220, on James Greenfield (1753–1812, New York), approved 30 October 1942, NSDAR. For Mary's birth year, see *Find A Grave* (https://www.findagrave.com/cgi-bin/fg.cgi), memorial 20981768, of Margaret Sweet Greenfield gravestone (Century Cemetery, Town of Russia, Herkimer Co.), digital image, 13 May 2011, by Steve Staruch. The marker says "his [James Greenfield's] wife" died on 20 September 1833, "in her 75th year." See Robert Lorick, contributor, "Century Cemetery: Town of Russia; Herkimer County, NY," transcription updated 27 August 2009, *Herkimer Co. NY: Genealogy, History, GenWeb* (http://herkimer.nygenweb.net/cemeteries/centcem.html). Lorick cited and updated "the original September 1928 list of the tombstone readings made by Mr. and Mrs. Charles E. Merritt and Mr. and Mrs. Harry P. Layton for the Genealogical Research Committee of the Oneida Chapter, N.Y.S. D.A.R."

- *Half brothers.* Siblings with one parent in common share less autosomal DNA than siblings with both parents in common. Therefore, genetic distances between half siblings' descendants average more than those between full siblings' descendants. If Nathaniel were Thomas's half brother, their fifth-generation descendants' genetic distances would average more than six generations to Nathaniel and Thomas's common parent. Besides the table-1 pairs' estimated genetic distances, no known evidence suggests one of Thomas's parents had a child outside their marriage.
- *Parents and child.* Thomas and Mary precede their traced fifth-generation descendants by five generations. If they were Nathaniel's parents, they would precede his fifth-generation descendants by six generations. The respective descendants would be fourth cousins, once removed—a relationship between five and six generations to common ancestors. Those generations' 5.5 midpoint resembles table 1's average estimated distances to common ancestors, 5.64 generations.

The DNA donors representing Nathaniel descend from three sisters: Esther, Ida, and Meribah. See figure 1. Seven pairs of identical DNA segments between a sister's descendant and a descendant of Thomas and Mary Greenfield indicate that one of the sisters' four grandparents was Thomas and Mary's child. Other candidates, including Thomas's and Mary's siblings and other relatives, are unlikely. The results do not, however, specify that Nathaniel Greenfield was Thomas's son.

The sisters' paternal grandparents can be eliminated. Neither Ebenezer Tucker nor Minerva Pierce was Thomas and Mary Greenfield's child.[55] Calista's mother is unknown, but no known document suggests one of Thomas's daughters married a Greenfield. This paper identifies Calista's father as Nathaniel Greenfield. He was the likely conduit of the DNA her descendants share with Thomas and Mary Greenfield's descendants.

Nathaniel apparently was Thomas and Mary Greenfield's son. At least seven pairs of their respective traced descendants inherited identical autosomal-DNA segments, including triangulations on two chromosomes. Those factors and the segments' measurements—centimorgans and SNP counts—support the relationship. One or two pairs would be insufficient, but seven pairings support the assertion that Thomas and Mary were Nathaniel's parents.

CONCLUSION

Along with scarce historical records, DNA testing helped identify Nathaniel Greenfield's children and parents. The only sources naming him—the 1830 federal census, an army enlistment record, and a court-martial file—identify no one related to him. Nevertheless, documentary and DNA evidence indicate that Nathaniel's children were Calista Jane (Greenfield) Tucker and Benjamin

55. For the sisters' paternal grandfather, see Michigan Division of Vital Statistics, Certificate of Death (1908) no. 506, George M. D. Tucker. For their paternal grandmother, see ibid., no. 518 (1902), Caroline [(Tucker)] Bonesteel, Osceola County. Also, E. L. Tucker, declaration for pension, 15 September 1876, in Ebenezer L. Tucker, father's pension no. 190,200, for service of Augustus P. Tucker (Co. C, 70th N.Y. Inf.), Civil War and Later Pension Files, RG 15, NA–Washington. Ebenezer wrote that he married Minerva Pierce on 31 October 1821, five years before George's birth. Minerva was the mother of Caroline, born six years after George.

Franklin "Frank" Greenfield and that Nathaniel's parents were Thomas and Mary (Walters) Greenfield.

APPENDIX: EVIDENCE THAT FRANK HAS NO LIVING DESCENDANTS

1. **Benjamin Franklin "Frank" Greenfield,** born in 1830 at Cayuga County, New York,[56] died of consumption on 23 December 1869 in the town of Hartland, Niagara County, New York.[57]

Frank married (1) in 1850–53 likely in Niagara County, **Christina Talcott,**[58] born in 1830–31 in Massachusetts and died apparently in 1860–65.[59] She had moved to the town of Hartland in 1847–48.[60] That date, her first name, and her birthplace—all given in 1855—agree she was Christina Talcott, apparent daughter of Israel F. and Julia (Barrett) Talcott, living in Hartland in 1850.[61] Also, in 1865 Christina's daughter Julia lived in a household with four of Christina's apparent brothers and sisters from the 1850 Israel Talcott household.[62] Christina was born perhaps in the town of Richmond in Berkshire County, Massachusetts, where Israel F. Talcott lived in 1830.[63]

---

56. For 1830, see 1850 U.S. census, Niagara Co., N.Y., pop. sch., Town of Somerset, p. 713, dwell. 179, fam. 183, Isaac "Hofman" household, for Franklin Greenfield. Also, 1860 U.S. census, Niagara Co., N.Y., pop. sch., Town of Newfane, pp. 26–27, dwell. 199, fam. 203, Franklin B. Greenfield household; NARA microfilm M653, roll 823.

57. 1870 U.S. census, Niagara Co., N.Y., mortality schedule, "Subdivision No46 Hartland," p. 1, fam. 387, Frank Greenfield. Also, notation on jacket, dated 2 May 1870, in Sarah Greenfield, widow's pension application no. 186,401 (Abandoned), for service of Benjamin F. Greenfield (12th Independent Battery, N.Y. Light Artillery), Civil War and Later Pension Files, RG 15, NA–Washington.

58. Franklin was unmarried in 1850. See 1850 U.S. census, Niagara Co., N.Y., pop. sch., Town of Somerset, p. 713, dwell. 179, fam. 183, Isaac "Hofman" household, for Franklin Greenfield. By 1855 he was married to Christina and had a two-year-old daughter, Julia. See 1855 N.Y. Census, Niagara Co., Town of Hartland, unpaginated, dwell. 96, fam. 98, Franklin Greenfield household.

59. Christina was not enumerated in the contiguous Niagara County towns of Hartland, Newfane, and Somerset in 1865, when one of her daughters was living with Christina's siblings and their spouses. See "New York, State Census, 1865," *FamilySearch* (https://familysearch.org/search/collection/1491284), database search for "Greenfield" in Niagara County and author's line-by-line reading. Also, "New York, State Census, 1865," *FamilySearch* > Niagara > Newfane, E.D. 01 > image 6, 1865 N.Y. census, Niagara Co., Newfane, ED 1, p. 9, visitation 61, fam. 65, Theodore W. Connor household.

60. 1855 N.Y. census, Niagara Co., Town of Hartland, unpaginated, dwell. 96, fam. 98, Franklin Greenfield household.

61. 1850 U.S. census, Niagara Co., N.Y., pop. sch., Town of Hartland, p. 616, dwell./fam. 16, Israel F. Talcott household. For "Barrett," see Ontario, Canada, Deaths: County of Kent, Ridgetown Division, p. 356, death record no. 20149 (1920), Joseph Francis Talcott; container 765 (unit 22); Deaths Registrations, series 80-8; RG 80: Office of the Registrar General; Archives of Ontario, Toronto; FHL microfilm 1,863,286, item 2. The informant was Joseph's son Fred.

62. 1865 N.Y. census, Niagara Co., Newfane, ED 1, p. 9, visitation 61, fam. 65, Theodore W. Connor household.

63. 1830 U.S. census, Berkshire Co., Mass., Richmond, p. 448, Israel F. "Talcot" household; NARA microfilm M19, roll 62.

At the bride's residence in Hartland on 27 April 1866 Frank married (2) **Sarah "Sally" (Van Orman) Thorn.**[64] She was born in 1828 at Saratoga County, New York, and died on 24 August 1870 at Hartland.[65] She had married (1) Nelson Thorn on 29 October 1843 at Ridgeway, Orleans County, New York.[66] Leaving Sally with nine children, Nelson died on 24 November 1861 at Hartland.[67]

In 1850 Franklin, a twenty-year-old single laborer, lived in the Isaac "Hofman" household in the town of Somerset in Niagara County.[68] In 1855, with Christina and a daughter, he lived in Hartland (just south of Somerset).[69] In 1860 they lived in Newfane (just west of Somerset and Hartland), Niagara County. Franklin, a day laborer, owned no reported real or personal property.[70]

On 8 October 1861 at Newfane, Frank—as "Benjamin F. Greenfield"—enlisted for three years as a private in the 12th New York Light Artillery. Giving his age as thirty-one, he was a "farmer; eyes blue; hair sandy; complexion light; height 5 ft. 6½ in." At Brandy Station, Virginia, on 24 December 1863 he re-enlisted for three more years. At Albany on 14 June 1865 he was mustered out.[71] Newfane's town clerk reported in 1865 "nothing known of him since he was mustered out; supposed to be in NYC."[72] Frank was back in Hartland in April 1866, when he married Sally.

64. Amasa Miller, affidavit, 24 July 1884, and Emma (Thorn) Ellis, Application for Arrears of Pension, 16 June 1883; in "Henry, Emma (now Ellis), and Carrie Thorn," pension no. 229,579 (service of Elias Thorn, Pvt., Co. D, 8th N.Y. Light Artillery), Civil War and Later Pension Files, RG 15, NA–Washington. For "Van Orman," see Ellis's application.

65. For 1827–28 and Saratoga County, see "New York, State Census, 1865," *FamilySearch* > Niagara > Hartland, ED 02 > image 13, 1865 New York census, Town of Hartland, ED 2, p. 20, dwell. 157 [should be 160], fam. 166, Sally Thorn household. For 1828–29, see 1860 U.S. census, Niagara Co., N.Y., pop. sch., town of Hartland, p. 6, dwell./fam. 41, Nelson Thorn household; NARA microfilm M653, roll 822. For Sarah's death, see A. H. Hill, affidavit, 11 March 1886; in "Henry, Emma (now Ellis), and Carrie Thorn," pension no. 229,579, Civil War, RG 15, NA–Washington. Dr. Hill attended Sarah "during h[e]r last sickness."

66. "Saly" Thorn, "Mother's Declaration for Pension," 20 September 1864; in "Henry, Emma (now Ellis), and Carrie Thorn," pension no. 229,579, Civil War and Later Pension Files, RG 15, NA–Washington.

67. For Nelson's death, see ibid. For nine children, see "New York, Probate Records, 1629–1971," *FamilySearch* > Niagara > Probates 1835–1970 box T2 > images 928–46, Niagara County Probate Records box T2, Nelson "Thorne" file, at image 943 for Sally Thorn, petition, 20 January 1862.

68. 1850 U.S. census, Niagara Co., N.Y., pop. sch., Town of Somerset, p. 713, dwell. 179, fam. 183, Isaac "Hofman" household.

69. 1855 N.Y. census, Niagara Co., Town of Hartland, unpaginated, dwell. 96, fam. 98, Franklin Greenfield household.

70. 1860 U.S. census, Niagara Co., N.Y., pop. sch., Town of Newfane, pp. 26–27, dwell. 199, fam. 203, Franklin B. Greenfield household.

71. "New York, Civil War Muster Roll Abstracts, 1861–1900 [comp. by New York Adjutant General]," *Ancestry* > 12th Independent Battery Light Artillery > A–Z > 812 > image 179, B. F. Greenfield.

72. "New York, Town Clerks' Registers of Men Who Served in the Civil War, ca 1861–1865," *Ancestry* > Niagara > Hartland–Somerset > image 53, Newfane, N.Y., Officers, Soldiers, Seamen . . . Town of Newfane, County of Niagara, 1865, pp. 40–41, Benjamin F. Greenfield. The entry omits his birth data and parents' names.

73. "New York, Probate Records, 1629–1971," *FamilySearch* > Niagara > General Index 1822–1928 A–K > image 222, Niagara Co., General Index to Surrogate's Records, p. 197, entries for Gre–.

Frank's death, in 1869, generated no Niagara County estate record.[73] On 11 May 1870 Sally applied for a Civil War widow's pension. She died three months later, and her application file was stamped "Abandoned."[74]

Frank and Christina had two daughters, born in Niagara County:

\+ 2 i. JULIA R. GREENFIELD, born in 1852.[75] Her last certain record is in Grand Rapids, Michigan, in 1894.[76] Julia married in Lamont, Ottawa County, Michigan, on 27 January 1870, Bethuel Rice.[77]

3 ii. HARRIET GREENFIELD, born in 1855–56.[78] Her only known record is in 1860, but an 1870 note is ambiguous about her death date.[79]

2. **Julia R. Greenfield** was born in 1852.[80] Her last certain record is in Grand Rapids, Michigan, in 1894.[81]

On 27 January 1870, when living in Grandville, Michigan, Julia married **Bethuel Rice** in the nearby village of Lamont, in Tallmadge Township, Ottawa County, Michigan.[82] She likely had moved to Grandville with her maternal

---

74. Sarah Greenfield, widow's pension application no. 186,401 (Abandoned), Civil War and Later Pension Files, RG 15, NA–Washington.

75. For 1852–53, see 1860 U.S. census, Niagara Co., N.Y., pop. sch., Town of Newfane, pp. 26–27, dwell. 199, fam. 203, Franklin B. Greenfield household, for Julia Greenfield, age seven. Also, 1880 U.S. census, Kent Co., Mich., pop. sch., Grand Rapids, ED 148, p. 3, dwell. 28, fam. 30, Elizabeth D. Smith household, for Julia Rice, age twenty-seven. For 1851–52, see 1870 U.S. census, Ottawa Co., Mich., pop. sch., Tallmadge Twp., p. 3, dwell./fam. 27, John Rice household, for Julia Rice, age eighteen; NARA microfilm M593, roll 697.

76. 1894 Mich. census, Kent Co., Grand Rapids, 2nd Ward, p. 79A, dwell. 30, fam. 88, Julia R. Rice; FHL microfilm 984,227, item 1. Julia, thirty-nine, was a widowed dressmaker who had lived in Michigan for twenty-four years. She had borne two children, of whom one was living. She was born in New York, her father in "England" and her mother in Massachusetts.

77. "Michigan, Marriages, 1868–1925," *FamilySearch*, digital film 004207597, image 184, Return of Marriages in the county of Ottawa for the Year Ending December 31st A.D. 1870, p. 61, Rice-Greenfield, 27 January 1870.

78. 1860 U.S. census, Niagara Co., N.Y., pop. sch., Town of Newfane, pp. 26–27, dwell. 199, fam. 203, Franklin B. Greenfield household, for Harriet Greenfield, age four.

79. Pension official's note, 20 May 1870, "Letter to Atty. for . . . children by former wife," in Sarah Greenfield, widow's pension application no. 186,401 (Abandoned), Civil War and Later Pension Files, RG 15, NA–Washington. The official's comment suggests the widow's attorney had mentioned "children by former wife." The file does not contain, however, what the attorney had written. Harriet's apparent absence from the 1865 and 1870 censuses suggests she died by 1865, but the pension annotation suggests a possibility she was alive in 1870.

80. 1860 U.S. census, Niagara Co., N.Y., pop. sch., Town of Newfane, pp. 26–27, dwell. 199, fam. 203, Franklin B. Greenfield household. Also, 1870 U.S. census, Ottawa Co., Mich., pop. sch., Tallmadge Twp., p. 3, dwell./fam. 27, John Rice household. Also, 1880 U.S. census, Kent Co., Mich., pop. sch., Grand Rapids, ED 148, p. 3, dwell. 28, fam. 30, Elizabeth D. Smith household.

81. 1894 Mich. census, Kent Co., Grand Rapids, 2nd Ward, p. 79A, dwell. 30, fam. 88, Julia R. Rice.

82. Return of Marriages in the County of Ottawa for the Year Ending December 31st A.D. 1870, p. 61, Rice-Greenfield, 27 January 1870.

83. 1870 U.S. census, Kent Co., Mich., pop. sch., Wyoming Twp., p. 6, dwell./fam. 50, Theodore W. Conner household; NARA microfilm M593, roll 682. Also, 1865 N.Y. census, Niagara Co., Newfane, ED 1, p. 9, visitation 61, fam. 65, Theodore W. Connor household.

uncle and aunt, Theodore and Harriet (Talcott) Connor, with whom she lived in Niagara County in 1865.[83] Julia divorced Bethuel in 1880.[84]

Julia and Bethuel had two children, born in Tallmadge Township:[85]

4 i. JOHN "JOHNNIE"[7] RICE, born on 21 November 1870;[86] died on 19 November 1952 at Grand Rapids, apparently single and childless.[87]

5 ii. HATTIE RICE, born on 28 December 1871;[88] died of cholera infantum on 3 August 1872 in Tallmadge Township.[89]

---

84. Kent Co., Chancery Calendar 2, case no. 6-4256, Julia Rice v. Bethuel Rice, complaint filed on 7 December 1879 and decree filed on 11 February 1880; Circuit Court, Grand Rapids; FHL microfilm 2,195,817. The file, like most Kent County chancery case files for 1862–80, is missing. See Kent County chancery cases finding aid, typescript; Regional History Collection, Western Michigan University, Kalamazoo.

85. Bethuel Rice, questionnaire 3-389, 19 March 1915; in Bethuel Rice (Co. C, 10th Mich. Cav.) Civil War pension application 391,687, certificate 896,609, RG 15, NA–Washington.

86. Ottawa Co., Mich., Record of Births 1:294, no. 403, John Rice, 21 November 1870; County Clerk, Grand Haven, Mich.; FHL microfilm 984,233.

87. In 1940, at age sixty-nine, John was single. See 1940 U.S. census, Kent Co., Mich., pop. sch., Grand Rapids, ED 41-18B, sheet 6A, household 87, John Rice; NARA microfilm T627, roll 1,774. Also, "Rice," *Press* (Grand Rapids, Mich.), 20 November 1952, page 44, col. 4. The funeral notice, identifying Lamont as John's former residence and burial place, mentions no survivors.

88. Ottawa Co., Record of Births 1:398, no. 565, Hattiece [*sic*] Rice, 28 December 1871.

89. Ottawa Co., Record of Deaths 1:72, no. 351 [blank] Rice (daughter of Bethuel Rice), 3 August 1872; County Clerk, Grand Haven; FHL microfilm 984,237.

Appendix B

Examples of Creating a Citation Using Waypoints to a Numbered Image

---

Note: This appendix is updated and adapted from Thomas W. Jones, "Genealogy > Citations > Waypoints: An Option for Locating and Citing Unindexed Numbered Online Images," *Association of Professional Genealogists Quarterly* 31 (June 2016): 71–79, specifically pp. 76–77.

Online researchers who find the image of Raymond Greenfield's original will can create a citation leading directly to it, bypassing 1,191 digital or microfilm images of more than six hundred papers in one probate box.

Looking at the image, researchers can craft the citation from back to front, starting with a description of the item of interest. This description shows the source qualities—an original record with a knowledgeable informant:

Raymond Greenfield, will, 10 October 1821.

Preceding the description, researchers insert the numbers of the images showing the will:

images 426–27, Raymond Greenfield, will, 10 October 1821.

Above the image, *FamilySearch* provides three waypoints to the image. The first waypoint also is the collection title, which researchers can cite at the citation's last step as a part of a publication. Researchers can copy and paste the other two waypoints into their citation:

> Cayuga > Estate papers 1799–1904 box 4 > images 426–27, Raymond Greenfield, will, 10 October 1821.

If the beginning of the URL (for example, *http://www.)* is not needed for functionality in a print environment, as in this example, researchers can truncate the collection's URL and paste it and their download date into the citation:

(familysearch.org/search/collection/1920234 : accessed 20 February 2017) > Cayuga > Estate papers 1799–1904 box 4 > images 426–27, Raymond Greenfield, will, 10 October 1821.

Placing the collection and publication titles at the beginning completes the citation. Counting the URL as a word and discounting the greater-than signs, this citation has the same number of words and numbers as a microfilm citation to the same image. Unlike the microfilm citation, the waypoints citation leads directly to an unindexed record:

> "New York Probate Records, 1629–1971," *FamilySearch* (familysearch.org/search/collection/1920234 : accessed 20 February 2017) > Cayuga > Estate papers 1799–1904 box 4 > images 426–27, Raymond Greenfield, will, 10 October 1821.

That citation shows the source qualities and where to find it. Readers using it can point their Web browsers to the URL and then click the off-putting link "Browse through 14,045,639 images." From there, they click the second waypoint ("Cayuga") and then the third ("Estate papers 1799–1904 box 4"). That third mouse-click downloads the collection's first image. Replacing number 1 with 426 opens the image of Raymond Greenfield's will's first page.

The preceding citation is a full reference-note citation, used to cite the source in a footnote or endnote at the source's first appearance in a genealogist's work. Researchers can easily adapt it to a shortened reference-note citation and a reference-list citation:

> "New York Probate Records, 1629–1971," *FamilySearch* > Greenfield, will, 10 October 1821.

> "New York Probate Records, 1629–1971." *FamilySearch*. Familysearch.org/search/collection/1920234 : 2017.

A software-based master-source citation template can point to the collection, rather than the entire website, making it expandable to cite specific items within the collection:

> "New York Probate Records, 1629–1971," *FamilySearch* (familysearch.org/search/collection/1920234) > New York Probate Records, 1629–1971.

For another example, Silas Cleaveland's Revolutionary War pension file contains twenty-three unnumbered pages in a collection of alphabetically arranged files. One paper helps document Richard Greenfield's naval service. In 1969 the National Archives published images of Silas's file in its microfilm publication M804. *Ancestry* and *Fold3* digitized that publication. *Ancestry* numbered its images, which do not have unique URLs, by starting with 1 as each microfilm roll's first image. Richard appears there on image 885 from microfilm roll 574. *Fold3* numbered the images by starting with 1 as each pension file's first image. On *Fold3*, Richard appears on "page" 7. The publishers' numbers differ, but both sets—based on the papers' primary contexts—are stable. The number of microfilm images, their sequences, and the number of pages in the file are unlikely to change.

Leading to the group where the image mentioning Raymond is uniquely numbered, *Ancestry* provides four waypoints:

> U.S., Revolutionary War Pension and Bounty-Land Warrant Application Files, 1800–1900 >
>
> C >
>
> Cleary, William - Colburn, Zeruiah >
>
> Cleary, William - Cleaveland, William >

The first waypoint is also the collection title. It has a home page with its own URL. That page offers a series of drop-down menus for researchers to click through the other waypoints. The second waypoint refers to the first letter of a surname group, and the third encompasses twenty-five microfilm rolls (numbers 574–98) in National Archives microfilm publication M804.

Those three waypoints help researchers narrow down to a specific subgrouping of images. The fourth waypoint corresponds to the contents of microfilm roll 574, containing 1,021 unnumbered images. Clicking the fourth waypoint opens image 1 of the sequence containing the image of interest. Changing 1 to 885 takes readers to the page mentioning Richard Greenfield.

Besides the publisher's waypoints, a clear and complete citation to the image mentioning Richard requires the image number and at least four other citation elements:

- The database title (a part of a publication), "U.S., Revolutionary War Pension and Bounty-Land Warrant Application Files, 1800–1900"
- The publication title, *Ancestry*
- The truncated URL, search.ancestry.com/search/db.aspx?dbid=1995, which opens a web browser at the collection's home page, where readers can click through the other waypoints
- The access date, 20 February 2017

A description of what image 885 shows is "Silas Cleaveland, amended declaration, 23 January 1833, in Silas Cleaveland (Conn. Navy) pension application file S.12,486." This description shows an original record with a knowledgeable informant.

The assembled citation contains forty-five words and numbers, discounting the greater-than signs and counting the URL as one word:

> "U.S., Revolutionary War Pension and Bounty-Land Warrant Application Files, 1800–1900," *Ancestry* (http://search.ancestry.com/search/db.aspx?dbid=1995 : accessed 20 February 2017) > C > Cleary, William–Colburn, Zeruiah > Cleary, William–Cleaveland, William > image 885, Silas Cleaveland, amended declaration, 23 January 1833, in Silas Cleaveland (Conn. Navy) pension application file S.12,486.

This citation, showing the offline source's qualities and where to find it, is a full citation for a footnote or endnote. Like the prior example, this citation can be modified into a shortened, reference-list, or master-source citation. The citation using waypoints is five words shorter than a citation to the microfilm, which requires readers to browse hundreds of images to find one page:

> *Revolutionary War Pension and Bounty–Land–Warrant Application Files,* microfilm publication M804, 2,670 rolls (Washington, D.C.: National Archives and Records Service, 1969), roll 574, Silas Cleaveland (Conn. Navy) pension application file S.12,486, for Silas Cleaveland, amended declaration, 23 January 1833.

Appendix C

Genealogy standard 5

Note: Genealogy standard 5 is central to this book's content and organization, and the book frequently cites and quotes parts of it. It is quoted here, with the permission of the Board for Certification of Genealogists, for the convenience of readers wishing to refer to the entire standard.

5. Citation elements. Complete citations use a standard format to describe at least four facets of each cited source:

- *Who*—the person, agency, business, government, office, or religious body that authored, created, edited, produced, or was responsible for the source; or, if identified, the source's informant
- *What*—the source's title or name; if it is untitled, a clear item-specific description
- *When*—the date the source was created, published, last modified, or accessed; in some cases, if the source is unpublished, the date of the event it reports
- *Where[is]*—if unpublished, the source's physical location; if a published book, CD-ROM, microfilm, or newspaper, its place of publication; if an online resource, a stable URL

Complete citations to information items documenting specific statements, facts, images, and conclusions (reference-note citations) describe a fifth facet:

- *Wherein*—the specific location within the source where the information item can be found [*or where the researcher looked for relevant information but did not find it*], for example, page, image, or sequence number; or—if the source is unpublished—its box number, folder or collection name, or similar identifying information.[1]

1. BCG, *Genealogy Standards*, 7–8, for standard 5, "Citation Elements." Quoted here with permission. *Wherein* is shorthand for *Where within the source*. The coined word *Whereis*, which does not appear in *Genealogy Standards*, is the present author's shorthand for *Where is the source*.

Glossary

The following terms are defined as they pertain to genealogical documentation. Italics denote words defined elsewhere in this glossary.

abbreviation	Letters representing a word, name, or phrase, including *acronyms* and *initialisms*
acronym	An *initialism* pronounceable like a word
article	An authored *narrative* that appears in a *journal, magazine, newsletter, newspaper,* or other *periodical publication*
author	Someone who writes a *narrative* or report
bibliography	See *reference list*
book	A group of *folios, leaves,* or *pages* bound or sewn together in a *volume* with a hard or soft cover; or the collected digital *images* of such a group
chapter	A numbered multi-*page* section of a book, usually with a *title*
citation	A *source* description in a standard format to communicate source qualities and location; used by genealogists in *reference lists, reference notes,* and *source labels*
complex citation	A *reference-note citation* structured to contain a *simple citation* and supplementary information partially describing an image's underlying version or an underlying version's image; analogous in structure to a complex sentence; also called a *layered citation;* compare to *compound citation* and *simple citation*

compound citation	A *reference-note citation* structured as two connected simple citations, one fully describing an image and the other fully describing its underlying version; analogous in structure to a compound sentence; also called a *layered citation*; compare to *complex citation* and *simple citation*
derivative record	A *record* created from a prior record by *(1)* transcribing the prior record or part of it by hand, keyboard, or optical-character-recognition, speech-to-text, or other technology, *(2)* abstracting information from it, *(3)* translating it from one language to another, or *(4)* reproducing it with alterations; a work created to expand accessibility to the prior record's information, or to some part of it; the opposite of *original record*
discursive note	A *reference note* containing discussion, usually along with one or more *citations*
document *(noun)*	A page, group of *pages*, or digital file containing writing, one or more images, or both
document *(verb)*	The processes of *recording* and showing the *sources* of concepts, evidence, images, words, and other material a researcher has used
documentation	The *sources* supporting genealogical conclusions and proof, *citations* to those sources, the genealogist's comments about them, and *formatting* showing the connections between the sources and specific statements and conclusions
edition	A *publication's* first form, or a reissue of a publication in which its content is altered; compare with *reprint*
endnote	A *reference note* placed at the end of an *article*, *book*, report, Web publication, or other work to *document* concepts, evidence, images, words, and other material a researcher has used; compare with *footnote*
et al.	The abbreviation of *et alii*, Latin for *and others*, used in *reference-note citations* after the first author's name when citing works with more than three authors
evidence	Information, or its lack, considered as it bears on the answer to a research question; can be right

	or wrong, complete or incomplete, or vague or specific; can be direct, indirect, or negative
facsimile	An *image* that shows researchers no less information and context than they would see when examining the *underlying source* that had been imaged
foliation	An obsolete system of numbering *leaves* in a *manuscript* or printed work; see *folio* and compare with *pagination*
folio	A sheet of paper folded for writing or printing on more than one side, or a *leaf* of a *manuscript* or *book* in which numbering appears on one side of a two-leaf *spread* or the same number appears on facing leaves; compare with *page*
footnote	A *reference note* appearing at the bottom of a *page* to *document* a statement on that page or two-page *spread*; compare with *endnote*
format/formatting	A *citation's* capitalization, punctuation, and sequencing; the placement of *documentation* in a written work and connections between that documentation and the narrative
full citation	A *sentence-style* format used for a written work's first *citation* to a *source* and providing all applicable citation details; compare with *shortened citation*
genealogy	A research field concerned primarily with accurately reconstructing forgotten or unknown identities and familial relationships in the past and present, typically covering more than one generation and including adoptive, biological, collateral, extramarital, marital, and other kinds of familial relationships; a narrative family history covering descendants of an ancestral couple
headline style	Capitalization of the first and last of a series of words, and most other words except some articles, conjunctions, and prepositions; the form of capitalization used for *titles*; compare with *sentence style*
image	A film, photocopy, photograph, scan, video, or another replication of an *underlying source*; compare with *facsimile*

independent clause	A group of words that could be a stand-alone sentence, if it was not joined to another independent clause with a conjunction
informant	Someone who provided one or more *information* items
information	Statements based on experience, fabrication, hearsay, intuition, observation, reading, research, or otherwise; a *source*'s surface content, including its physical characteristics; what researchers see or hear when they examine a source, not what they interpret; can be *primary, secondary,* or undetermined
initialism	An *abbreviation* formed from a name or phrase, with no concluding period and often in all capital letters; compare with *acronym*
joint authors	Two or more people who—with ostensibly similar roles or contributions—write a *narrative* or report
journal	A *periodical publication* containing *articles* with professional or scholarly content
layered citation	See *complex citation* and *compound citation*
leaf	A sheet of paper or other material folded for writing on more than one side or bound into a book; compare with *folio* and *page*
long-form citation	See *full citation*
magazine	A *periodical publication* containing *articles* for general readers
manuscript	A *document* written by hand; also a *typescript*
medium	A means of showing *facsimiles* or *images* of *sources,* including digital images, film, microfiche, microfilm, photocopies, photographs, and video
multivolume set	A collection of *volumes* published simultaneously or sequentially
narrative	A written work that describes multiple events, synthesizes information from prior *sources,* and presents an *author*'s conclusions, interpretations, and thoughts

negative search	A search that yields no useful evidence
original record	A report in a fixed form of an action, observation, utterance, or other event, often—but not always—made during the event or soon after and not based on a prior record; the opposite of *derivative record* and one of three kinds of genealogical *source*; see *record*
page	A *leaf* within a *manuscript* or print *publication* or one side of such a leaf; compare with *folio*
pagination	*Page* numbering where each side of each *leaf* is numbered sequentially; compare with *foliation*
periodical publication	A *titled publication* issued at scheduled intervals; includes *journals, magazines,* and newspapers
primary information	Information about an event provided by an eyewitness remembering the event; the opposite of *secondary information*
printer	A business, machine, or person that produces or reproduces printed works
provenance	The history of a source's custody
publication	A *source* made available for distribution to people and libraries wishing a copy; the opposite of *unpublished source*
publish	To make a *source* available to the public for private ownership, subscription, or consultation
publisher	A business or person that handles a *publication*'s initial distribution to the public and to libraries, if not also later distributions
record *(noun)*	An account, usually written, of an action, observation, utterance, or other event, typically intended to describe, memorialize, or note the action, observation, utterance, or other event; can be *original* or *derivative;* a broad subcategory of genealogical *source*
record *(verb)*	To make a *record*
recto	The front side of a *foliated leaf;* when bound, a two-page *spread*'s right-hand page; compare with *verso*

reference list	An alphabetical or categorical grouping of citations showing research scope, providing the general documentary basis for the content of a lecture, lesson, presentation, or written work, or directing others to sources related to such content; also called a *bibliography* or *source list*
reference-list citation	A *citation* in a paragraph format, customarily with a hanging indent, used to identify a *source* fully but not to *document* a specific item, and typically not referring to specific information or pages within the source
reference note	A section of a genealogical work written sentence style and containing one or more *citations,* discussion of an researcher's *sources,* or both
reference-note citation	A *citation* in a sentence format, customarily numbered, usually referring to a specific or information or pages and used to *document* concepts, evidence, images, words, and other material a researcher has used; can be an *endnote* or *footnote* and *full* or *shortened*
repository	An agency, building, or office housing source material, like an archive (personal, private, or public), courthouse, historical society, library, museum, or town hall, and business, governmental, personal, religious, and other kinds of office
reprint	A reissue of a *publication* in which its content is not altered; compare with *edition*
secondary information	Information reported by someone who obtained it from someone else; hearsay; the opposite of *primary information*
sentence style	A form of capitalization that involves lowercasing all words in a group of words except the group's first word and any proper nouns, including formal titles, and ending the group with a period; the form of capitalization and punctuation used in *reference-note citations* and *source labels;* compare with *headline style*
serial	A *titled* work with *volumes* or parts issued at different times; includes *periodicals* and *series*
series	*Volumes* compiled or published sequentially under a series title, series number, or both

shortened citation	A *sentence-style* format used for all but a work's first *reference-note citation* to a *source* and providing only enough detail to trigger recall and identification of the prior *full citation* and to document the statement to which it is attached; compare with *full citation*
simple citation	A *reference-note citation* structured to answer the five citation questions once, describing one source or one version of a source and containing no supplementary information about an image or underlying version; compare to *complex citation* and *compound citation*
source	A container of information; can be a *publication*, *unpublished* artifact or manuscript, *record*, recording, or written material; can be used and cited as an *image* or as the material underlying the image
source label	A *citation* resembling a *reference-note* citation affixed to a container or image of a source
source list	See *reference list*
spread *(noun)*	Two facing *leaves*, *folios*, or *pages*
subsequent note	See *shortened citation*
title	The designated name of a source or a part of a *source*, including most *publications*, many *unpublished sources*, and their parts
titled set	A collection of numbered or lettered untitled *volumes*, *published* or *unpublished*, under a shared *title*
typescript	An *unpublished document* written with a keyboard
underlying source	A *source* viewed via a *medium*
unpublished source	A *source* for which only one or a few copies exist, or a source for which distribution is limited to select people or places; the opposite of *publication*
verso	The back side of a *foliated leaf;* when bound, a two-page *spread*'s left-hand page; compare with *recto*
volume	A *book*, often a numbered or titled element of a *serial* or *series*

Reading and Source List 1:

References and supporting material

Board for Certification of Genealogists. *Genealogy Standards*. Nashville, Tennessee: Ancestry.com, 2014. Also available as a Kindle e-book.

The Chicago Manual of Style, 16th ed. Chicago: University of Chicago Press, 2010.

The Chicago Manual of Style Online. http://www.chicagomanualofstyle.org /home.html : 2017.

Jones, Thomas W. "Genealogy > Citations > Waypoints: An Option for Locating and Citing Unindexed Numbered Online Images." *Association of Professional Genealogists Quarterly* 31 (June 2016): 71–79.

———. "Getting the Most from Case Studies in the National Genealogical Society Quarterly." *NGS Magazine* 41 (October–December 2015): 47–53.

———. *Mastering Genealogical Proof*. Arlington, Virginia: National Genealogical Society, 2013. Also available as a Kindle e-book.

———. "Roots of Today's Standards for Amateur and Professional Genealogy." *CrossRoads* 11 (Spring 2016): 4–9.

Mills, Elizabeth Shown. *Evidence Explained: Citing History Sources from Artifacts to Cyberspace*, 3rd ed. Baltimore: Genealogical Publishing Company, 2015. Also available as a Kindle e-book.

———. *Evidence Explained: Historical Analysis, Citation, and Source Usage*. https://evidenceexplained.com/ : 2017.

———. *QuickSheet: Citing Genetic Sources for History Research Evidence! Style*, laminated folder. Baltimore: Genealogical Publishing Company, 2015.

———. *QuickSheet: Citing Online Historical Resources Evidence! Style*, laminated folder, revised edition. Baltimore: Genealogical Publishing Company, 2007.

Reading and Source List 2:

Selected guides for learning about American genealogical sources

Bettinger, Blaine T., and Debbie Parker Wayne. *Genetic Genealogy in Practice*. Arlington, Va.: National Genealogical Society, 2016.

Eakle, Arlene, and Johni Cerny. *The Source: A Guidebook of American Genealogy*. Salt Lake City: Ancestry, 1984 [best used with the third edition, cited under Szucs].

Eales, Anne Bruner, and Robert M. Kvasnicka. *Guide to Genealogical Research in the National Archives of the United States*, 3rd ed. Washington, D.C.: National Archives and Records Administration, 2000.

FamilySearch. *Research Wiki*. https://familysearch.org/wiki/en/Main_Page : 2017.

Freilich, Kay Haviland, and William B. Freilich. *Genealogy and the Law: A Guide to Legal Sources for the Family Historian*. Arlington, Va.: National Genealogical Society, 2014.

Greenwood, Val D. *The Researcher's Guide to American Genealogy*, 3rd ed. Baltimore: Genealogical Publishing Company, 2000.

Mills, Elizabeth Shown. *Evidence Explained: Citing History Sources from Artifacts to Cyberspace*, 3rd ed. Baltimore: Genealogical Publishing Company, 2015.

Rubincam, Milton, ed. *Genealogical Research: Methods and Sources*, vol. 1, 2nd ed. Washington D.C.: American Society of Genealogists, 1980.

"Skillbuilding." *Board for Certification of Genealogists*. http://www.bcgcertification.org/skillbuilders/index.html : 2017.

Stevenson, Noel C. *Genealogical Evidence: A Guide to the Standard of Proof Relating to Pedigrees, Ancestry, Heirship, and Family History*. Laguna Hills, Calif.: Aegean Park, 1979.

Szucs, Loretto Dennis, and Sandra Hargreaves Luebking. T*he Source: A Guidebook to American Genealogy*, 3rd ed. Provo, Utah: Ancestry, 2006.

Note: *Exercise answers for all seventeen chapters appear in regular type except where italics are required (publication titles, for example). In contrast, each exercise's directions or description appears in italics or, where italics would normally appear, in* reverse italics.

Chapter 1 exercise answers

1. *What is a citation?*

   A citation is a description of a source. *[page 1]*

2. *What are the purposes of citations?*

   A citation shows a source's qualities and where to view that source. A group of citations shows the research scope. *[pages 3–4]*

3. *Why should genealogists want to document their research?*

   Documentation requires researchers to understand their sources. This gives them a research advantage: compared to people who do not fully understand their sources, genealogists who document understand more about the people they are researching and they get more from the sources they use. Documentation can show that the underlying research was thorough, the researcher's sources are credible, and the conclusions are valid. Should researchers need to reexamine information within a source, clear and complete documentation enables them to turn to that information. Habitual documentation also prevents genealogists from committing plagiarism. *[pages 2–3]*

4. *What is the meaningful difference between poor documentation and documentation with poor sources?*

   Poor documentation means that documentation is missing or too scant to support all the researcher's statements and conclusions. Readers cannot tell whether the conclusions are valid or not.

Documentation with poor sources means the researcher provided documentation, but it shows that the sources are vulnerable to error or otherwise not strong enough to support the researcher's statements and conclusions. *[page 4]*

5. *How does "right" documentation differ from "wrong" documentation?*

   "Right" documentation shows readers the qualities and locations of the researcher's sources and it points to the relevant information they contain. It also shows research scope. It does this so clearly that readers share the researcher's understanding of the qualities and locations of the researcher's sources and information. "Right" documentation enables readers to assess the presence or absence of source and information qualities associated with accuracy.

   "Wrong" documentation confuses readers about sources the researcher used, or it causes readers to understand something different from what the researcher intended about source and information qualities and locations. *[pages 3–4]*

6. *How do researchers learn about their sources?*

   They study the white pages in *Evidence Explained,* archival guides to research materials, laws and regulations governing their sources, and online and offline guides to genealogical sources. They study their sources in context, comparing and contrasting them with similar sources. *[page 7]*

7. *What are the risks of blindly using citation models and templates?*

   The researcher will bypass the advantages of analyzing sources and crafting citations. (See answer 3, above.) Because template-based citations might not be tailored to fit the researcher's source, they could yield citations that might miscommunicate information about the source or confuse readers. *[page 7]*

8. *What are the genealogy field's primary guides to documentation?*

   They are *The Chicago Manual of Style, Evidence Explained,* and *Genealogy Standards. [page 5]*

9. *What is the major difference between* Mastering Genealogical Documentation *and* Evidence Explained*?*

   Evidence Explained mostly gives guidance and examples for citing many specific kinds of sources. *Mastering Genealogical Documentation* is not source based. It describes documentation purposes, source and citation contexts, and citation structures and elements. It emphasizes the patterns and logic in genealogical documentation. *[page 9]*

Chapter 2 exercise answers

10. *What are the four components of genealogical documentation?*

    (a) Sources and specific information within them; *(b)* citations; *(c)* narratives discussing sources, and tables and other enhancements showing researcher assessments and interpretations; and *(d)* formatting showing the connections between citations and what they document. *[pages 11]*

11. *What should genealogists document?*

    Genealogists use documentation to identify the sources of all substantive information and images they gather, use, or plan to gather or use, except sources of "common knowledge" beyond dispute, like the years of major historical events. [*pages 11–12, quoting genealogy standard 1*]

12. *In what kinds of written works do genealogists provide documentation?*

    Genealogists document research plans, logs, notes, works in progress, and similar materials. They use documentation in classroom and lecture materials. They also use documentation, usually in footnotes, in all kinds of finished genealogical-research products, including articles, blogs, books, case studies, charts and forms, educational materials, family histories, other kinds of histories, applications to lineage societies, reports, trees in any format, and various kinds of written projects. *[pages 12–13]*

13. *Why do experienced genealogical readers prefer footnotes over endnotes?*

    Footnotes lie conveniently near the information they document, enabling readers to glance at the bottom of the page to see the researcher's sources and their qualities. Readers do not need to hunt for footnotes or turn pages to find them. *[page 13]*

14. *When are endnotes a good choice?*

    In electronic publications, where readers can mouse over or click a reference-note number, letter, or symbol and see the note [page 16]

15. *In the Greenfield article in this book's appendix A, find examples of citations documenting the following:*

    a. *Specific data items (dates, places, and relationships)*

       Footnote 3, both citations, document the statement about the date and place of George and Calista's marriage. Many other citations in this article document specific data items.

    b. *Statements of fact (more than dates, places, and relationships)*

       The citations in footnotes 4 and 5 document statements about family heads. Many other citations in this article document statements of fact.

    c. *Quotations*

       Footnote 23 documents a block quotation. Other citations in this article document quotations.

    d. *Paraphrases*

       The citations in footnote 2 document a paraphrase. (The citation says that the segment of narrative is a paraphrase.) Other citations in this article document the researcher's paraphrases of other writers' and researchers' words.

    e. *Elements within a table or figure*

       Citations in the footnotes in figure 1 and figure 2 document the relationships represented by the figures' vertical lines. The citation in table 1's sole footnote documents the DNA test results that the table shows.

16. *Dissect footnote 1 in the Greenfield article:*

    a. *How many citations does the footnote contain?*

       The footnote contains four citations. They reference *(1)* a family record, *(2)* a death record, *(3)* the 1880 U.S. census, and *(4)* the 1900 U.S. census.

    b. *What devices did the researcher use to separate the citations?*

       Each citation ends with a period. A sentence and a lead-in phrase separate the first two citations. Another sentence and "Also" separate the second and third citations. A lead-in phrase to the fourth citation helps separate it from the third citation.

c. *Which respective data item or statement of fact does each citation document?*

The first citation documents Calista's specific birth date. The second and third citations corroborate her birth year. The fourth citation corroborates her birth month.

d. *What noncitation components does this footnote contain?*

Besides its four citations, the footnote contains two sentences that are not citations. It also contains lead-in phrases and words.

e. *What are those components' roles within the footnote?*

The first sentence, naming the informant, helps readers assess the validity of the source's information. The second sentence, providing information about the source, helps readers and researchers avoid confusion, should they examine the source. The lead-in phrases specify what each citation documents.

17. *Dissect Greenfield footnote 58:*

a. *How many citations does the footnote contain?*

Greenfield footnote 58 contains two citations.

b. *What devices did the researcher use for separating the citations?*

The first citation ends with a period, a sentence separates the citations, and the second citation begins with a lead-in word, "See."

c. *Which respective data item or statement of fact does each citation document?*

The first citation documents the footnote's first sentence, "Franklin was unmarried in 1850." That citation implies that his household shows no candidate for his wife.

The second citation documents the footnote's second sentence, "By 1855 he was married to Christina and had a two-year-old daughter, Julia." That citation implies that the cited state census names Christina and Julia, states their ages, and gives their relationship to Franklin.

d. *What noncitation components does this footnote contain?*

Besides two citations with lead-in words ("See"), the footnote contains two sentences.

e. *What are those components' roles within the footnote?*

Those two sentences explain the statement in the narrative that Frank married Christina in 1850–53 in Niagara County. Those documented sentences form a proof summary supporting that statement. The lead-in words join the sentences and citations into a cohesive footnote.

18. *Why is note-number 58 in the Greenfield article's narrative not at the end of the sentence?*

    The footnotes use different sources to document unrelated facts. Footnote 58 documents Franklin's marriage to Christina. The statement and the documentation focus on Franklin. Footnote 59 documents Christina's death. The phrase and the documentation focus on Christina. Because of the footnotes' different focuses, combining them would require more words than the two separated footnotes. Attaching each footnote to the information its respective citation documents requires placing note-number 58 within the sentence.

19. *How many citations does Greenfield footnote 31 contain? How are they separated? What noncitation content does this footnote contain? Why might the author have chosen to include that content in the citation?*

    Footnote 31 contains two citations. The first cites a DNA report, and the second cites an online article. The first citation ends with a period, two sentences separate the citations, and the second citation begins with the lead-in word "See."

    The text leading up to footnote-number 31 states a relationship based on DNA test results. The second noncitation sentence in footnote 31 states two cutoffs used in establishing that relationship.

20. *In the Greenfield article's narrative portion, what examples do you find of mentioning or discussing sources? Why are these discussions not in the footnotes?*

    One example appears in the last paragraph on page 186, where the narrative mentions three state censuses. Mentioning the censuses simplifies the discussion of Calista and Franklin's birthplace and the absence of information from sources that might show it. Another example appears in the first paragraph on page 187. Mentioning the sources puts the discussion in the context of reliable sources.

    This article contains other examples of sources mentioned or discussed in the narrative.

21. *Which sentences in the two following paragraphs need documenting?*

    Three years later Mary married the widower, Fred Guker. Marinda might have brought them together. The marriage might never have occurred had Mary not walked to Red Bud through the snow with two children.

    Mary and her brother, Jacob, apparently never reconciled. In 1921 some fifty guests attended the fiftieth-anniversary celebration of Jacob and his wife, Lena. Coming from St. Clair County and St. Louis, most were Lena's relatives. Not one represented Jacob's side of the family.

In the first paragraph, only the first sentence requires documenting. A marriage record documents that sentence. That paragraph's second and third sentences do not require documenting because their wording—"might have" and "might never have"—shows they are the writer's opinions.

The second paragraph's first sentence is a topic sentence, foreshadowing what the paragraph will establish. It does not require documenting, because the paragraph's content will be documented. The paragraph's second and third sentences summarize a newspaper article reporting on the fiftieth-anniversary celebration. The last sentence is an inference drawn from that article. Because the same source documents all three sentences, the number of the footnote citing the article would appear only at the end of the last sentence.

22. *Below are two undocumented paragraphs. Within them, place note numbers 1–7 at the ends of sentences, or groups of sentences, requiring documentation. Below the two paragraphs are seven citations in random order. Number them to correspond with the seven note numbers you placed in the two paragraphs.*

In 1767 Archibald Greenfield bequeathed to "my grandson James Greenfield the Son of Starr Archibald Greenfield a Silver Spoon."[1] This grandson's birth, on 7 January 1752[/3], was recorded at Lyme.[2] The date is consistent with the calculated birth year of James Greenfield who died at the town of Russia, New York, on 15 January 1812 "in the 59 year of his age."[3] Nonetheless, these men of one name and similar age are distinguishable.

James Greenfield,"aged 92 years, a soldier of the Revolution," died at Lyme on 26 November 1843.[4] Living there in 1832 at age eighty, he applied for a pension. Citing Lyme's town records, he said he had lived there since his birth, on 7 January 1752. He recalled serving five terms during the war, totaling twenty-nine months while based at Lyme.[5] Other Lyme-native veterans confirmed that James was born there and "ever since lived there."[6] He received the pension in Connecticut through September 1843.[7]

---

7 "U.S., Revolutionary War Pensioners, 1801–1815, 1818–1872," *Ancestry* (http://ancestry.com/search/db.aspx?dbid=1116 : viewed 20 February 2017) > T718: 1818–1872 > 08: Revolutionary War, 1831–1848 > image 90, Treasury Department pension payment ledger for 1831–48, p. 99, James Greenfield.

5 "U.S., Revolutionary War Pension and Bounty-Land Warrant Application Files, 1800–1900," *Ancestry* (http://search.ancestry.com/search/db.aspx?dbid=1995 : viewed 20 February 2017) > G > Graham, Joseph–Gregory, Joseph > Greenelsh, Edward–Greenslit, John >

image 131, James Greenfield, claim for a pension, 6 August 1832, in James Greenfield pension application file S13192.

6 "U.S., Revolutionary War Pension and Bounty-Land Warrant Application Files, 1800–1900," *Ancestry* (http://search.ancestry.com/search/db.aspx?dbid=1995 : viewed 20 February 2017) > G > Graham, Joseph–Gregory, Joseph > Greenelsh, Edward–Greenslit, John > image 147, Seth Miner, deposition, 15 December 1832; image 149, John Mather, deposition, 7 December 1832; and image 151, John Lay, deposition, 8 December 1832, in James Greenfield pension application file S13192.

4 "Died," *People's Advocate* (New London, Conn.), 13 December 1843, page 3, col. 3.

1 Essex Co., Mass., Probate Records (Old Series Books) 45, fols. 255–56, will of Archibald Greenfield, 1 November 1767, proved on 4 September 1769; Registry of Probate, Salem, Mass.; microfilm 875,028, Family History Library, Salt Lake City.

3 *Find A Grave* (https://www.findagrave.com/cgi-bin/fg.cgi : viewed 20 February 2017), memorial 20981767, for James Greenfield gravestone (Century Cemetery, Russia, N.Y.), digital image, 13 May 2011, by Steve Staruch.

2 Lyme, Conn., vital records 1:65, James Greenfield birth, 7 January 1752[/3]; Town Clerk, Lyme; microfilm 1,311,111, Family History Library, Salt Lake City.

Chapter 3 exercise answers

23. *In the Greenfield article in this book's appendix A, footnote 1 announces three acronyms or initialisms and uses other abbreviations. What are the acronyms and initialisms, and what do all the abbreviations stand for?*

    FHL is an initialism for *Family History Library*, and *ED* is an initialism for *enumeration district*. *NARA* is an acronym for *National Archives and Records Administration.*

    The abbreviations include *Co.* for *County, Mich.* for *Michigan, no.* for *number* (from *numero,* the Latin word for *number*), *U.S.* for *United States, Twp.* for *Township, Ind.* for *Indiana, pop. sch.* for *population schedule, dwell.* for *dwelling,* and *fam.* for *family.*

24. *In the Greenfield article, compare the second citation in footnote 18 (the atlas) with the last citation in footnote 35. What similarities and differences do you see between the full and the shortened reference-note citations?*

    The similarities are the author's surname (*Burr*) and four words from the title (*Atlas of New York*). The content in the shortened citation follows the same order as it appears in the full citation. Four differences are apparent:

    - The author's full name in the full form; only his surname in the shortened form
    - The full eight-word title in the full form; a four-word title in the shortened form
    - The parenthetical publication information in the full form; omitted in the shortened form
    - A map number, county, and year in the full form; only the county name (a different county) in the shortened form

25. *Why is the last citation in Greenfield footnote 34 a shortened citation and not a full citation?*

    Because the 1830 U.S. census of Cayuga County was first cited in full in footnote 12

26. *In the Greenfield article, compare the last citation in footnote 4 with the first citation in footnote 55. These full and shortened citations to the same source document different statements. What similarities and differences do you see between those citations?*

    Similarities:

    Citing the same death record, both citations name the same creator (Michigan Division of Vital Statistics), give the same record title, year, and number, and name the same person.

    Differences:

    The shortened form omits the county and all the information about the digital image (digital collection title, website title, URL, and the words "digital image").

27. *Greenfield footnote 11 contains two* ibids. *What does each of them refer to? What does each of them replace?*

    Each *ibid.* refers to the prior citation.

    The first *ibid.* replaces everything in the prior citation except the identifications of the image, page, dwelling, and family numbers, and the name of the household head.

    The second *ibid.* replaces everything in the respective prior citation except the identifications of the image, dwelling, and family numbers, and the name of the household head. Because the prior citation says the source is "unpaginated," the citation with the second *ibid.* contains no replacement page number.

28. *The first citation in footnote 22 omits the author's or creator's name. What is it, and why is it omitted?*

    The creator of the microfilm publication is the National Archives and Records Administration (NARA). It also is the publisher. When a source's institutional creator and a publisher have the same name, omitting the answer to the *Who* citation question is customary.

29. *Using this book's tables 1–5, convert each full reference-note citation to* (a) *a shortened reference-note citation and* (b) *a reference-list citation.*

    Note that the following give just one of several examples of acceptable citations. Other content choices and arrangements are acceptable.

Shortened reference-note citations omit information at the writer's discretion, but they usually answer the *Wherein* citation question.

Reference-list citations typically show the first author's name as last-name first, separate the citation answers with periods, and usually do not answer the *Wherein* citation question.

FULL: Jane Fletcher Fiske, transcr., *Rhode Island General Court of Trials: 1671–1704* (Boxford, Mass.: privately printed, 1998), 223.

SHORTENED: Fiske, *Rhode Island General Court of Trials,* 223.

LIST: Fiske, Jane Fletcher. *Rhode Island General Court of Trials: 1671–1704*. Boxford, Mass.: privately printed, 1998.

FULL: Gerald W. McFarland, *A Scattered People: An American Family Moves West* (New York: Pantheon, 1985), 26.

SHORTENED: McFarland, *A Scattered People,* 26.

LIST: McFarland, Gerald W. *A Scattered People: An American Family Moves West*. New York: Pantheon, 1985.

FULL: "Died," *People's Advocate* (New London, Conn.), 13 December 1843, page 3, col. 3.

SHORTENED: "Died," *People's Advocate,* 13 December 1843, page 3, col. 3.

LIST: *People's Advocate*. New London, Conn.

FULL: Marya Myers and Donald W. James Jr., "The Family of William[1] and Susannah (Martin) James of Portsmouth and Newport, Rhode Island: New Discoveries," *New England Historical and Genealogical Register* 147 (October 1993): 334, footnote 5.

SHORTENED: Myers and James, "The Family of William[1] and Susannah (Martin) James," 334, footnote 5.

LIST: Myers, Marya, and Donald W. James Jr. "The Family of William[1] and Susannah (Martin) James of Portsmouth and Newport, Rhode Island: New Discoveries." *New England Historical and Genealogical Register* 147 (October 1993): 334, footnote 5.

or

New England Historical and Genealogical Register.

FULL: First Church of Christ (New London, Conn.), records 1:157, James Greenfield, 5 November 1738; Connecticut State Library (CSL); microfilm 1,011,944, Family History Library (FHL), Salt Lake City.

SHORTENED: First Church of Christ, records 1:157, James Greenfield, 5 November 1738.

LIST: First Church of Christ. New London, Conn. Records. Microfilm 1,011,944. Family History Library. Salt Lake City.

FULL: Lyme, Conn., Land Records 6:70, Roulin-"Greenfeald" marriage, 1 May 1736, recorded on 17 December 1736; Town Clerk, Lyme; FHL microfilm 4680.

SHORTENED: Lyme, Land Records 6:70, Roulin-"Greenfeald" marriage, 1 May 1736.

LIST: Conn. Lyme. Land Records. Microfilm 4680, Family History Library, Salt Lake City. [*Note:* Either the punctuation shown here for the FHL microfilm number or that in the example above (First Church of Christ) is acceptable.]

FULL: 1790 U.S. census, Albany Co., N.Y., "Stephen Town," pp. 281 (Raymond Greenfield), 285 (Bethuel Greenfield), and 287 (Archibald Greenfield); microfilm M637, roll 6, National Archives and Records Administration (NARA).

SHORTENED: 1790 U.S. census, Albany Co., N.Y., "Stephen Town," pp. 281 (Raymond Greenfield), 285 (Bethuel Greenfield), and 287 (Archibald Greenfield).

LIST: 1790 U.S. census. Albany Co., N.Y. Microfilm M637, roll 6, National Archives and Records Administration.

FULL: *Find A Grave* (https://www.findagrave.com/cgi-bin/fg.cgi : viewed 20 February 2017), memorial 20981767, for James Greenfield gravestone (Century Cemetery, Russia, N.Y.), digital image, 13 May 2011, by Steve Staruch.

SHORTENED: *Find A Grave,* memorial 20981767, for James Greenfield gravestone.

LIST: *Find A Grave.* https://www.findagrave.com : 2017.

FULL: "Massachusetts, Town Clerk, Vital and Town Records, 1626–2001," *FamilySearch* (https://familysearch.org/search/collection/2061550 : viewed 20 February 2017) > Essex > Salem > Marriages 1695–1815 vol 4 > image 25, Salem, Mass., Book of Marriages 4:44, Greenfield-Bacon, 31 May 1733, return "By the Rev^{d}. M^{r}. Wm Jenison."

SHORTENED: Salem, Book of Marriages 4:44, Greenfield-Bacon, 31 May 1733.

LIST: "Massachusetts, Town Clerk, Vital and Town Records, 1626–2001." *FamilySearch.* https://familysearch.org/search/collection/2061550 :2017. Images of original records.

Chapter 4 exercise answers

30. *What questions must genealogy citations answer?*

    What is the source, who created it, when was it created, where within it is the information that documents, and where is the source. *[page 40]*

31. *How does learning about sources advance genealogical research goals?*

    Learning about sources helps researchers understand the people named in sources. Knowledge about sources often reflects research subjects' actions and can reveal their motivations. *[page 37]*

32. *For groups a–d of unsequenced citation elements, follow the models to complete tasks 1 and 2:*

    Group a, completed task 1: The question each element answers

    - Standard Certificate of Death no. 38796 *(What)*
    - State of Illinois *(Who)*
    - Department of Health, Springfield, Ill. *(Whereis)*
    - Mary Margaretta Guker *(Wherein)*
    - (1934) *(When)*

    Group a, completed task 2: The elements logically sequenced

    - State of Illinois
    - Standard Certificate of Death no. 38796
    - (1934)
    - Mary Margaretta Guker
    - Department of Health, Springfield, Ill.

    Group b, completed task 1: The question each element answers

    - searched on 20 February 2017 *(When)*
    - search for "Jac* Gros*" in Illinois and Missouri *(Wherein)*
    - http://search.ancestry.com/search/db.aspx?dbid=6742 *(Whereis)*
    - "1880 United States Federal Census," *Ancestry (What)*

Group b, completed task 2: The elements logically sequenced

- "1880 United States Federal Census," *Ancestry*
- http://search.ancestry.com/search/db.aspx?dbid=6742
- searched on 20 February 2017
- search for "Jac* Gros*" in Illinois and Missouri

Group c, completed task 1: The question each element answers:

- 313–14 *(Wherein)*
- "Biographical," in *Portrait and Biographical Record of Randolph, Jackson, Perry, and Monroe Counties, Illinois* (What)
- 1894 *(When)*
- Chicago: Biographical Publishing *(Whereis)*

Group c, completed task 2: The elements logically sequenced

- "Biographical," in *Portrait and Biographical Record of Randolph, Jackson, Perry, and Monroe Counties, Illinois*
- Chicago: Biographical Publishing
- 1894
- 313–14

Group d, completed task 1: The question each element answers:

- Belleville, Ill. *(Whereis)*
- page 3, col. 1 *(Wherein)*
- "Jacob Gross and Wife Wed Half Century: Freeburg Couple celebrate Golden Wedding at Singer Hall in that City Sunday," *Belleville News-Democrat* (What)
- 1 August 1921 *(When)*

Group d, completed task 2: The elements logically sequenced

- "Jacob Gross and Wife Wed Half Century: Freeburg Couple celebrate Golden Wedding at Singer Hall in that City Sunday" *Belleville News-Democrat*
- Belleville, Ill.
- 1 August 1921
- page 3, col. 1

Chapter 5 exercise answers

33. *In the Greenfield article in appendix A, footnotes 8, 18, 30, 65, 88, and 89, what are the functions of the paired square brackets and the content between them?*

    In Greenfield footnote 8, the square brackets surround an author addition to the title of an online record collection. The addition shows that the source is not a modern database.

    In Greenfield footnote 18, square brackets surround clarifying words that the author inserted into a quotation.

    In Greenfield footnote 30, square brackets surround the spelled-out meanings of initialisms within a quotation. The square brackets signify that those meanings are not in the quoted material. Instead, they are the author's additions.

    In Greenfield footnote 65, square brackets surround the author's correction to a dwelling number recorded incorrectly.

    In Greenfield footnote 88, square brackets surround the Latin word *sic* (meaning *thus*), showing that the illogical spelling appears in the cited record.

    In Greenfield footnote 89, square brackets surround the word *blank*. This shows that the record keeper did not fill in the space for the child's first name.

34. *For the citations in Greenfield footnotes 2, 3, 10, and 23, explain why the capitalized and uncapitalized words appear the way they do.*

    In Greenfield footnote 2 the first words of citations, person's names, and a month are capitalized. All other words are the author's descriptions and comments.

    In Greenfield footnote 3 the first word, proper nouns (names and places), initialisms, and the formal titles of records, collections, and military units are capitalized headline style. The researcher's descriptive words, including *questionnaire* and *pension no.*, are lowercased.

    In Greenfield footnote 10 names of places and people are capitalized. The other words are the author's, showing the source bears no page numbers and giving his generic descriptions of what numbers refer to.

In Greenfield footnote 23 the formal titles of the record, the record collection, and the record group are capitalized headline style, as are the repository's initialism and city. Lowercased are prepositions and conjunctions in headline-style capitalization, the identification of CC 462 as a folder and a description of folder CC 462's form.

35. *In Greenfield footnote 18, line 8, what are the punctuation marks around* tons *and why are they there?*

    Those are single quotation marks, used in footnote 18 because they surround a quotation within a quotation. The cited source uses double quotation marks around the word *tons*. Changing the original double quotation marks to single quotation marks avoids confusing what the article's author quoted (the passage) with what the source creator quoted (the word *tons*).

36. *For the citations in Greenfield footnote 22, explain why the capitalized and uncapitalized words appear as they do.*

    Names of people, places, and publishers are capitalized, and formal titles of publication and collections are capitalized headline style. Lowercased are conjunctions and prepositions within titles and the author's words used generically.

37. *What is the purpose of the colons in the citations in Greenfield footnote 30?*

    The first colon in footnote 30 separates a publication title from its subtitle. The second colon is part of a waypoint's name, and the third colon indicates that something (a quotation, in this example) is to follow. The fourth colon appears within the quotation, where it has a similar function (signifying that something is to follow). The fifth and sixth colons separate article titles from their subtitles.

38. *In Greenfield footnote 1, what are the functions of the commas and semicolons in the first citation?*

    The semicolons divide the citation's segments into three groups: a description of the source; a comment on the original record's unknown location; and the form, date, and location of a copy. Commas in the first segment set off an introductory phrase, an appositive ("two handwritten pages" and the title refer to the same item), and a phrase about the date. In the third segment, commas set off the date from what precedes it and what follows it.

39. *In Greenfield footnotes 3 and 72, what are the functions of the ellipsis dots?*

    In footnote 3, the ellipsis dots show that the author omitted part of the title of a collection. In footnote 72, they show that he omitted part of the title of a source.

40. *Explain the greater-than signs in Greenfield footnote 71.*

    The greater-than signs separate waypoints—descriptions of clickable titles leading from a website to a numbered image.

41. *What is the first footnote in the Greenfield article that cites a publication title? How can you easily find it?*

    Footnote 4 cites the publication titled *Seeking Michigan*. It is easy to find because the citation contains italics (signifying a publication's title).

42. *What are the functions of the dashes, hyphens, and semicolons in Greenfield footnote 23?*

    En dashes separate inclusive page numbers (16–21) and inclusive years (1809–1894). They also create a hyphenated term where at least one side contains more than one word. (In this example, the initialism *NA* represents the words *National Archives*.) The hyphens in this citation join word pairs into phrasal adjectives, *sixty-seven* and *Court-Martial*. Jointly, not separately, those hyphenated words modify, respectively *unbound paginated folios* and *Case Files*.

    The four semicolons group the citation into five segments. The segments reflect nested levels ranging from a six-page source up to a city. The segments are *(a)* the title of the source and its relevant page numbers, *(b)* the title and description of the folder containing that source, *(c)* the title and dates of the collection containing that folder, *(d)* the number and title of the record group containing that collection, and *(e)* the initialism for the building containing that record group and the city where it is located.

43. *What are the functions of the parentheses in the citations in Greenfield footnotes 1, 2, 3, 4, and 17?*

    In footnote 1 parentheses announce three initialisms: *FHL* for *Family History Library*, *ED* for *enumeration district*, and *NARA* for *National Archives and Records Administration*. Only the initialisms will appear in the article's subsequent citations.

    In footnote 2, parentheses set off married women's maiden names.

    In footnote 3, parentheses set off a description of George's military service. The parentheses keep the description's four parts together. (Commas instead of parentheses could cause confusion). Because no punctuation precedes the opening parenthesis, the parenthetical information clearly applies to George.

    In footnote 4, the first two parentheses surround a URL, answering the *Whereis* citation question. The second pair of parentheses set off the year of a death certificate. This is a common format for state vital records grouped by year.

In footnote 17, the parentheses surround the source's publication details, as they do in footnote 4. Because the publication cited in footnote 17 is an offline book, the parenthetical information gives publication place, publisher name, and year.

44. *What are the purposes of the quotation marks in the citations in Greenfield footnote 18?*

    The first set surrounds a long quotation. The second set surrounds the title of a part of a publication.

45. *What are the purposes of the slashes in the citations in Greenfield footnote 7?*

    They separate segments of a web page's URL.

46. *The following citations are capitalized and punctuated:*

    Randolph Co., Ill., Birth Record 1:120, no. 1537, Edgar F. Guker; County Clerk, Chester, Ill.; FHL microfilm 973,995.

    St. Michael's Roman Catholic Church (Paderborn, Ill.), Deaths, Marriages, unpaginated, 1871 marriages, no. 4, Gross-Hausman, 3 August 1871; Diocese of Belleville, Belleville, Ill.

    1900 U.S. census, City of St. Louis, Mo., pop. sch., ED 6, sheet 5A, dwell. 76, fam. 102, Andrew Clark household; NARA microfilm, T623, roll 889.

    Note: Without seeing those records, this book's readers would not know whether or not to capitalize *birth record, deaths, marriages,* and *census.*

Chapter 6 exercise answers

For each kind of source listed below, find at least two citation examples.

47. *Published book*

    Footnote 17, *New York Family History Research Guide and Gazetteer*; and many others

48. *Published microfilm*

    Footnote 22, *Register of Enlistments in the U.S. Army, 1798–1914;* and others

49. *Unpublished microfilm*

    Footnote 1, Antrim Co., Mich., Records of Deaths 3:69; FHL microfilm 980,363—and other citations

50. *Unpublished material viewed on-site*

    Footnote 3, questionnaire 3—402; and others

51. *Unpublished material in personal files*

    Footnote 2, interview notes in author's files; and others

52. *Previously unpublished material viewed as published images*

    Footnote 4, *Seeking Michigan;* and many others, including most of the *FamilySearch* citations

53. *Source material created for online publication*

    Footnote 18, *Google Maps, The USGenWeb Project;* and many others

Chapter 7 exercise answers

54. *Identify the titles of sources, the titles of source parts, and any subtitles in Greenfield footnote 30.*

    "GEDmatch forums," *GEDmatch: Tools for DNA and Genealogy Research* (part's title, source's title and subtitle)

    "GEDmatch.com: DNA One-to-One Comparison Entry Form," *GEDmatch* (part's title and subtitle, source's title)

    "Category: Glossary," *ISOGG Wiki* (part's title and subtitle, source's title)

    (Other elements in these citations answer the *Who, When, Wherein,* and *Whereis* citation questions.)

55. *In Greenfield footnote 36, what are the answers to the* What *citation question?*

    "New York, Probate Records, 1629–1971," *FamilySearch*

    estate papers, file 02871, James Greenfield

    inventory

    (Other elements in these citations answer the *Who, When, Wherein,* and *Whereis* citation questions.)

56. *In Greenfield footnotes 23 and 43, what is the purpose of the quotation marks?*

    In footnote 23, the quotation marks surround the title of an unpublished narrative. This is a common usage of quotation marks in citations.

    In footnote 43, the quotation marks surround the title of a record book. This is not a common usage of quotation marks in citations. This example, however, is an unusual title for a record book. The quotation marks tell readers that the given title, although unusual, is correct.

57. *In Greenfield footnote 52, what is the first source cited? Is this a title or description? How do you know?*

The first source cited is a membership application. This is a description because it is capitalized sentence style. (Headline style capitalization would signal that it is the application's formal title.)

58. *What is the last source cited in Greenfield footnote 52?*

    The last source cited is a letter. Pease's membership application file answers the *Whereis* citation question; "letter to Mrs. Edward Cooch (Registrar General, NSDAR)" answers the *What* question.

59. *In Greenfield footnote 7, how are the three citations' answers to the* What *citation question similar?*

    All three cite a publication and a part of a publication. The first citation, using sentence-style capitalization, describes a source viewed as an image on the *FamilySearch* website. The second citation, using headline style capitalization, gives *FamilySearch's* title of a searchable database. The third citation, also using sentence-style capitalization, cites the title on *Ancestry* for one of its collections of images.

60. *Greenfield footnotes 1 and 2 cite photocopies made for personal use. What might be the reasons for citing them instead of the underlying sources?*

    In footnote 1, the original record's whereabouts are now unknown. Because the photocopy can be cited in full, including a repository where researchers can view the photocopy, it is the better source to cite. Citing the original record, in a place where it no longer exists, would be unhelpful.

    In footnote 2, the holder of the original letter does not welcome contact from researchers. Thus, the accessible photocopy is cited.

Using sources consulted in your own genealogical research, answer the What citation question for one or more sources of each of the following types. Include any descriptive words that might be helpful.

61. *Published books*

    Check your examples against these guidelines:

    Book titles will be italicized and capitalized headline style. A colon will separate a book title from its first (or only) subtitle (if any). Semicolons will separate any subsequent subtitles.

    Titles of parts of books will appear between quotation marks and not in italics. A colon will separate the part's title and subtitle (if any). In citations, titles of book parts usually precede book titles, but they sometimes appear after book titles (and any parenthetical information after book titles) or after the page numbers answering the *Wherein* citation question.

Descriptive words and abbreviations (for example, 2nd. ed., 18 vols.), and other information can follow the title of a book title or its part. Capitalized sentence style, the descriptive information follows what it describes.

62. *Print periodicals*

    Check your examples against these guidelines:

    Periodical titles will be italicized headline style. A colon will separate a periodical title from its subtitle (if any).

    Cited article titles appear between quotation marks and not in italics. They usually appear before the periodical title.

    Rarely do descriptive words precede or follow a journal or article title.

63. *Online publications*

    Check your examples against these guidelines:

    Website titles will be italicized and capitalized headline style. A colon will separate a website title from its first (or only) subtitle (if any). Semicolons will separate any subsequent subtitles.

    Titles of web pages will appear between quotation marks and not in italics. A colon will separate a web page's title from its subtitle (if any). Cited web page titles most often precede the website title, but they sometimes appear after the website title and any parenthetical information after that title.

    Descriptive words and abbreviations (for example, blog, digital images), and other information can follow the title of a website or web page. Capitalized sentence style, the descriptive information follows what it describes.

64. *CD-ROM publications, microfilm publications, or both*

    Check your examples against these guidelines:

    CD-ROM titles will be italicized and capitalized headline style. A colon will separate a CD-ROM's title from its first (or only) subtitle (if any). Semicolons will separate any subsequent subtitles.

    Titles of parts of a CD-ROM's content will appear between quotation marks and not in italics. A colon will separate the part's title from its subtitle (if any). In citations, titles of parts of CD-ROMs most often precede the title, but they sometimes appear after the title (and any parenthetical information after that title).

    Descriptive words, abbreviations (for example, *CD-ROM*), and other information can follow a CD-ROM title.

65. *Untitled sources*

Check your examples against these guidelines:

If the source does not bear a title, describe it briefly but unambiguously. Readers should be able to understand from your description what the source is and to recognize it when they see it.

Your description should be capitalized sentence style.

Chapter 8 exercise answers

66. *In the Greenfield article, footnote 2, what is the answer to the* Who *citation question for both citations? How do you know what those persons' roles were in creating the cited sources?*

    Bernice (Leach) Turner, as informant, and Fern (Leach) Dr'y, as letter writer, are the creators of both cited sources. Their names appear first in each citation, the usual position for the answer to the *Who* citation question.

67. *Greenfield footnote 3, second citation, shows a source within a source. What is the answer to the* Who *citation question for each?*

    George M. D. Tucker, is the creator of the information on the filled-in form. That form is part of pension file no. S.C. 874,447, created by the Pension Bureau, now the Department of Veterans Affairs (DVA). Its historical records, like those of most federal agencies, are at the National Archives.

68. *In Greenfield footnote 23, what is the answer to the* Who *citation question?*

    The Office of the Judge Advocate General (Army) created the cited record.

69. *In Greenfield footnote 38, who is the informant? How is the informant's identity shown?*

    Probably Laura (Greenfield) Au. Discussion in the footnote identifies her and suggests she provided the information in the cited article.

70. *Greenfield footnote 36 cites an image and describes the source underlying the image. How does the citation answer the* Who *citation question?*

    Herkimer Co., N.Y., created the estate papers file. FamilySearch created a digital image of the papers within the file. Stephen Greenfield, James Greenfield, and Thomas Greenfield created the inventory within the file.

Use sources from your own genealogical research to answer the Who *citation question for the source categories listed in exercises 71–73. Include any descriptive words that might be helpful.*

71. *Sources created by organizations that are not governments*

    The organization's name should be capitalized like it appears on the source. If the organization's role in producing the source is unclear, you can add clarifying words, capitalized sentence style, after the organization's name.

72. *Sources created by private individuals*

    The answer would be a person's name. This could be an article or book author, letter writer, photographer, or interviewee. Descriptive words (or abbreviations) might be compiler, editor, translator, or transcriber. If the source is unpublished, you also could include the person's address, or just the city and state, in parentheses after the person's name.

73. *Sources created by governments*

    Governmental sources used by genealogists usually are created by governments from national to local levels. The answer to *Who* would be the name of the government that created the official record.

74. *Under what circumstances could you omit the answer to the* Who *question in a citation you are crafting?*

    When the creator's name is an organization, not a person, and it is also the source title or the publisher's name; also when the creator's name is unknown. *[page 87]*

Chapter 9 exercise answers

75. *Greenfield footnotes 1 (its first citation), 2 (its second citation), and 18 (within the .5quotation), cite unknown dates in different ways. What are those ways, and why do they differ?*

    Footnote 1 says *probably late 1880s,* footnote 2 says *probably 1972,* and footnote 18 says *in the 1940s.* These estimates show different degrees of specificity ranging from a probable single year to a decade. The wording of all three shows they are estimates.

76. *Greenfield footnote 18, the last citation, has two answers to the* When *citation question. What does each refer to?*

    January 2007 refers to the date of the cited report. The URL access date, cited generically before footnote 1, was *13 December 2015.*

77. *Explain the answer to the* When *citation question in Greenfield footnote 44, the second citation.*

    The cited marriage date spans four days. They encompass the dates of the application, issuance of the license, and date of the marriage. Also, above footnote 1, the author cited the image viewing date for all the online sources supporting the Greenfield article.

78. *How many answers to the* When *citation question appear in Greenfield footnote 52? What do they tell you?*

    The membership application was approved on 30 October 1942. The transcription is dated 4 September 1942; a letter, 21 January 1928; the sworn statement, 2 February 1942; and a letter, 4 September 1942. Together they give the provenance of material supporting a DAR application.

Using materials from your own research, answer the When *citation question for the kinds of sources listed in exercises 79–83:*

79. *One or more books*

    Your answer is the book's copyright year. If it is a federal government publication, it has no copyright year and you cite the publication year.

80. *One or more journals or magazines*

    Your answer will be the month or season plus year, or the exact date, whichever appears on the journal or magazine. If no season, month, or date appears on the issue, you cite the issue number.

81. *One or more websites.*

    This will be your access, downloading, or viewing date. If the website shows a "last updated" date or a copyright year, you may cite it as well.

82. *One or more unpublished sources for which only one answer to* When *is helpful.*

    This will be either the event date or the recording date. If the date is not specified, you should estimate it, if at all possible, and use wording indicating that you made an estimate.

83. *One or more unpublished sources for which more than one answer to* When *is helpful.*

    This will be the dates your source shows as the event date, recording date, or another date. You also may cite any other dates (like a court appearance date) that might help you and your readers understand and evaluate the unpublished source. Do not, however, cite dates "just because they are there."

84. *Under what circumstances is it acceptable to not give a date as the answer to the* When *question in a citation you are crafting?*

    When the source shows no date and no date can be reasonably estimated. *[pages 92–93]*

Chapter 10 exercise answers

85. *In Greenfield footnote 3, second citation, what are the source's nested levels? How are they sequenced in the citation? What are the citation's answers to the* What *and* Wherein *citation questions?*

    The levels are sequenced from specific to general. They are a record, file containing it, collection of case files, series of collections, record group containing the series, building housing the record group, city, and district.

    The answer to *What* is *questionnaire 3—402*. Because this is a single printed form, the specific line or item does not need to be cited. The other nested levels answer the *Wherein* citation question.

86. *In Greenfield footnote 4, first citation, what are the source's nested levels? How are they sequenced in the citation? What are the citation's answers to the* What *and* Wherein *citation questions?*

    The levels, sequenced roughly from general to specific, are the 1850 U.S. census as a whole, county (and its state), town, pages, dwelling/family numbers, and household name. The answer to the *What* citation question is 1850 U.S. census. The other levels answer the *Wherein* question.

87. *In Greenfield footnote 24, what are the source's nested levels? How are they sequenced in the citation?*

    The levels, sequenced from general to specific, are title of a multi-volume set, one volume's number, a page within that volume, a law ("chapter") on that page, and a section within that law.

88. *In Greenfield footnote 30, first citation, what are the source's nested levels? How are they sequenced in the citation?*

    Sequenced from general to specific, they are the website and its titled part, three waypoints leading to discussion-thread subject, and a numbered message in that thread.

89. *Greenfield footnote 39 uses nested levels to cite two unpublished sources. What are each source's levels, and how are they sequenced in the citation?*

    In the first source, the levels—cited from specific to general—are a record, file containing that record, office housing the file, city, and state.

    In the second source, the levels—cited from specific to general—are a widow's declaration, bounty-land-warrant file containing that paper, collection containing that file, record group (RG) containing that collection, building housing that record group (*NA* for *National Archives*), and its city.

90. *Greenfield footnote 61, second citation, references an unpublished image of an unpublished archival record. What are the nested levels in this source? How are they arranged in the citation? How does the citation answer the* What *and* Wherein *citation questions?*

    The levels follow two sequences. After the source creator, the citation continues with a volume of death records, page within that volume, and record on that page—a general-to-specific sequence. Then the citation continues in a specific-to-general sequence: the volume's numbered container, series including that container, record group containing the series, building housing the record group, its city, and its province. The FHL microfilm information is supplementary.

91. *Arranged for a citation to a publication:*

    The Great Migration: Immigrants to New England, 1634–1635

    vol. 1

    p. 92

    Alice Ashby [item]

92. *Arranged for a citation to a publication:*

    New York Historical Manuscripts: English [series title]

    vol. 22

    Administrative Papers of Governors Richard Nicolls and Francis Lovelace, 1664–1673 [volume title]

    p. 76

93. *Arranged for a citation to an unpublished source:*

    "1779 Land Tax list of the South East Quarter of the Manor of Ranselear District in the County of Albany"

    folder 7

    box 2

New York Treasurer's Office Account and Tax Assessment Lists, series A3210

New York State Archives

Albany

94. *Arranged for a citation to an unpublished source:*

    Claim no. 283, pension for Enos Greenfield

    Final Payment Vouchers, 1818–1864

    Record Group 217: Records of the Accounting Officers of the Department of the Treasury

    National Archives

    Washington

    D.C.

95. *Arranged for a citation to a multivolume set:*

    "The Story of the Vessels Built in Connecticut for the Continental Navy: II, The Confederacy"

    in *Records and Papers of the New London County Historical Society*

    vol. 1

    p. 61

96. *Sequence an answer to the* Wherein *citation question for books used in your own research. Include at least one example of each of the following:*

    - *Titled multivolume set with volume numbers and no volume titles*
    - *Titled multivolume set with volume numbers and titles*
    - *A multivolume set with numbered series and volume number (could be a book series or a journal series)*
    - *A multivolume set with volume titles and a series title*

    Refer to table 15 for the essential and optional elements for each kind of multivolume set.

97. *Sequence an answer to the* Wherein *citation question for at least one offline unpublished source with nested levels used in your own genealogical research.*

    Your citation likely will show the levels in a specific-to-general sequence. Other sequences are acceptable, if they are easy to understand. See table 12.

98. *Sequence an answer to the* Wherein *citation question for serials used in your own genealogical research. Include at least one example of each of the following:*

- *Journal*
- *Newspaper*

The answer to *Wherein* for a journal or a newspaper will be one or more page numbers. For a newspaper, the answer typically includes a column number.

Chapter 11 exercise answers

99. *In Greenfield footnote 4, second citation, what is the answer to the* Wherein *citation question? What information does the citation imply but does not state? Is that information necessary to cite? Why or why not?*

    The answer to *Wherein* is the certificate year and number. The implied information is that citation users have to search within the website to find the record. Because that becomes obvious from the page at the cited URL, adding the information to the citation seems to add little value.

100. *In Greenfield footnote 5, second citation, what is the answer to the* Wherein *citation question? Which of the six options in table 16 does the citation use? Why do you think the author chose that option and not one of the others?*

    Two waypoints, leading from the online collection to the images, answer the *Wherein* question. This citation uses option 6, waypoints (citing what the researcher used and what the reader is likely to use). Formatted like a standard one-part citation for a publication, that citation enables readers to turn directly to the cited information. Waypoints often are more stable than links and URLs.

101. *In Greenfield footnote 5, second citation, is the cited source an original record, derivative record, or authored narrative? How do you know? What information does this citation document? Who provided that information? How do you know? Is that information primary or secondary? How do you know? What is that citation's answer to the* Whereis *question?*

    The citation refers to a published image of an original record, an estate distribution in a probate file. The record is dated 1853, according to the citation, which indicates it is an original record. The waypoints show it was filed with a court with jurisdiction over a county. The citation documents the Huffman surname and composition of Isaac's family. The source does not name its informant-creator, but the administrator or executor of Isaac Huffman's estate would have prepared a record with this record's title. Thus, the information likely is primary.

This citation's answer to *Whereis* is the URL for the image collection's home page.

102. *The first citation in Greenfield footnote 7 (1855 census) and the citation in footnote 10 refer to different information in the same source. How do you describe the difference between the two citations' formats? Is the absence of an image number in footnote 10 a problem? Why or why not? What else is intentionally omitted from the citation in footnote 10?*

    Footnote 7, the first citation, uses a full reference-note citation format, and footnote 10 uses a shortened reference-note citation format, for citing a previously cited source.

    The dwelling and family numbers cited in footnote 10 appear on the image cited in footnote 7. That makes repeating the image number unnecessary for footnote 10. The citation also omits the information about the images' online publication, since that would be the same information as in footnote 7.

103. *In Greenfield footnote 7, which of the six options for answering the* Wherein *citation question for an online information item does the citation show? What answer does the citation give?*

    Greenfield footnote 7, the last citation, uses option 6, waypoints, for citing information from online sources. It answers *Wherein* with the three waypoints between the cited collection and the image. The citation's last two lines specify the underlying source and information that the image shows.

104. *The second citation (1865 census) in Greenfield footnote 7 documents a negative online search. How does this citation differ from one that documents a specific information item (like the first citation, to the 1855 census, in footnote 7)?*

    The second citation is a one-part citation to a FamilySearch database. Giving the online collection title, the website title, and a summary of the search, the citation uses the format for citing a page in a book's titled chapter. The first citation provides a series of waypoints to navigate from the collection to specific information.

105. *In Greenfield footnote 18, third citation (*Google Maps*), what is the answer to the* Wherein *question? Is further information needed? Why or why not? If yes, what could be added to the citation? What is that citation's answer to the* Whereis *question?*

The citation's answer to *Wherein* describes a search. Readers using the citation would click on the map's "Directions" icon (an arrow) and then enter the two places cited. This would be obvious to most readers using the citation, and citations usually do not give directions for using a research tool. If readers might not understand that the modern addresses are the sites of the poorhouse and Isaac Huffman's land, that information could be added.

The citation's answer to *Whereis* is the URL for the website's home page.

106. *The author used an online image for the source cited in Greenfield footnote 24, but the published citation does not acknowledge it. What might be his rationale? Where is this source online? The citation appears differently in the author's working notes. What differences would you expect?*

   The citation references a published book. The website merely shows images of that publication. It has not modified what the book shows or created a new edition. Researchers and readers have many options for locating the publication online and in brick-and-mortar libraries. Thus, citing the place where one researcher viewed the book is not helpful information.

   Images of this book, or PDF downloads of it, appear on the websites *Archive.org, The Constitution Society,* the Library of Congress, *Wikisource,* and elsewhere. The author's working notes are likely to cite both the offline book and the place he viewed its images. That expanded citation makes it possible for him to check his work without repeating his original search. The citation in footnote 24, in a printed work, is more concise.

107. *In Greenfield footnote 28, first citation, what is the answer to the* Wherein *citation question? Referring to table 16, identify the option the author used for answering the* Wherein *question about online information. What is that citation's answer to the* Whereis *question?*

   The URL answers the *Wherein* citation question because it points to the cited web page. This is option 4 from table 16. The URL also answers the *Whereis* question.

108. *Greenfield footnote 30, first citation, includes a sentence after the citation. Does it help answer the* Wherein *citation question, even though it is separate from the citation? Why or why not?*

   The sentence quotes a sentence from a short message-board posting. It helps the citation document a statement in the narrative, but it is not needed to help answer the Wherein *citation* question.

109. *Answer the* Wherein *citation question for online sources from your own genealogical research with the following sets of characteristics:*

- *Simple search terms lead directly to the information of interest.*

  Your answer likely will resemble the examples under option 3 on pages 117–18.

- *Digital images or cited information items have stable URLs, and the website structure makes cited information easy to find.*

  Your answer likely will resemble the example under option 4 on pages 118–19.

- *An indexed or unindexed collection shows titled or numbered collections without waypoints.*

  Depending on characteristics of the source you choose, your answer likely will resemble the examples under options 4 and 5 on pages 118–19.

- *An indexed or unindexed collection shows numbered images in titled or numbered collections with waypoints*

  Your answer likely will resemble the example under option 6 on page 120.

Chapter 12 exercise answers

110. *The two citations in Greenfield footnote 2 give a cryptic answer to the* Whereis *citation question. Why are no repository, city, and state cited in this context? Also, why is the* Wherein *citation question not answered?*

    The author's name and contact information appear above footnote 1. A finished product need not repeat this information in each citation to the same author's files or collections. Page numbers are the likely answer to *Wherein* for interview notes and a letter. Their absence in footnote 2 suggests the notes and letter are brief, perhaps one page each, or the pages are unnumbered. In the latter case, citing them as "unpaginated" would be conventional.

111. *In Greenfield footnote 3, what is the answer to the* Whereis *citation question?*

    The answer is the National Archives building in Washington, D.C.

112. *In Greenfield footnote 6, second citation (the questionnaire), what locations does the cryptic answer to the* Whereis *citation question refer to? Where is the short initialism announced? Why does it differ from the more familiar initialism NARA?*

    The *Whereis* answer refers to the National Archives building in Washington, D.C. Footnote 3, in its last line, announces that initialism. *NARA*, an acronym for *National Archives and Records Administration*, refers to the name of a federal agency. The initialism *NA* refers to the buildings housing that agency.

113. *In Greenfield footnote 17, what is the answer to* Whereis*?*

    The answer is the publisher's location and name—New York: New York Genealogical and Biographical Society

114. *In Greenfield footnote 18, second citation (the atlas), who was the publisher? How do you know?*

    David H. Burr published the book. *Privately published* usually means the author self-published the book.

115. *In Greenfield footnote 22, first citation, decode the information in parentheses.*

    The abbreviation *D.C.* refers to the *District of Columbia;* the acronym *NARA* refers to the *National Archives and Records Administration;* and the abbreviation *n.d.* means *no date,* showing that the publication bears no publication date.

116. *In Greenfield footnote 37, first citation, citing the book as "privately published" or "privately printed" could mislead readers. Why?*

    Citing the book as privately published or printed would tell readers, incorrectly, that the author was the publisher. The church published the book.

117. *In Greenfield footnote 39, first citation, explain the capitalization in the answer to the* Whereis *citation question.*

    Mather file and Cayuga Co. historian's office are capitalized sentence style. That capitalization signals that those phrases are the author's descriptions, not formal titles.

118. *What answer does Greenfield footnote 43 give to the* Whereis *citation question? What does that answer tell you about the creator? Why is that answer omitted from the citation in footnote 46?*

    The citation's answer to *Whereis* is First Baptist Church of North Utica, North Utica, N.Y. The name of the creator, Deerfield Baptist Church, could have changed to First Baptist Church of North Utica, or the Deerfield church could have closed and the First Baptist Church acquired its records. The *Whereis* answer is omitted from the citation in footnote 46 because that subsequent citation to the same source is a shortened citation.

119. *Greenfield footnote 52, first citation, gives a fifteen-word answer to the* Whereis *citation question. Why is it so long?*

    The fifteen words are the seven-word name of the building, its initialism, the five-word name of the office within the building, the city, and the city's location. Omitting any of the words might cause confusion.

120. *The second citation in Greenfield footnote 61, like many other citations to GSU/FamilySearch microfilm, includes a repository. Because the source was viewed on microfilm elsewhere, why does this kind of citation include the repository?*

GSU/FamilySearch microfilm is unpublished, which means its availability is limited to designated places. Citing the underlying source's repository gives researchers and readers another option for accessing the record.

121. *In Greenfield footnote 84, last citation (the finding aid), why does the answer to the* Whereis *citation question omit the state?*

    Western Michigan University would be only in Michigan. Telling readers that a Michigan university is in Michigan is unnecessary.

122. *In Greenfield footnote 87, last citation (the newspaper), what is the answer to the* Whereis *citation question?*

    Grand Rapids, Mich., the publisher's location.

123. *Why does the citation in Greenfield footnote 88 not answer the* Whereis *citation question?*

    The citation in footnote 86 tells where the cited volume is located. Repeating that information in a later citation is unnecessary.

124. *From your own research, answer the* Whereis *citation questions for one or more published sources in each of six categories:*

    - *Book*

      Your answer will be a publisher name and its city and state. If the author self-published the book, however, your answer will be *privately published* or *privately printed.*

    - *CD-ROM*

      Your answer will be a publisher name and its city and state.

    - *Microfilm*

      Your answer will be a publisher name and its city and state.

    - *Journal*

      Your answer will be the journal title.

    - *Newspaper*

      Your answer will be the newspaper title and its city and state or province.

125. *From your own research, answer the* Whereis *citation question for one or more unpublished sources in each of six kinds of repositories:*

    - *Archive*

      Your answer will be the name of the archive and its city and state or province.

- *County, state, or provincial government building or office*

  Your answer will be the name of the agency or office and its city and state or province.

- *Local government building or office*

  Your answer will be the name of the agency or office, its city, and its state or province.

- *National government building or office*

  Your answer will be the name of the agency or office and its city and state or province.

- *Religious organization location or office*

  Your answer will be the name of the organization (for example, church, diocese, mosque, parish, or synagogue) and its city and state or province.

- *Anyone's personal files*

  Your answer will be the name of the person and the person's e-mail and postal addresses. If the person does not want you to share any of that information, you will remove it before sharing and note that information was removed.

126. *Describe the provenance of one or more privately held or online sources used in your own genealogical research.*

    Your answer will describe the source's "chain of title" from its place of creation to its present repository.

Chapter 13 exercise answers

127. *What is the first example in the Greenfield article of a citation to original online content? How does that citation answer the* Wherein *citation question? What statement or information does the cited source document?*

   Footnote 7, the second citation, cites a negative search of an online database. The specified search term answers *Wherein.* The citation documents the statement that Franklin "was not enumerated in 1865."

128. *Greenfield footnote 18, last citation, describes original online information. Referring to page 137, devise two different ways for that citation to point precisely to specific information of interest.*

   Describe where the information is on the page (option 2):

   > See Christine J. Spengler, "A Report With Some Photo Images From County House Cemetery: Town Of Sennett—Cayuga County, New York," January 2007, at *The USGenWeb Project* (http://www.rootsweb.ancestry.com/~nycayuga/cem/cem197a/index.htm : viewed 20 February 2017), fourth paragraph.

   Give a unique phrase to search for (option 3):

   > See Christine J. Spengler, "A Report With Some Photo Images From County House Cemetery: Town Of Sennett—Cayuga County, New York," January 2007, at *The USGenWeb Project* (http://www.rootsweb.ancestry.com/~nycayuga/cem/cem197a/index.htm : viewed 20 February 2017), search for "I was told by."

129. *Does Greenfield footnote 54, last five lines, cite original online content? Why or why not?*

   The cited web page mentions a reading in 1928. The online transcription of that reading, which could contain accidental omissions and typographical errors. The web page last updated that content in 2009. The keyboarding and apparently some of the content differ from the 1928 record, suggesting that the website presents a mixture of new online content and previously unpublished content.

130. *Create a free account online at https://familysearch.org/register/, sign in, and then cite the original online information at this* URL:

    https://familysearch.org/wiki/en/Genealogical_Society_of_Utah

    Your citation should resemble—not necessarily match—this one:

    "Genealogical Society of Utah," *FamilySearch* (https://familysearch.org/wiki/en/Genealogical_Society_of_Utah : viewed 20 February 2017).

131. *Create a free account at https://www.gedmatch.com/. Then, using* GEDMatch's *default settings, run a "'One-to-one' compare" analysis on kits T829710 and T316184. Finally, cite the resulting report.*

    Your citation should resemble—not necessarily match—this one:

    "GEDmatch.Com Autosomal Comparison - V2.1.1(c)," *GEDmatch* (https://www.gedmatch.com/ : viewed 20 February 2017), comparison of kits T829710 (Thomas Wright Jones) and T316184 (Raymond Leach).

132. *Cite a negative "Descendants" search at this* URL:

    http://services.dar.org/Public/DAR_Research/search/

    Your citation should resemble—not necessarily match—this one:

    "Descendants Search," *DAR: Daughters of the American Revolution* (https://services.dar.org/Public/DAR_Research/search/ : used on 20 February 2017), search for "[the name that you searched for]."

133. *From your own research, cite at least three* Find A Grave *resources:*

    - *A memorial essay only*
    - *A grave-marker image only*
    - *An entry with both a memorial essay and a grave-marker image*

    Your answers should resemble the examples on pages 139–40.

134. *From your own research, cite negative searches on the* Ancestry *or* FamilySearch *website or both.*

    Your answers should resemble the example at the bottom of table 19, on page 141.

Chapter 14 exercise answers

135. *Which of the five options listed in table 20 would you use for your working notes or works in progress? Why is that your choice?*

    Any answer other than number 1 is correct, especially for working notes. Your answer, however, might resemble this one:

    Option 1 is not recommended, and option 2 offers few advantages over other options. Option 3, the most concise option, is acceptable for citations in print media. Option 4 could be best for working notes, if it points to the image. Option 5, which points to the image and includes all the details the working researcher might need to cite the source in any venue, seems the best choice.

136. *Which of the five options listed in table 20 would you use for your BCG portfolio, ICAPGen materials, journal submission, or family history book? Why is that your choice?*

    Option 1 could confuse, so it should be avoided. The other options are acceptable, but citations in print should avoid excessive length, eliminating option 5. The remaining options are acceptable, but option 3 is the most concise.

137. *In Greenfield footnote 18, the first two citations refer to books that were viewed online. The citations do not acknowledge that online viewing. In this article's context, is that a problem? Why or why not? If it is not a problem in this context, in what context might it be a problem? Why or why not?*

    The cited images show facsimiles, so the citations meet the standard of citing what was used. Citations containing working links, however, would be convenient in working notes and when the citations appear in an electronic medium. If the images were not facsimiles or the book was difficult to find, omitting the online information could be a problem.

138. *Greenfield footnote 22, first citation, references a source with a page number viewed but not cited as image 305 of an* Ancestry *collection with a title similar to the title of the cited microfilm publication. That collection's* URL *is http://ancestry.com/search/db.aspx?dbid=1198. The waypoints forming a path from the collection to the image are > 1835–1839 > A–Z >. Suppose you*

want to cite this source in your working notes. Select an option from table 20 and craft the citation. Explain why you chose the option you used.

Your citations should resemble—not necessarily match—these:

1. "U.S. Army, Register of Enlistments, 1798–1914," *Ancestry* (http://search.ancestry.com/search/db.aspx?dbid=1198 : accessed 20 February 2017) > 1835–1839 > A–Z > image 305.

2. "U.S. Army, Register of Enlistments, 1798–1914," *Ancestry* (http://search.ancestry.com/search/db.aspx?dbid=1198 : accessed 20 February 2017) > 1835–1839 > A–Z > image 305; citing Register of Enlistments in the U.S. Army, 1798–1914, National Archives microfilm publication M233, n.d.

3. *Register of Enlistments in the U.S. Army, 1798–1914,* microfilm publication M233, 81 rolls (Washington, D.C.: NARA, n.d.), roll 20, for Descriptive and Historical Register of Enlisted Soldiers of the Army, p. 77, no. 42, Nathaniel Greenfield.

4. *Register of Enlistments in the U.S. Army, 1798–1914,* microfilm publication M233, 81 rolls (Washington, D.C.: NARA, n.d.), roll 20, for Descriptive and Historical Register of Enlisted Soldiers of the Army, p. 77, no. 42, Nathaniel Greenfield; digital image, *Ancestry* (http://search.ancestry.com/search/db.aspx?dbid=1198 : accessed 20 February 2017), image 305.

5. "U.S. Army, Register of Enlistments, 1798–1914," *Register of Enlistments in the U.S. Army, 1798–1914,* microfilm publication M233, 81 rolls (Washington, D.C.: NARA, n.d.), roll 20, for Descriptive and Historical Register of Enlisted Soldiers of the Army, p. 77, no. 42, Nathaniel Greenfield; online at *Ancestry* (http://search.ancestry.com/search/db.aspx?dbid=1198 : accessed 20 February 2017) > 1835–1839 > A–Z > image 305.

5. "U.S. Army, Register of Enlistments, 1798–1914," *Ancestry* (http://search.ancestry.com/search/db.aspx?dbid=1198 : accessed 20 February 2017) > 1835–1839 > A–Z > image 305; digital image of *Register of Enlistments in the U.S. Army, 1798–1914,* microfilm publication M233, 81 rolls (Washington, D.C.: NARA, n.d.), roll 20, for Descriptive and Historical Register of Enlisted Soldiers of the Army, p. 77, no. 42, Nathaniel Greenfield.

Option 1 is not recommended and option 2 offers few advantages over other options. Option 3, the most concise, is acceptable for citations in print. Option 4, when it points to the image, could be best for working notes. Either option 5 always will point to the image and includes all the details the working researcher might need to cite the source.

139. *Using links at https://memory.loc.gov/ammem/amlaw/lwsllink.html, locate the publication cited in Greenfield footnote 24. Using option 5 in table 20 and*

noting that you will need to gather information beyond that one image, cite this online resource.

Your citation should resemble—not necessarily match—this one:

> 5. United States, *The Statutes at Large*, vol. 17 (Boston: Little, Brown, 1873), 261, chapter 316, section 2; digital image, The Library of Congress, "A Century of Lawmaking for a New Nation: U.S. Congressional Documents and Debates, 1774–1875," *American Memory* (https://memory.loc.gov/cgi-bin/ampage?collId=llsl&fileName=017/llsl017.db&recNum=2 : viewed 20 February 2017), image 261.

140. *What strategies might you use to locate the book cited in Greenfield footnote 38? Once you found it, how would you cite it? Why would you cite it that way?*

Googling the book title leads to at least three websites providing facsimile images of the book online or in downloadable PDFs. The first of these is *Archive.org*. If you choose to cite that source, your citation will resemble some or all the parts of this one, using option 5:

> "A Centennial biographical history of Richland county, Ohio," *Archive.org* (https://archive.org/details/centennialbiogra00baug : viewed 20 February 2017); digital images and downloadable PDF of A. J. Baughman, ed., "Captain Christopher Au," in *Centennial Biographical History of Richland County, Ohio* (Chicago: Lewis, 1901), 425.

Option 1 is not recommended, and option 2 is not as good as option 3, which is ideal for print products. Option 4 shows one place to view the source, and option 5 provides complete information about the underlying publication and the online image.

141. *Using options 3, 4, and 5 from table 20 and noting that you will need to gather information beyond one image, cite each of the following in a full reference-note format:*

a. *Point your Internet browser to archive.org and search for "History of the Starr Family of New England. . . ."*

Your three citations should resemble these:

> 3. Burgis Pratt Starr, *A History of the Starr Family of New England* (Hartford, Conn.: Case, Lockwood, & Brainard, 1879), 6.
>
> 4. Burgis Pratt Starr, *A History of the Starr Family of New England* (Hartford, Conn.: Case, Lockwood, & Brainard, 1879), 6; digital image, *Archive.org* (https://archive.org/ : viewed 20 February 2017).
>
> 5. Burgis Pratt Starr, *A History of the Starr Family of New England* (Hartford, Conn.: Case, Lockwood, & Brainard, 1879), 6; digital image, "A history of the Starr family of New England . . . ," *Archive.org*

(https://archive.org/details/historyofstarrfa1879star : viewed 20 February 2017), 6.

b. *Point your Internet browser to memory.loc.gov/ammem/amlaw/, navigate to "Statutes at Large," . . .*

Your three citations should resemble these:

3. United States Congress, *The Statutes at Large*, vol. 9 (Boston: Little, Brown, 1862), 428–36, "An Act providing for the taking of the seventh and subsequent Censuses of the United States . . . ," approved 23 May 1850.

4. United States Congress, *The Statutes at Large*, vol. 9 (Boston: Little, Brown, 1862), 428–36, "An Act providing for the taking of the seventh and subsequent Censuses of the United States . . . ," approved 23 May 1850; digital image, *American Memory* (http://memory.loc.gov/ammem/amlaw/lwsllink.html : viewed 20 February 2017).

5. United States Congress, *The Statutes at Large*, vol. 9 (Boston: Little, Brown, 1862), 428–36, "An Act providing for the taking of the seventh and subsequent Censuses of the United States . . . ," approved 23 May 1850; digital image, Library of Congress, "Statutes at Large, 1789–1985," *American Memory* (http://memory.loc.gov/ammem/amlaw/lwsllink.html : viewed 20 February 2017), for vol. 9, images 428–36.

c. *Point your Internet browser to http://chroniclingamerica.loc.gov . . .*

Your three citations should resemble these:

3. "Army Rolls," *Manning Times* (Manning, S.C.), 24 February 1904, 4th page, col. 2.

4. "Army Rolls," *Manning Times* (Manning, S.C.), 24 February 1904, 4th page, col. 2; digital image, *Chronicling America: Historic American Newspapers* (http://chroniclingamerica.loc.gov/lccn/sn86063760/1904-02-24/ed-1/seq-4/ : viewed 20 February 2017).

5. "Army Rolls," *Manning Times* (Manning, S.C.), 24 February 1904, 4th page, col. 2; digital image, Library of Congress, *Chronicling America: Historic American Newspapers* (http://chroniclingamerica.loc.gov/lccn/sn86063760/1904-02-24/ed-1/seq-4/ : viewed 20 February 2017), *Manning times*, 24 February 1904, image 4.

d. *Point your Internet browser to davidrumsey.com. . . .*

Your three citations should resemble these:

3. David H. Burr, *Map of the County of Cayuga* (Albany: Surveyor General of New York, 1829).

4. David H. Burr, *Map of the County of Cayuga* (Albany: Surveyor General of New York, 1829); digital image, *David Rumsey Map Collection* (http://www.davidrumsey.com/ : viewed 20 February 2017).

5. David H. Burr, *Map of the County of Cayuga* (Albany: Surveyor General of New York, 1829); digital image, *David Rumsey Map Collection* (http://www.davidrumsey.com/ : viewed 20 February 2017), search for "Cayuga 1829."

e. *Log into FamilySearch, click "Search" and then "Books". . . .*

Your three citations should resemble these:

3. Hosea Starr Ballou, *Early Starrs in Kent and New England* (Boston: Starr Family Association, 1944), 137.

4. Hosea Starr Ballou, *Early Starrs in Kent and New England* (Boston: Starr Family Association, 1944), 137; digital images, *ExLibrisRosetta* (https://dcms.lds.org/deliveryDeliveryManagerServlet?dps_pid =IE1018811&from=fhd : viewed 20 February 2017).

5. Hosea Starr Ballou, *Early Starrs in Kent and New England* (Boston: Starr Family Association, 1944), 137; digital images, "Early Starrs in Kent and New England," *ExLibrisRosetta* (https://dcms.lds.org /delivery/DeliveryManagerServlet?dps_pid=IE1018811&from=fhd : accessed 20 February 2017), image 142.

f. *Point your Internet browser to news.google.com/newspapers. . . .*

Your three citations should resemble these:

3. "Genealogical," *Boston Evening Transcript*, 26 February 1906, p. 14, col. 2, query no. 8498.

4. "Genealogical," *Boston Evening Transcript*, 26 February 1906, p. 14, col. 2, query no. 8498; digital image, *Google News* (https://news.google.com /newspapers : viewed 20 February 2017).

5. "Genealogical," *Boston Evening Transcript*, 26 February 1906, p. 14, col. 2, query no. 8498; digital image, *Google News* (https://news.google .com/newspapers?nid=sArNgO4T4MoC : viewed 20 February 2017) > Boston Evening Transcript – Feb 26, 1906 > image 14.

g. *Point your Internet browser to hathitrust.org. . . .*

Your three citations should resemble these:

3. *Records of the First Church in Huntington, Long Island, 1723–1779: Being the Record Kept by the Rev. Ebenezer Prime, the Pastor During Those Years* (Huntington, N.Y.: Moses L. Scudder, 1899), 75.

4. *Records of the First Church in Huntington, Long Island, 1723–1779: Being the Record Kept by the Rev. Ebenezer Prime, the Pastor During Those Years* (Huntington, N.Y.: Moses L. Scudder, 1899), 75; digital image, *HathiTrust* (https://www.hathitrust.org/ : viewed 20 February 2017).

5. *Records of the First Church in Huntington, Long Island, 1723–1779: Being the Record Kept by the Rev. Ebenezer Prime, the Pastor During Those Years* (Huntington, N.Y.: Moses L. Scudder, 1899), 75; digital image, *HathiTrust*

(https://babel.hathitrust.org/cgi/pt?id=loc.ark:/13960/t5s75nk1k;view=1up;seq=11 : viewed 20 February 2017), image 75.

h. *If you are a member of the National Genealogical Society, visit the society's website. . . .*

Your three citations should resemble these:

3. Laurel T. Baty, "Aaron Strickland's North Carolina Origin," *National Genealogical Society Quarterly* 104 (March 2016): 21–37.

4. Laurel T. Baty, "Aaron Strickland's North Carolina Origin," *National Genealogical Society Quarterly* 104 (March 2016): 21–37; digital image, *National Genealogical Society* (http://www.ngsgenealogy.org/cs/ngsq_archives : viewed 20 February 2017).

5. Laurel T. Baty, "Aaron Strickland's North Carolina Origin," *National Genealogical Society Quarterly* 104 (March 2016): 21–37; digital image "NGSQ Archives," *National Genealogical Society* (http://www.ngsgenealogy.org/cs/ngsq_archives : viewed 20 February 2017), for vol. 104, no. 1, March 2016, PDF.

i. *Point your Internet browser to digitalcollections.nypl.org. . . .*

Your three citations should resemble these:

3. S. N. Beers and D. G. Beers, cartographers, "Galway," in *New Topographical Atlas of Saratoga Co., New York* (Philadelphia: Stone and Stewart, 1866), map 31.

4. S. N. Beers and D. G. Beers, cartographers, "Galway," in *New Topographical Atlas of Saratoga Co., New York* (Philadelphia: Stone and Stewart, 1866), map 31; digital image, *The New York Public Library Digital Collections* (https://digitalcollections.nypl.org : viewed 20 February 2017).

5. S. N. Beers and D. G. Beers, cartographers, "Galway," in *New Topographical Atlas of Saratoga Co., New York* (Philadelphia: Stone and Stewart, 1866), map 31; digital image, *The New York Public Library Digital Collections* (https://digitalcollections.nypl.org/items/510d47e3-c111-a3d9-e040-e00a18064a99 : viewed 20 February 2017).

Chapter 15 exercise answers

142. *Which option in table 21 did the Greenfield article's author choose for footnote 4, the last citation (to a death certificate)? How does this citation answer the* Whereis *citation question? What might you add to the citation to answer that question more explicitly?*

    The citation uses option 3. It answers the *Whereis* citation question with information about the online image publication. Information about the repository of the underlying certificate is not needed. The citation includes, however, the creator and date of the certificate, showing readers that the online publication shows an image of an original official record. A more explicit answer could describe the search terms.

143. *Greenfield footnotes 5 (second citation, to the probate record) and 7 (first and third citations, to the 1855 census and 1870 mortality schedule) use similar formats for citing previously unpublished material. How are they the same?*

    All three citations use option 3 for the citation content. Each gives information about the online publication first and adds information about what the image shows, identifying it as an original official record containing primary information. Each citation's information about the offline source is incomplete, because their only answer to the *Whereis* citation question refers to the online publication. Information about the underlying source's repository is unnecessary.

144. *In Greenfield footnote 8, what is the purpose of the information in square brackets? Which option in table 21 does this citation use?*

    This is option 3 from table 21. The added information is in the square brackets. That information helps establish that the source is a record created by a state official and clarifies that it is not a modern database transcription.

145. *Which option in table 21 does the citation in Greenfield footnote 13 use? Re-craft this citation using another option.*

This citation uses option 3, the variant with information about the underlying source first. Here are four options, including the other option-3 variant:

> 1. "New York, Land Records, 1630–1975," *FamilySearch* (https://familysearch.org/search/collection/2078654 : viewed 20 February 2017) > Cayuga > Deeds 1839–1840 vol 61–62 > image 120.
>
> 2. Cayuga Co., N.Y., Deeds 61:152–53, Huffman to Rathbun, recorded 7 June 1839; County Clerk, Auburn, N.Y.
>
> 3. "New York, Land Records, 1630–1975," *FamilySearch* (https://familysearch.org/search/collection/2078654 : viewed 20 February 2017) > Cayuga > Deeds 1839–1840 vol 61–62 > image 120, Cayuga Co., N.Y., Deeds 61:152–53, Huffman to Rathbun, recorded 7 June 1839.
>
> 4. Cayuga Co., N.Y., Deeds 61:152–53, Huffman to Rathbun, recorded 7 June 1839; County Clerk, Auburn, N.Y.; digital image, "New York, Land Records, 1630–1975," *FamilySearch* (https://familysearch.org/search/collection/2078654 : viewed 20 February 2017) > Cayuga > Deeds 1839–1840 vol 61–62 > image 120.

146. *Why does the citation in Greenfield footnote 36 omit the URL? Would you do this in your working notes? Why or why not?*

This is a shortened citation. The URL appears in footnote 5, second citation. That is the first citation to the image collection cited in footnote 36. Shortened citations are not necessary in working notes, where space factors affecting printing and mailing costs are unlikely. Also, having the URL with the notes could help the researcher turn or click to the image.

147. *Which of the four options listed in table 21 would you use for your working notes or works in progress? Why is that your choice?*

Option 3. It answers all the citation questions clearly and completely for the online image. It shows the underlying source's qualities as a provider of genealogical evidence. Option 4 also does this, but it includes unnecessary information, making the citation longer than it needs to be. Options 1 omits information essential to understanding the source's qualities. Options 1 and 2 risk misleading researchers about the source the researcher used and its context.

148. *Which of the four options listed in table 21 would you use for your BCG portfolio, ICAPGen materials, journal submission, or family history book? Why is that your choice?*

Option 3. It answers all the citation questions clearly and completely for the online image. It shows the underlying source's qualities as a provider of genealogical evidence. Option 4 also does this, but it includes unnecessary information, making the citation longer than it needs to be. Option 1 omits information essential to understanding the source's qualities. Options 1 and 2 risk misleading researchers about the source the researcher used and its context.

149. *Remembering that you will need to gather citation information from places other than an image you are viewing, cite sources a–g, listed below. Use options 3 and 4 (both variants) from table 21 to create three full reference-note citations. Then identify which versions you prefer, and explain your choice.*

Your citations should resemble—not necessarily match—the examples.

a. *Point your Internet browser to https://familysearch.org/ark:/61903/1:1:KMCQ-M24. . . .*

3. Jennings Co., Ind., Marriage Record 5:570, Donohue-Lanahan license, 4 September 1858; viewed at "Indiana Marriages, 1811–2007," *FamilySearch* (https://familysearch.org/search/collection/1410397 : viewed 20 February 2017) > Jennings > 1850–1858 Volume 5 > image 350.

3. "Indiana Marriages, 1811–2007," *FamilySearch* (https://familysearch.org/search/collection/1410397 : viewed 20 February 2017) > Jennings > 1850–1858 Volume 5 > image 350, Jennings Co., Marriage Record 5:570, Donohue-Lanahan license, 4 September 1858.

4. Jennings Co., Ind., Marriage Record 5:570, Donohue-Lanahan license, 4 September 1858, County Clerk, North Vernon, Ind.; viewed at "Indiana Marriages, 1811–2007," *FamilySearch* (https://familysearch.org/search/collection/1410397 : viewed 20 February 2017) > Jennings > 1850–1858 Volume 5 > image 350.

The second option 3 is more concise than the others. Answering all five citation questions and showing the source qualities, it contains all the information that would be needed for working notes or a printed work. The first option 3 and option 4 contain redundancy, and the offline repository information in option 4 is unhelpful.

b. *Point your Internet browser to https://familysearch.org/search/collection/1388122 . . . navigate through St. Clair. . . .*

3. "Illinois, Diocese of Belleville Parish Records, 1729–1956," *FamilySearch* (https://familysearch.org/search/collection/1388122 : viewed 20 February 2017) > St. Clair > Paderborn > St. Michael Archangel > 1861–1898 Marriages, Death > image 38, Gross-Hausman marriage, 3 August 1871.

3. St. Michael Archangel Parish (Paderborn, Ill.), "Deaths, Marriages 1861–," under 1871 marriages, Gross-Hausman marriage, 3 August 1871; viewed at "Illinois, Diocese of Bellville Parish Records, 1729–1956," *FamilySearch* (https://familysearch.org/search/collection/1388122 : viewed 20 February 2017) > St. Clair > Paderborn > St. Michael Archangel > 1861–1898 Marriages, Death > image 38.

4. St. Michael Archangel Parish (Paderborn, Ill.), "Deaths, Marriages 1861–," under 1871 marriages, Gross-Hausman, 3 August 1871, Diocese of Belleville, Belleville, Ill.; viewed at "Illinois, Diocese of Bellville Parish Records, 1729–1956," *FamilySearch* (https://familysearch.org/search/collection/1388122 : viewed 20 February 2017) > St. Clair > Paderborn > St. Michael Archangel > 1861–1898 Marriages, Death > image 38.

The first option 3 is more concise than the others. Answering all five citation questions and showing the source qualities, it contains all the information that would be needed for working notes or a printed work. The second option 3 and option 4 contain redundancy, and the offline repository information in option 4 is unhelpful.

c. *Point your Internet browser to http://s1.sos.mo.gov/records/archives/archivesdb/deathcertificates/Default.aspx, search for Cordelia Ziegler. . . .*

3. "Missouri Death Certificates, 1910–1965," *Missouri Digital Heritage* (http://s1.sos.mo.gov/records/archives/archivesdb/deathcertificates/Default.aspx : viewed 20 February 2017), search for "Cordelia Ziegler," for Standard Certificate of Death, no. 39479 (1949), PDF.

3. The Division of Health of Missouri, Standard Certificate of Death, no. 39479 (1949), Cordelia Ziegler; PDF from "Missouri Death Certificates, 1910–1965," *Missouri Digital Heritage* (http://s1.sos.mo.gov/records/archives/archivesdb/deathcertificates/Default.aspx : viewed 20 February 2017), search for "Cordelia Ziegler."

4. The Division of Health of Missouri, Standard Certificate of Death, no. 39479, Cordelia Ziegler, 14 November 1949; Missouri State Archives, Jefferson City; PDF from "Missouri Death Certificates, 1910–1965," *Missouri Digital Heritage* (http://s1.sos.mo.gov/records/archives/archivesdb/deathcertificates/Default.aspx : viewed 20 February 2017), search for "Cordelia Ziegler."

The first option 3 is more concise and contains less redundancy than the others. Answering all five citation questions and showing the source qualities, it contains all the information that would be needed for working notes or a printed work. The second option 3 and option 4 contain redundancy, and the offline repository information in option 4 is unhelpful.

d. *Create a free account at mdlandrec.net, log in, and select Queen Anne's County . . . .*

3. Queen Anne's Co., Md., deeds, Liber RT, B:53–54, Beath to Greenfield, 23 August 1737; PDF, *MDLANDREC* (https://mdlandrec.net/main/dsp_search.cfm?cid=QA : viewed 20 February 2017).

3. *MDLANDREC* (https://mdlandrec.net/main/dsp_search.cfm?cid=QA : viewed 20 February 2017), for Queen Anne's Co., Md., deeds, Liber RT, B:53–54, Beath to Greenfield, 23 August 1737, PDF.

4. *MDLANDREC* (https://mdlandrec.net/main/dsp_search.cfm?cid=QA : viewed 20 February 2017), for PDF, Queen Anne's Co., Md., deeds, Liber RT, B:53–54, Beath to Greenfield, 23 August 1737; Maryland State Archives, Annapolis.

The option-3 variations are nearly identical. They answer all five citation questions, show the source qualities, and contain all the information that would be needed for working notes or a printed work. The option-4 citation contains redundancy, and its offline repository information is unhelpful.

e. *Point your Internet browser to http://www.virginiamemory.com/collections/petitions. . . .*

3. Citizens of Stafford Co., Va., to the General Assembly of Virginia, petition, 1 December 1785; PDF, Library of Congress, *American Memory* (http://www.virginiamemory.com/collections/petitions : viewed 20 February 2017), search for keyword "1785-12-01" and locality "Stafford County."

3. Library of Congress, "Early Virginia Religious Petitions," *American Memory* (http://www.virginiamemory.com/collections/petitions : viewed 20 February 2017), search for keyword "1785-12-01" and locality "Stafford County," for Citizens of Stafford Co., Va., to the General Assembly of Virginia, petition, 1 December 1785, PDF.

4. Citizens of Stafford Co., Va., to the General Assembly of Virginia, petition, 1 December 1785; Legislative Petitions collection, Library of Virginia, Richmond; PDF, Library of Congress, "Early Virginia Religious Petitions," *American Memory* (http://www.virginiamemory.com/collections/petitions : viewed 20 February 2017).

The option-3 variations are nearly identical. They answer all five citation questions, show the source qualities, and contain all the information that would be needed for working notes or a printed work. The option-4 citation contains redundancy, and its offline repository information is unhelpful.

f. *Point your Internet browser to http://vault.georgiaarchives.org/cdm/landingpage/collection/TestApps. . . .*

3. Simon W. Overton, sworn statement, 5 January 1788; digital image, Georgia Archives, "Confederate Pension Applications," *Georgia's Virtual Vault* (http://vault.georgiaarchives.org/cdm/landingpage/collection/TestApps : viewed 20 February 2017).

3. Georgia Archives, "Confederate Pension Applications," *Georgia's Virtual Vault* (http://vault.georgiaarchives.org/cdm/landingpage/collection/TestApps : viewed 20 February 2017), for Simon W. Overton, sworn statement, 5 January 1788.

4. Simon W. Overton, sworn statement, 5 January 1788; in Application for Allowance no. 513, Simon W. Overton; Confederate Pension Applications; Georgia Confederate Pension Office, RG 58-1-1; Georgia Archives, Morrow; digital image, Georgia Archives, "Confederate Pension Applications," *Georgia's Virtual Vault* (http://vault.georgiaarchives.org/cdm/landingpage/collection/TestApps : viewed 20 February 2017).

The option-3 variations are nearly identical. They answer all five citation questions, show the source qualities, and contain all the information that would be needed for working notes or a printed work. The option-4 citation contains redundancy, and its offline repository information is unhelpful.

g. *Point your Internet browser to http://www.archivesindex.sc.gov/online archives/search.aspx, search Record group "All" for Collier. . . .*

3. Civil Works Administration and Works Progress Administration, South Carolina Will Transcripts, 1782–1868, typescript, 1930s, pp. 38–40, will of Joseph Collier; digital images, "On-Line Records Index," *South Carolina Department of Archives and History* (http://www.archivesindex.sc.gov/onlinearchives/Thumbnails.aspx?recordId=301635 : viewed 20 February 2017).

3. "On-Line Records Index," *South Carolina Department of Archives and History* (http://www.archivesindex.sc.gov/onlinearchives/Thumbnails.aspx?recordId=301635 : viewed 20 February 2017), digital images, from Civil Works Administration and Works Progress Administration, South Carolina Will Transcripts, 1782–1868, typescript, 1930s, pp. 38–40, will of Joseph Collier.

4. Civil Works Administration and Works Progress Administration, South Carolina Will Transcripts, 1782–1868, typescript, 1930s, pp. 38–40, will of Joseph Collier; call no. S 108093; South Carolina Department of Archives and History, Columbia; viewed at "On-Line Records Index," *South Carolina Department of Archives and History* (http://www.archivesindex.sc.gov/onlinearchives/Thumbnails.aspx?recordId=301635 : viewed 20 February 2017), digital images of undated typescript of will of Joseph Collier).

The option-3 variations contain nearly identical content. They answer all five citation questions, show the source qualities, and contain all the information that would be needed for working notes or a printed work. The option-4 citation contains redundancy, and its offline repository information is unhelpful.

Chapter 16 exercise answers

150. *In the Greenfield article in appendix A, find at least two examples of citations demonstrating each of these pairings of an image with an underlying-source:*

    - *Published image + unpublished underlying source*

      Footnote 4, second citation; footnote 5, second citation

      Footnote 22, first citation

    - *Unpublished image + unpublished underlying source*

      Footnote 1, first and second citations

151. *Give a rationale for the absence of examples in the Greenfield article of these pairings of an image with an underlying source:*

    - *Unpublished image + published underlying source*
    - *Published image + published underlying source*

    Unpublished images of published sources are rare. When images show facsimiles of publications and when crafting citations for a printed work, the Greenfield author takes the option of citing only the underlying source. This is consistent with the image-provider's functioning as a library.

152. *What are some examples from your own research of the following pairings of an image with an underlying source?*

    - *Unpublished image + published underlying source*
    - *Published image + published underlying source*
    - *Published image + unpublished underlying source*
    - *Unpublished image + unpublished underlying source*

    Your answers will apply information you learned in chapter 6 about differences between published and unpublished sources and images.

153. *In the Greenfield article find at least two examples of each of the following varieties of citation content and structures:*

- *A citation to an image supplemented with selected information about the underlying source (complex citation structure)*

  Footnote 5, second citation

  Footnote 22, first citation

  The citation in footnote 71

- *A citation to only an underlying source (simple citation structure)*

  All this article's citations to federal censuses refer to microfilm publications, but the author viewed the online images. The images are available on multiple websites, and the microfilm publications are available in brick-and-mortar libraries and archives. Another example is all the citations to out-of-copyright books and maps, which cite the books and maps, not the images. Although the author viewed them as online images or downloaded PDFs, they are available on multiple websites and brick-and-mortar libraries.

- *A citation to an underlying source supplemented with selected information about the image (complex citation structure)*

  Examples include the citations in footnotes 45 and 76.

154. *Explain why you find no examples of the following varieties of citation content and structure in the Greenfield article:*

- *Citations to an image only with no supplementary information (simple citation structure)*
- *Citations that fully cite both the image and the underlying source with both parts connected (compound citation structure)*

Citations to images with no information about the underlying source rarely provide enough information to assess the source's qualities. Full citations to both image and underlying source contain unnecessary redundancy, which add to a printed work's printing and mailing costs. They can be useful, however, for working notes and works in progress.

155. *From your own research, provide examples of the following varieties of citation content and structure:*

- *A citation to an image supplemented with selected information about the underlying source (complex citation structure)*
- *A citation to only an underlying source (simple citation structure)*
- *A citation to an underlying source supplemented with selected information about the image (complex citation structure)*

- *A citation that fully cites both the image and the underlying source with both parts connected (compound citation structure)*

Your citations will reflect the citation options for source-content and source-structure discussed in this chapter and shown in table 24.

156. *Referring to table 24, select a recommended or acceptable option for citing each of five given sources. Craft the citation and give the specified information.*

a. *The first volume of Norwich, Vermont, town records. . . . Cite the information documenting the younger daughter's birth.*

That is a pairing of a published image with an unpublished underlying source. Citation options 2, 4, and 5 in table 24 are acceptable choices:

2. "Vermont, Town Clerk, Vital and Town Records, 1732–2005," *FamilySearch* (https://familysearch.org/search/collection/1987653 : accessed 20 February 2017) > Windsor > Norwich > Town records 1761–1895 vol 1–3 > image 154, Norwich, Vt., town records 1:264, birth of Lydia Burton, 14 August 1769.

4. Norwich, Vt., town records 1:264, birth of Lydia Burton, 14 August 1769; Town Clerk, Norwich; viewed at *Family Search* (https://familysearch.org/search/collection/1987653 : accessed 20 February 2017), image 154.

5. Norwich, Vt., town records 1:264, birth of Lydia Burton, 14 August 1769; Town Clerk, Norwich; digital image, *FamilySearch* (https://familysearch.org/search/collection/1987653 : accessed 20 February 2017) > Vermont, Town Clerk, Vital and Town Records, 1732–2005 > Windsor > Norwich > Town records 1761–1895 vol 1–3 > image 154.

5. "Vermont, Town Clerk, Vital and Town Records, 1732–2005," *FamilySearch* (https://familysearch.org/search/collection/1987653 : accessed 20 February 2017) > Windsor > Norwich > Town records 1761–1895 vol 1–3 > image 154, Norwich, Vt., town records 1:264 birth of Lydia Burton, 14 August 1769; Town Clerk, Norwich.

The above choices are acceptable, but this book recommends option 2. Both versions of option 5 are long and contain unnecessary information. Option 4 is concise, but readers must figure out how to navigate from the collection level to the images. Also, option 4 cites the underlying source in its primary context, where the researcher did not examine it.

b. *That image also is available on Family History Library microfilm. Cite it.*

That is a pairing of an unpublished image with an unpublished underlying source. Citation options 2 and 4 in table 24 are acceptable choices, but this book recommends only option 4:

4. Norwich, Vt., town records 1:264, birth of Lydia Burton, 14 August 1769; Town Clerk, Norwich; microfilm 28,587, Family History Library (FHL), Salt Lake City.

That is the only option that this book recommends for citing unpublished images of unpublished underlying sources.

c. *Archive.org provides online images and downloadable* PDFs *of many books, including one titled* Descendants of Elijah B. Cook and Charity Lockwood Cook. *Cite the information for this family: "11—Joseph Lockwood Cook."*

That is a pairing of a published image with a published underlying source. Citation options 2, 3, 4, and 5 in table 24 are acceptable choices:

2. "Elijah B. Cook, born Sept. 11, 1759, and his wife, Charity Lockwood Cook, born June 27, 1762," *Archive.org* (https://archive.org/details/elijahbcookborns00cort : viewed 20 February 2017), digital image of *Descendants of Elijah B. Cook and Charity Lockwood Cook* (1916), family no. 11.

3. Mrs. William H. Cortright, *Descendants of Elijah B. Cook and Charity Lockwood Cook* (Homer, Mich.: Index Press, 1916), family no. 11.

4. Mrs. William H. Cortright, *Descendants of Elijah B. Cook and Charity Lockwood Cook* (Homer, Mich.: Index Press, 1916), family no. 11; digital image, *Archive.org* (https://archive.org/details/elijahbcookborns00cort : viewed 20 February 2017).

5. Mrs. William H. Cortright, *Descendants of Elijah B. Cook and Charity Lockwood Cook* (Homer, Mich.: Index Press, 1916), family no. 11; digital image, "Elijah B. Cook, born Sept. 11, 1759, and his wife, Charity Lockwood Cook, born June 27, 1762," *Archive.org* (https://archive.org/details/elijahbcookborns00cort : viewed 20 February 2017).

5. "Elijah B. Cook, born Sept. 11, 1759, and his wife, Charity Lockwood Cook, born June 27, 1762," *Archive.org* (https://archive.org/details/elijahbcookborns00cort : viewed 20 February 2017); showing images from Mrs. William H. Cortright, *Descendants of Elijah B. Cook and Charity Lockwood Cook* (Homer, Mich.: Index Press, 1916), family no. 11.

The above choices are acceptable. Option 2 and both versions of option 5, however, are long and contain unnecessary information. Option 3 is concise, and this book recommends it, especially for citations to appear in print. Option 4 seems the most useful for working notes and works in progress.

d. *The Cayuga County, New York, probate file for Jonathan Tucker has disappeared. . . . Cite the only record that the file contains.*

This is a pairing of a published image with a missing underlying source. Citation options 2 and 4 are applicable and acceptable choices:

2. "New York Probate Records, 1629–1971," *FamilySearch* (https://familysearch.org/search/collection/1920234 : viewed 20 February 2017) > Cayuga > Estate Papers 1799–1905 box 5 > images 1080–83, for Phillip King and Samuel Tucker, "Inventory of the Personal Estate of Jonathan Tucker Deceased," 9 January 1823, in Jonathan Tucker probate file, 1823.

4. Phillip King and Samuel Tucker, "Inventory of the Personal Estate of Jonathan Tucker Deceased," 9 January 1823, Cayuga Co., N.Y., in Jonathan Tucker probate file, 1823; digital images, "New York Probate Records, 1629–1971," *FamilySearch* (https://familysearch.org/search/collection/1920234 : viewed 20 February 2017) > Cayuga > Estate Papers 1799–1905 box 5 > images 1080–83.

When the image of a missing source is published, like that example, options 2 and 4 contain nearly identical information. In this case, conciseness tips the scale in favor of option 2.

e. *The Burton genealogy file in the library of this book's author in Monroe, New York, contains a photocopy of a publication titled* The Life of Asa Burton. *Cite page 8.*

That is a pairing of an unpublished image paired with an underlying publication. Citation options 2, 3, and 4 in table 24 are acceptable choices:

2. Photocopy of Asa Burton, *The Life of Asa Burton* (Thetford, Vt.: First Congregational Church, 1973), 8; Burton file of Thomas W. Jones, Monroe, N.Y.

3. Asa Burton, *The Life of Asa Burton* (Thetford, Vt.: First Congregational Church, 1973), 8.

4. Asa Burton, *The Life of Asa Burton* (Thetford, Vt.: First Congregational Church, 1973), 8; photocopy, Burton file of Thomas W. Jones, Monroe, N.Y.

Although the book is out of print, it is available in libraries and for sale. Citing the photocopy, while acceptable, adds little value (except in the working notes of the person who holds the photocopy). Option 3 is the best option, especially for a citation that will appear in print.

Chapter 17 exercise answers

157. *Imagine you inherited a linen dish towel from your great-grandmother. Embroidered on it is her birth date, the only known source for that information. Imagine the dish towel's appearance, qualities, and location. Then, cite it in a full reference-note citation.*

Your citation might resemble this one:

1. Celia (Lanahan) Leach, embroidered birth date on a linen dish towel, ca. 1920s; author's collection.

158. *Transform that reference-note citation into* (a) *a shortened reference-note citation and* (b) *a reference-list citation.*

Your citations might resemble these:

11. Leach, embroidered birth date on a linen dish towel, ca. 1920s.

Leach, Celia (Lanahan). Embroidered birth date on a linen dish towel. Ca. 1920s. Author's collection.

159. *Imagine that you lost the dish towel after you had digitally photographed it and put the image on your (perhaps imaginary) website or blog. Craft another reference-note citation citing that source for your great-grandmother's birth date.*

Your citation might resemble this one:

3. William C. Leach, "Images of Family Artifacts," *Leach Family History* (http://www.WilliamLeach.com : viewed 20 February 2017), for image of Celia (Lanahan) Leach, embroidered birth date on a linen dish towel, ca. 1920s.

160. *Transform that reference-note citation into* (a) *a shortened reference-note citation and* (b) *a reference-list citation.*

Your citations might resemble these:

33. Leach, "Images of Family Artifacts," linen dish towel, ca. 1920s.

Leach, William C. *Leach Family History*. http://www.WilliamLeach.com : 2017.

Index